THE WORLD UPTURNING
ELSIE HENRY'S IRISH WARTIME DIARIES, 1913-1919

THE WORLD UPTURNING

ELSIE HENRY'S IRISH WARTIME DIARIES, 1913-1919

EDITED BY
CLARA CULLEN

MERRION

Dublin & Portland, Oregon

First published in 2013 by Merrion
an imprint of Irish Academic Press

8 Chapel Lane
Sallins
Co. Kildare

920 NE 58th Avenue, Suite 300
Portland, Oregon,
97213-3786 USA

British Library Cataloguing in Publication Data
Henry, Elsie.
The world upturning : Elsie Henry's wartime diaries,
1913-1919.
1. Henry, Elsie--Diaries.
2. World War, 1914-1918--Ireland--Dublin--Sources.
3. World War, 1914-1918-- Personal narratives, Irish.
4. Ireland--History--1910-1921--Sources.
5. Nationalism--Ireland--History- 20th century--Sources.
I. Title II. Cullen, Clara.
941.8'350821'092-dc23

978-1-908928-14-6 (cloth)

978-1-908928-15-3 (paper)

978-1-908928-17-7 (e-book)

Typeset by www.sinedesign.net
Printed by CPI Group (UK) Ltd, Croydon, CR0 4YY

To my family

and

for my grandmother Clara Louise Collins,
one of the millions of women who 'kept the home
fires burning' while her husband served with the
Royal Artillery in France 1914–18

CONTENTS

ACKNOWLEDGEMENTS

My first thanks must go to Dr Ciarán Wallace of Trinity College Dublin (TCD) who not only made me aware of Elsie and her diaries but also made his own research available to me in the true spirit of academic collegiality.

The family of Elsie Henry in Canada, James Brunton and Nancy Willson, gave me permission to use these diaries and also were very generous with their memories of their family. This work would not have been possible without them. I must also sincerely acknowledge the generosity of other members of Elsie and Augustine's extended family, Barbara Phillips and Sandra Lefroy, who searched through their family papers and shared their memories of Elsie with me.

In the course of my research I had the opportunity to meet many wonderful people in archives and libraries. The staff of the National Library of Ireland, especially those in the department of manuscripts, have been superb in supporting my work on Elsie Henry and I most sincerely thank them. Also very deserving of my heartfelt thanks are the staff of the Library of the National Botanic Gardens in Glasnevin and also Seamus O'Brien of the Botanic Gardens, who very kindly shared his knowledge of Augustine and Elsie Henry with me. The library of University College Dublin, especially Avril Patterson, also deserves my heartfelt thanks.

Professor Mary E. Daly of University College Dublin (UCD) was the academic supervisor for my PhD and she mentored me in the rigours of historical scholarship. In reality she was much more than that and she deserves my most sincere thanks.

Dr Margaret Ó hÓgartaigh and Dr Anne Mac Lellan bravely and

generously read drafts of the manuscript and made very helpful comments and suggestions. To them my most sincere thanks.

I must also thank those who were so supportive of this project. They are too numerous to mention but include Professor Ciaran Brady (TCD), Professor Mary O'Dowd (Queens University Belfast), Professor Mary E. Daly (UCD), Professor Maria Luddy (University of Warwick), Professor Tom Bartlett (University of Aberdeen), Dr Lindsey Earner-Byrne (UCD) and Dr Eimear O'Connor. My thanks to all of them and all the others who offered me encouragement.

I must also acknowledge the UCD Humanities Institute of Ireland, who gave me the facilities to conduct this research.

Lisa Hyde, Conor Graham, Peter O'Connell and Colin Eustace deserve my special thanks. They have been enthusiastic about Elsie and her diaries since I first suggested their publication.

Finally my most sincere and heartfelt thanks to all my family, who have been unfailingly supportive in every way possible.

LIST OF PLATES

1. Elsie Henry as an infant (Courtesy of James Brunton and Nancy Willson).

2. Elsie Henry's introduction to her diaries (Courtesy of the National Library of Ireland).

3. Elsie Henry, Nance Brunton, Dorothy Stopford and Kathleen Dickinson in the garden of 5, Sandford Terrace Ranelagh, c.1913 (Courtesy of the National Library of Ireland).

4. Castle Shane, Ardglass 1913, Elsie Henry's diary, September 1913 (Courtesy of the National Library of Ireland).

5. Letter from Roger Casement to Elsie Henry, 26 October 1913 (Courtesy of the National Library of Ireland).

6. Letter from Eoin MacNeill to Elsie Henry, 15 December 1913 (Courtesy of the National Library of Ireland).

7. Letter from Alice Stopford Green to Elsie Henry, 31 March 1914 (Courtesy of the National Library of Ireland).

8. 'Artists and ecclesiastics' by AE, Elsie Henry's diary, 8 July 1914 (Courtesy of the National Library of Ireland).

9. Elsie Henry's diary, 4, 8 July 1914 (Courtesy of the National Library of Ireland).

10. (l. to r.) Paul Heger, Elsie and Augustine Henry, 20 July 1914, Oisquerque, Belgium (Courtesy of the National Library of Ireland).

11.   Elsie and Augustine Henry with Sir Jocelyn Gore-Booth at Lissadell, June 1915 (Courtesy of the National Library of Ireland).

12.   Birthday card from her brother Ted Brunton to Elsie, August 1915 (Courtesy of the National Library of Ireland).

13.   Reverse of Ted's birthday card to Elsie, August 1915 (Courtesy of the National Library of Ireland).

14.   Grave registration card of Ted Brunton, October 1915 (Courtesy of the National Library of Ireland).

15.   Dublin, Easter 1916, from Weekly Irish Times *Sinn Fein Rebellion Handbook: Easter 1916* (Dublin, 1917) (Courtesy of the National Library of Ireland and the *Irish Times*).

16.   Elsie Henry's diary, 25-26 April 1916 (Courtesy of the National Library of Ireland).

17.   Elsie Henry diary, 30 April 1916, with Augustine Henry's travel permit into Dublin from Dun Laoghaire (Courtesy of the National Library of Ireland).

18.   Elsie Henry's diary, 3 May 1916 (Courtesy of the National Library of Ireland).

19.   Elsie Henry's diary, 13 May 1916 (Courtesy of the National Library of Ireland).

20.   'Conference' by AE, Elsie Henry's diary, 26 May 1916 (Courtesy of the National Library of Ireland).

21.   Elsie Henry's diary, April 1917 (Courtesy of the National Library of Ireland).

1

Introduction:

Elsie Henry and her Diaries

*E*lsie Henry (1881–1956) was born in London in August 1881and christened Alice Helen, the elder daughter of a successful London physician, Thomas Lauder Brunton[1] and his wife Louisa Jane, Stopford. She was one of four children[2], Alice Helen ('Elsie'), Stopford ('Top'),[3] Anne ('Nance')[4] and Edward ('Ted')[5].Throughout her diaries, both in diary entries and in correspondence, Elsie's siblings are referred to by the shortened versions of their names. Through her mother, Elsie was connected to the large Anglo-Irish family of Stopfords.[6] She was especially close to one of her mother's sisters, the nationalist historian Alice Stopford Green,[7] who is referred to in the diaries as either Aunt Alice or Mrs Green, and also to her cousins, Dorothy,[8] Robert,[9] Alice[10] and Edith Stopford,[11] the children of her uncle Jemmett Stopford and his wife Constance (née Kennedy), who had moved to London after the death of their father in 1902.

In 1908 Elsie married Augustine Henry (1857–1930),[12] an Irishman who was then lecturing on forestry in Cambridge. In 1913 the couple moved to Dublin, following Augustine's appointment as Professor of Forestry at the Royal College of Science for Ireland (RCScI). Their Dublin home, in the suburb of Ranelagh, soon became a meeting place for a wide variety of people from across Dublin's nationalist, administrative and literary circles. In Dublin Augustine already had a circle of colleagues and friends (including many of the leaders of the Gaelic revival, such as George Russell[13] and Evelyn Gleeson[14]) and Elsie had Stopford relatives[15] living in the city. Her aunt Alice Stopford Green made their home her base when she visited Ireland, and the Henrys entertained numbers of her friends from across the political spectrum – many of whom were to play prominent roles in twentieth-century Irish history. Elsie's sister Nance described their home at 5 Sandford Terrace, Ranelagh[16] as:

> It was a little, grey stone house with a buddleia which Augustine had brought back from his travels in China and introduced into Great Britain, growing in front.
>
> There was a wide hall running through the house and a large garden at the back, with a little green house where Elsie raised Augustine's seedlings for him, and fields and trees behind.
>
> The house was beautifully furnished, handmade carpets from Glasnevin, made by Miss Gleeson; a beautiful picture of an apple tree in the dusk by AE, and another by him, of a kneeling woman embracing two children as they ran to her out of the sea in the golden light of dawn. A polished yellow table made of a single section of a tree, given them as a wedding present by Mr. Elwes[17] who was joint author with

Augustine of *Great trees of Great Brittain [sic] and Ireland*, a standard work now. A little dining room with Mother's writing desk in it, and a little old fashioned dresser from Fleet.

Everything was so dainty and so interesting; the little Tanagra figure under a glass case and the [really] red glass jar from Bohemia on the mantelpiece in the drawing room.

I think everyone interesting in Dublin was in that room; AE, Sir Horace Plunket [*sic*],[18] James Stephens[19] (whose children Elsie god-mothered), Miss Purser[20] who made stained glass windows, all the botanists and foresters, Augustine knew them all, and they flocked to him, for he was a great teacher and Elsie a very good hostess.[21]

The Ireland to which Elsie and Augustine moved in 1913 was a country in the process of change. The main political concern was Home Rule, although Dublin, by the end of 1913, was crippled by a General Strike and Lockout. In 1912 the third Home Rule Bill, which would grant Ireland its own parliament and a degree of domestic autonomy, had been introduced in the House of Commons by the prime minister Herbert Asquith,[22] passed and was guaranteed to be enacted in 1914. However, the Unionists' determined opposition to any break of the Union with Britain led to the emergence of a militant unionist movement in Ulster, and the possibility of a partition of the island of Ireland in order to achieve the passing of the Home Rule Bill in Westminster. By the summer of 1914, the main concern in Ireland and the government in Britain was the very real threat of a civil war in Ireland. Events in continental Europe, including the assassination of an Austrian archduke, were far less important than potential conflict in Ireland.

THE DIARIES OF ELSIE HENRY

In August 1914, when war was declared on Germany, many thousands of men in Britain and Ireland were recalled to their regiments or volunteered to join the armed forces. They left behind them wives, sisters and daughters. Alice ('Elsie') Henry was one of these women. Although her husband Augustine (who was 57 in 1914) did not join any of the armies but continued with his own research work and advised on forestry policies in Ireland, a number of her family served during the First World War. One of her brothers, Stopford ('Top') Brunton was in Canada and joined a Canadian regiment. Her younger brother, Edward ('Ted') Brunton, having completed his medical training, went to France in 1915 with the Royal Army Medical Corps. A cousin, George Stopford, was already in the British army and in 1913 was seconded to the recently formed Royal Flying Corps (RFC). Another Stopford cousin, Robert Jemmett Stopford, who was due to begin university, instead joined a Friends Ambulance Corps and by the end of 1914 was serving with them in Belgium. Bob Venables, another cousin, spent the years from 1914 to 1917 in a prisoner-of-war camp in Germany.[23]

Like so many other women during the First World War Elsie wrote to her relatives and friends serving in the various theatres of war, sending them parcels of 'comforts' as well as news of home. Living in Dublin, she attended a First Aid class, and joined the Voluntary Aid Detachment (VAD) in the Royal College of Science for Ireland (RCScI). From 1915 to 1919 she was Quartermaster of the Sphagnum Department of the Irish War Supply Organisation at the RCScI acting as the Central Sphagnum Depot for Ireland.[24] In 1918 she was awarded an OBE for her contribution to the war effort.

Elsie also decided to keep a record of her experiences of the war. The volumes of her diaries,[25] now in the National Library of Ireland (NLI), reflect her life and are a record of one woman's experiences on the Irish Home Front during the First World War. Her introduction to these diaries summarizes her intentions:

> This diary was kept by Alice Helen, elder daughter of Sir Lauder Brunton, Bt. and wife of Augustine Henry. It was begun in the first year of their residence in Ireland; it was continued as a war record, showing the information received daily by the ordinary citizen; and it was kept up later until the end of the war, for the sake of Edward Lauder Brunton, that it might be complete, of its kind, for him in after years. A.H.B. Henry.[26]

In common with many other women on the Home Front during the First World War, Elsie obtained much of her information about what was happening in the war from the letters she and her family received from relations and friends serving in Belgium and France. A number of these have been included in this publication.[27] Also included are other letters from her family, her aunt Alice Stopford Green in particular, but also from her father in London. The text is Elsie's own, but minor corrections and changes have been made to conform with current publishing practice.

As Elsie emphasized in her introduction, her diaries are based on the information available to the ordinary citizen, either through the newspapers or from friends. The frustration at the lack of official information is a continuing theme throughout the diaries, most especially during the confusion of Dublin in April and early May1916. Throughout the years from 1913 to early 1919 Elsie recorded her descriptions and opinions of the places she visited, the people she met and her experiences in an Ireland that changed out of all recognition during the First World War. Her diary entries display her common sense, a realistic view of people and a robust sense of humour.

It has been a joy to edit them!

2

The Last Days of World Peace but Conflict in Ireland:

The Diaries 1913–14[1]

INTRODUCTION

Elsie's first diary, covering the period from August 1913 to 21 August 1914, records meetings, excursions, visitors to the Henrys' home at 5 Sandford Terrace, Ranelagh, and all the significant events in Ireland in the first twelve months of her life in Ireland. Although superficially peaceful, the concerns over Home Rule and Ulster militarism were not far below the surface in Ireland in 1913 and 1914, and by the summer of 1914 the situation had reached a crisis with the imminent threat of a civil war in Ireland. Elsie, through her Aunt Alice, met and entertained a significant number of men and women across the political spectrum and, as 1914 wore on, was witness to some of the events. More immediately for the Henrys, a few months after their arrival in Dublin the city's best remembered and bitterest labour dispute began – the Dublin Lock-out of 1913.[2]

❋

21 AUGUST 1913

Drove up from 'Bahama' [a guest house near Enniskerry, Co. Wicklow] 5 miles. The carman talked of the *Titanic*[3] and said that it was doomed before ever it sailed, for it was built in a Belfast dockyard and hadn't the workmen carved 'To hell with the Pope' on every plank of it? ... sharp fine showers stinging and singing through the heather. Mountains in view – Great Sugar Loaf, Little Sugar Loaf, Bray Head, War Hill and Djouce.

22 AUGUST 1913

Joined Mr. Laird, Lord Powerscourt's forester ... Descended into the valley, crossed the Dargle and climbed the other side ... Crossing the Dargle again came to an ancient circle of hoary hawthorns and granite blocks in the middle of a field. Mr L. wd. have it away, but the farmer wd. defend it with his life for the Fairies and Witches dance round it every night and one year when the farmer cut down a few branches, he suffered the loss of 3 cows by untimely deaths in consequence.

An old woman inhabiting a neighbouring cottage, was to have a new roof, and the agent proposed one of corrugated iron. She came hurrying up to Powerscourt, and fell on Lord P. with wrath declaring she would have no 'tin Tambourine' over <u>her</u> head. And she did not.

20 SEPTEMBER 1913

Arrived at Ardglass[4] 3 p.m. from Castlewellan. The red flag of the hand [*sic*] of Ulster shaking from windows of nearly every house and from the masts of the fishing fleet in the harbour. A throng of gay people to meet the pipers, and all pouring up to the Castle. 800 years has it stood and nearly 400 yrs empty till Mr Bigger[5] took it in 1911. Himself – people of Ardglass signalling a welcome from the roof, pigeons fluttering from

St Columba's Tower, and the Red Hand waving a triumphant blessing over all.

The year's fishing is just over, piles and piles of barrels are stacked on the quays of the harbour, but the inhabitants are all moving about in the Gaelic festivity which is to accompany the unveiling of the new church windows tomorrow.

Pike-men and girls, a 'Wee Willie' and all and sundry are climbing up and down the stairs. We scrambled up to the roof where the pipers were playing and children dancing. F.J.B. [Bigger] welcomed us and invited us hospitably to tea. Lord Ashbourne,[6] Mrs J.R. Green, Sir Roger Casement[7] and ourselves – A cosy tea with oat cake and home-made current loaf, off fine hand-woven linen of the 17th century. Irish material and Irish workmanship of every age furnish his room, old oak furniture, a magnificent bronze candelabra, incense burning in ancient copper flares, banners on the walls, fine old glass, metal: a great log fire blazing; rugs, books, and red flowers. In one corner a long blue curtain through which glimmer the candles of the turret oratory, with its rush strewn floor, its stone candlesticks, its saffron linen hangings and a pure white altar cloth and its flowers kept fresh all the year round, by unknown hands. Everyone contributes. One old woman, just after Castle Séan was opened, brought a priest's box, of the penal times, and presented it. She had kept it a dead secret, and even Father Donnelly did not know she possessed it, nor does he yet know who she is who gave it.

At dusk F.J.B. gave the signal and we all trooped up to the roof; the Red Hand came down at sunset and up went the green flag of the Harp, piped up into the air by the pipers standing on the topmost turret.

By 7.30 it was quite dark and the pipers met before the Castle and played in a circle to call up the procession; presently it formed. Two standard-bearers, four pike-men, 5 or 6 pipers, all in kilts, 2 drums and a big drum, and 20 or 30 small boys carrying flares. The pipers swayed gently, the 'Wearing of the Green' burst forth triumphantly and the whole procession swung off up the village. Swelling as it went it passed along; hardly a cottage on either side but showed a brave illumination of candles. Presently from behind there resounded the boom of the brass band from Dunsford and thenceforward they and the pipes shared 'A Nation once Again', 'God save Ireland', 'Tipperary', etc., throughout the march. Down by the harbour, back past the Castle, until the entire circuit had been made, and on into the village [hall], where Lord Ashbourne gave them a Gaelic address. F.J.B. offered us a magnificent supper of kingly lobsters, oat-cake and whiskey, and then marshalled the faithful on to their knees to return thanks; twelve or fourteen boys came up for their evening devotions, and then they drew aside and one alone standing in the oratory sang the infinitely sweet Gaelic lullaby that the Virgin crooned to her son.

21 SEPTEMBER 1913

The sun rose clear and red and piercing straight out of the sea, and presently sweet shrill pipes exhorted All [*sic*] the Faithful to come. The official Mass was at 10, and after that Augustine and I walked to Ballyroe, round by the salt flats of Killough, to see the ancient circles of stones in a hollow of ancient forts. Were they places of worship, or more likely burial-grounds? Dunsford, the Parish of Ardglass we didn't see, but there is the famous cross, restored by F.J.B. and Mrs Green and the following is its story. Himself and herself, together with Dr Starkie and others came once on a while to spend the day there and walked on what is now the golf-links.

F.J.B. saw a stone – looked at it and turned it over and looked again. No-one heeded him but Mrs J.R.G. [John Richard Green] and he came back to look. This was the first piece of that cross for which search had vainly been made during the preceding 50 ys. That piece F.J.B. replaced in its original position and a few days later he had it conveyed to the house of Father Donnelly, the priest, whom he did not then know; with instructions to house it until further orders. Two more pieces were found on the rockery of Bone Castle and two more built into a Presbyterian church, but the method of their recovery is a secret. Thus was the cross restored, and later under the glow of that omen did F.J.B. proceed into his heritage.

At 4 in the afternoon the priest came to the castle and held a Rosary service. Five hundred people poured themselves into every cranny of the castle. The service was held in Mr. Bigger's room, and he stationed his pike-men and pipers up and down the staircase, to catch up the responses after the priest, and send them on. The result was that the castle from ground to roof was a simultaneous hum. When the service was finished, the procession formed and marched with piping to the village church. The windows presented by Mr. Bigger and picturing people in Irish dress, were unveiled by Lord Ashbourne, and a sermon in Irish followed. Mr. Bigger marched to the forefront of the church, where right at the altar rails stood a special *prie-dieu*; the pipers knelt along the altar rails, and Mr. Bigger flopped on his knees in pomp, flanked by two standing pike-men. As a staunch Presbyterian Mr. Bigger must feel that he stands alone at the head of all powers spiritual and temporal, in Ardglass. We returned in solemn procession.

Singing and piping went on in the castle. Sir Roger sang the 'Wearing of the Green', in the Guard room; a tiny boy sang a long and lively song, and the village idiot took out some pennies to give him, but the child drew himself proudly away refusing it indignantly.

A cailedhe [sic] took place in the evening in the village hall and dancing and singing till 1 or 2 a.m.

The police the night before, being very weary by midnight, had heard the pipers discussing whether they would or wd. not start processing and piping around the village afresh, and the police had suggested that they should not. That clinched the matter, and the boys promptly processed for another hour, with the weary police at their heels. So this evening, the police said nothing at all, but they stole into the guard-room, where the boys found them sitting sheepishly round on benches. Mr. B. [Bigger] was appealed to as to whether this might be, and Mr. Bigger came down. Before long they were processing round the room, Mr. B. with a policeman's helmet on his head and baton in his hand, the 3 police solemnly after him and the pipers. Then there followed great Ulster speeches, F.J.B. demanding in stentorian 'Will the sun <u>never</u> set on the Empire?' 'NEVER, NEVER' was the solemn fervent response.

The police showed off their dancing, and the pipers declared they out did them in steps, and the sergeant laughed till he ached and went home at 2 a.m. in blissful delight!

One policeman had had his head cut some hours before in a tussle with some roughs. F.J.B. dressed it for him, and the policeman said apologetically 'You see, sorr [*sic*] the mistake I made was to get knocked down' but he never mentioned that the roughs were 5 to 1.

16 OCTOBER 1913

Augustine lectured at the D.B.C.[8] in Dame Street to the Forestry Society, a modest little violet, as societies go. A few hours before it began, a telegram arrived stating the Lord Lieutenant[9] would be present. Accordingly a blazing red carpet was spread over the pavement and their Excellencies made a royal progress between tea-urns and buns. They scuffled up the stairs, scrambled through the chairs and plumped on a fat sofa in the front row. The *Gemütlich* assemblage dropped their tea cups and slabs of light refreshment, and hurried to their seats, and every aperture was then hermetically sealed, as the Lord Lieutenant 'is Very Sensitive to Draughts'. The heat was appalling, and some of A.'s lantern slides melted shamelessly. A fatuous youth with a natty head and shiny hair and white spats took notes for Lady Aberdeen, and obliged Augustine with his silver topped cane as a pointer, and the lecture proceeded. A. rose to the occasion, and acquitted himself valiantly. He showed the rope made of bog fir, saying that it was an [wralt?] industry, and that one old man in Coleraine, with a sign over his door 'Fir Rope Maker'[10] still turns it out, and that it is an industry that should be encouraged and not let die. At this point the L.L. [Lord Lientenant] pointed his finger at Lady A. who acknowledged it with a graceful bow.

The proceedings ended with a string of ancient anecdotes *à propos* of nothing in particular from the L.L. and a flowery and melodramatic harangue from Mr Dawson,[11] their Excellencies exeunt through a honeyed mist, and the entire staff of the D.B.C. rushed off with tea-pots to 'wet fresh tea' in honour of the occasion.

MONDAY 20 OCTOBER 1913

Aunt Alice and Sir Roger Casement here, very agitated as to the chances of the meeting at Ballymoney on Friday; a Protestant Nationalist meeting, the first of its kind in Ulster, to protest against the lawless methods of Carsonism.

The 'Provisional Government'[12] has held a special meeting to consider the Ballymoney meeting, and has decided to allow it to proceed!

Postcard from Alice Stopford Green to Elsie about meeting in Ballymoney –

'Meeting an astonishing success in the best sense – I never heard to [*sic*] high a level of [squabbling?], nor saw so deep and sustained an enthusiasm. This is the beginning of much. We ended after 11 and drove to Ballycastle arriving 2.30 a.m. No chance of a telegram last night. I go [to] Belfast tomorrow, and Monday morning Dundalk to see house. On then to London. If I can get up by 6 to Dublin we might dine at Jammet's[13] – I'll telegraph. ASG'].

Letter from Roger Casement on Marine Hotel Ballycastle writing paper, to Elsie, 26 October 1913 –
'Dear Mrs Henry,
We had a great meeting. Splendid in every way and Mrs G. [Green] excelled herself and captured the house. A splendid audience – all Presbyterians! Or nearly all – a few Church of I [Church of Ireland] ones too and not a single R.C. [Roman Catholic]! We motored on at midnight to Ballycastle, getting there at 2 am and then yday [*sic*], Saturday we came over to Rathlin and spent the night on it, and now return today to Ballycastle and motor round the coast road to Belfast. Mrs G. will (D.V.) return to London on Monday covered with laurels and the friend of hundreds [more] up here in the [illegible] North. I did a dreadful thing: I forgot that postcard for Mrs Bickerdike[14] the night I dined with you and posted it only from Belfast (with a letter of explanation) only some days after. Forgive me,
    Yours sincerely,
    Roger Casement'

28 OCTOBER TO 9 NOVEMBER 1913
Top and Betty here.[15]

2 NOVEMBER TO 9 NOVEMBER 1913
Ted here.

WEDNESDAY 12 NOVEMBER 1913

AE and Susan Mitchell[16] came to lunch at Jammet's. AE tapped a meringue and said 'This is the first nice thing that has happened to me since the Albert Hall'. He thinks great good will come from the present disturbances. He says that hitherto only three sides of the 'everlasting square in the Universe' have had a turn uppermost [Diagram of the four sides –God, power, wealth and labour]. In the ancient civilisations of Assyria and Egypt, the King was divine representative, then Power in the hands of a body, as the Greek aristocracy. Wealth is the present day; and whichever side has been uppermost, it has always been loyally supported by the other two against the fourth. Now is coming a new era when the fourth will have its turn uppermost. His hope of the future is in co-operation, first to teach the people to divide Dublin up into squares, and have a co-operative branch in each, and then to go on to co-operative building and housing. AE went over to London in Oct. and spoke at the Albert Hall in support of Larkin[17] and the strike. On his return all Dublin, Ireland and the Plunkett House[18] rose up and abused him.

SUNDAY 16 NOVEMBER 1913

AE, William Rothenstein,[19] Miss Cunningham of Trinity Hall and Commissioner W.F. Bailey to lunch

17–20 NOVEMBER 1913

W. Rothenstein gave the Hermione lectures at Alexandra College.[20]

Letter from W. Rothenstein to Elsie, 24 November 1913 –
'My dear Mrs Henry –
believe me it was a real disappointment to me not to have one quiet evening with you both in Dublin. Your presence gave me a sense of

intimacy nothing else quite did. I believe the knowledge that you were sitting somewhere in that large anonymous audience did actually hearten me – the Bishops I had to meet nearly took all the courage out of me before I faced it. Many thanks indeed for the noble gift. I shall value it and when I see the flowers come I will remember I have a promise to redeem.

My very warm regards to your husband,

Yours, etc.,

W. Rothenstein'

WEDNESDAY 26 NOVEMBER 1913

Visited the National Schools in John's Lane where Miss Laird[21] has introduced voluntary feeding during the play hour. Nearly 300 children, boys, girls and infants, in a condemned building of an appalling description. Marching is forbidden on the first story as the ceiling below is giving way, and marching would bring the structure down on the boys' heads beneath! A good school is in building opposite, and was to be finished by Xmas, but no work has been done since the beginning of the strike (this is the fourteenth week). The children get breakfast now since the strike and dinner at 12 all the year round: Irish Stew prepared by the Penny Dinner kitchen, and rice and jam on fast days.

The infants were taught the Lord's Prayer in class, in chorus, the teacher going round afterwards to hear had they grasped it individually, and one infant began 'Our Father who worked in Heaven'.

FRIDAY 28 NOVEMBER 1913

AE and Susan brewed steak and coffee and set forth pears and nuts in a lordly dish at Plunket [sic] House. AE took me to Liberty Hall.[22] Three thousand are [receiving] relief. Miss Larkin was there superintending. They have kitchens downstairs, and a roomful of sewing machines working at clothing. The desolation and feebleness of the men swarming over and round the building is terrible.

Professor Davis of Harvard lectured at the College of Science on Normal and Glacial Sculpturing of Mountains, giving his theory of Geographical Cycles.

Dined with the de Montmorencys, Captain White[23] was there (son of Sir George White of Ladysmith). He is organising and drilling the 'Citizen army',[24] mainly Larkin's men and has about 10,000 of them drilling at Croydon Park, Clontarf.

SATURDAY 29 NOVEMBER 1913

John MacNeil [*sic*][25] came in after dinner, Professor of Ancient Irish at the National University. He was asked for an article on Ulster by one of the papers. He wrote 6 and destroyed them, and then suddenly produced an article on national defence, with the immediate result that a committee was formed, and within a fortnight there was a 'national army'[26] in the drilling stage. He hopes the Citizen army will amalgamate, when the strike is settled, and possibly the army of the North, Carson's, after Home Rule comes in.

Letter from Lauder Brunton in London to Elsie, 30 November 1913 –
'Dearest Elsie,

Stopford and Betty came back on Tuesday and they both seem to have enjoyed their stay in Ireland and Scotland very much. The portrait came on Friday. They both think I should have been painted in my best frock coat. Mrs Jaffé[27] has reserved any expression of opinion on the subject since the picture appeared. The others all approve of the picture and I say the likeness is excellent. One and all however, they say the colouring of the face is too grey. Originally it was much brighter and Herkomer[28] had taken an immense deal of trouble with it but Nancy went down with me to look at the portrait and colouring seemed too bright. Herkomer unluckily accepted her criticism and everyone else is disappointed. I am very much better indeed, that nurse has left this morning. I am looking forward to the night with some dread but I think I am sufficiently well to go along by myself and it is time I made a trial. Are the strikes in Dublin affecting you? Sir William Whitla[29] of Belfast came in for an hour on Tuesday evening. He is full of stories but I think is very apprehensive of civil war. If any attempt is made to coerce Ulster he will I think fight to the death and willingly sacrifice not only his own life but that of his wife and also all his property. The position is very [poor]. Uncle Jack is very far from well and I am very anxious about him but his brain is as clear as ever and he has given me a paper he has written on Civil War as a Court of Appeal which I think admirable. I am sorry that George cannot come to the family dinner on the 4th but he has been selected to fly with a maxim gun and cannot get leave.

With kindest regards to Augustine, Yours, etc,

Lauder Brunton'

MONDAY 1 DECEMBER 1913

Miss Malecka [*sic*] held forth at Sackville Hall on her Polish race and her imprisonment in Russia. She received letters for and visits of a member of the Polish Socialists while in Cracow. Whereupon the Russian Government arrested her, and as many of her friends as they could find, and as many of their friends again, and swept them all into prison. Miss Malecka made a great uproar as a British subject, and Sir Edward Grey was forced to intervene on her behalf, and £2,000 bail was collected, whereupon she was let out, but there is no word of all her friends. (At least I listened to her for an hour and three quarters and there was no word then). £200 was collected in Cambridge while we were there, Mrs Kennedy going round for signatures, and completely upsetting the Master of Magdalene, the Vice-Chancellor by the audacity of such a request.

WEDNESDAY 3 DECEMBER 1913

Bea[30] went to Croydon Park on Sunday to see the Citizen Army drilled by Captain White, and came back to Dublin with it. She says the great game of the Army is to march as fast as ever it can. It is escorted by battalions of police 6ft 6 [inches] and in long skirted coats. The faster the army marches the hotter do the panting police become, and the whole joy of the Army is to give them 'a run for their money'!

FRIDAY 2 [5] DECEMBER 1913

With Augustine, AE and Susan Mitchell to lunch in Grafton Street. AE said that [after] much pressure he expressed his views in the *Homestead* (while remarking that the I.A.O.S.[31] forbade Politics) saying 'The arguments for Home Rule are the intolerant stupidity of the politicians on the one side, and the stupid intolerance of the politicians on the other'.

SATURDAY 6 DECEMBER 1913

To lunch Mr and Mrs de Montmorency,[32] Dr Douglas Hyde[33] (founder of the Gaelic League), Mr and Mrs Campbell (Agricultural Department). Mrs de Montmorency was standing in a porch of the Commercial Buildings with a friend sheltering from the rain this morning when a man came out of the house and said 'It's all bust up'. He was one of the English delegates come over to try and settle the strike and he was coming out from the sitting. Dr Douglas Hyde is administering Sir Roger Casement's fund for feeding the school children in the fever districts of the West, Lettermullen, etc. 120 children and on fine days 180 are fed. They get cocoa and biscuits, and they say grace in Irish, speak Irish while eating and sing an Irish hymn at the end. The priests objected, saying 'Wud ye mak schlaves of us [*sic*]?' But Dr Hyde produced a threatening letter from Sir R.C. (with which he had previously armed himself) saying the fund would continue on those terms, so the priests gave in.

MONDAY 8 DECEMBER 1913

The Strike is partially settled today. Larkin is still in England. But the coal, cement, etc. etc. is no longer conducted by military with rifles, or 4 police on a car for every wagon of stuff.

[DECEMBER 1913]

James Stephens was awarded the Royal Literary Society's prize for literature last week, and went to London to receive it.

Letter from James Stephens in Paris to Elsie, 5/7 December 1913 –

'Dear Mrs Henry,

Many thanks for your letter, and enclosure. I have only returned from London but I will read the speech you sent me tomorrow. Dublin does seem to be wakening up. For myself, I think that this strike (and all the questions which it will raise months or years hence) is the most valuable thing which has happened in Ireland in 100 years. Our respects to yourself and your husband until March next when we hope to shake your hands,

Sincerely yours,

James Stephens'

Cutting from the *Irish Times*, 10 December 1913, with a report of Roger Casement's letter supporting the intention of the Hamburg-Amerika line to make Queenstown [Cobh] a port of call after the Cunard company had decided to abandon the Irish town as a port of call – with handwritten comment by Elsie:

'Sir Roger Casement has put his ideas through. He was speaking of it at Ardglass when the Cunard Co. refused to come into Queenstown Harbour, on the plea that it was not deep enough for their boats. Winston Churchill visited it in Spring and declared it large and deep enough for the biggest dreadnoughts of the British navy.'

WEDNESDAY 10 DECEMBER 1913

Annual meeting of the I.A.O.S., Father Finlay[34] in the chair, Sir Horace Plunkett in America.

Professor Yendo came to dinner. He grows seaweed as an economic asset, food, gelatine, manure, etc. for the Japanese Government, and apparently increases the area of the country by filling the sea up with rocks and covering them with wealth producing seaweed. He has every social and philosophic problem under the sun and [has] written a treatise on Suffrage from the Biological point of view. He declares that no one should receive a vote except a married couple, for the unit of the state is a married couple. Either faction having been in prison, or not having completed the educational curriculum of the country, should be deprived of the vote. And in no case should it be given to man or woman separately.

SUNDAY 14 DECEMBER 1913

Aunt Alice arrived. Augustine went for the weekend to Lord and Lady Headfort at Headfort, Kells. Aunt Alice's first dinner party was there.[35] The party was 13, so the carriage was sent back for her. In those days the menu was handed round, and she saw 'Duck' and pointed to that, and was then covered with confusion because she saw other people had chosen other things first, and that 'they did not bring around the last dish first because you chose it'! The Lady Headfort of that time had been a girl in a china shop, and ran away because her master beat her. She went to sea as a stewardess, and everyone fell in love with her. She married 3 times, the second man was a MacNaughten in the Indian army. There had been a rising in the hills and the Indians cut off the retreat of MacNaughten and his men. He was killed, and they cut off his head and carried it to where his wife was staying and threw it into her carriage while she was out driving. The sergeant who brought her home lived at Kells, and used to relate the story to the Stopfords. Aunt Alice heard it from him. The treasures in Headfort House delighted the Stopford children; silver and gold, and a silver four-post bed, presents from Indian princes. The doors and floors were mahogany, brought back as ballast from the West Indies, by ships exporting Irish slaves in 1750.

MONDAY 15 DECEMBER 1913

Augustine went to a doctor this morning with an unaccountable pain in his arm, and a fine sewing needle was extracted from his arm-pit, after a possible residence of many years. Horas Kennedy[36] suggests it might be congenital.

Professor MacNeil [*sic*] to dinner and AE, to meet Aunt Alice. MacNeil [*sic*] said he gave the meeting 'too strong a dose' in asking for cheers for the Ulster Volunteers, though this had been quite successful at other meetings. At the first disturbance all the reporters, but one, took flight, and apparently ran home to write up this lurid account. The chairman[37] was locally unpopular, and the rowdy element seized the excuse to fall upon him. He sat firmly in his chair behind the table, but the table was on castors, and under pressure began to run. It ran over him and knocked him and his chair clear to the ground, and when he was recovering himself he was thumped on the head. But the uproar subsided very rapidly and nobody paid the slightest attention to either Mr McNeil [*sic*] or R.C. [Roger Casement]

Letter from Eoin MacNeill from Herbert Park Dublin to Elsie,
15 December 1913 –
'Dear Mrs Henry,
I shall go very gladly to dine with you and Mrs Green this evening. Sir Roger has stayed in Cork to interview the important people about the Hamburg-Amerika steamers, and is not likely to leave Cork today. He is staying at the Imperial hotel there. Neither Sir Roger nor I was hustled or assaulted, and after the disturbance the meeting was resumed, and an excellent speech was made by Sir Roger, and about 700 young men gave their names as volunteers.

Yours faithfully,
Eóin MacNéill'

18 DECEMBER 1913

Augustine returned from Kerry 4.45 a.m. Aunt [Alice], Sir Roger Casement and John MacNeil at lunch. They are worried that the Government has withdrawn an Irish Post Office from the [Home Rule] Bill, especially as there cannot have been time to get the agreement of the House of Lords, and a Bill must go up a third time in precisely the same form as the first time. Sir Roger is also anxious that the Foreign Office may step in to make Germany refuse to send the N.G. Lloyd Alice ships to Queenstown, although that company has already accepted. He is out now for a French line to call at Belfast and take the pilgrimages direct to Lourdes.

Captain White was to have come, but didn't.

SUNDAY 11 JANUARY 1914

To visit Mr and Mrs T.P.Gill[38] at Kingstown [Dun Laoghaire] and then to Sir William and Miss Barrett.[39] Sir W. reminiscent of an Irish instrument maker, Lambert, who was the finest mechanic in Grubb's works.[40] He made an instrument for Sir William which he used at a lecture before the Society of Engineers in London. Lord Kelvin was in the chair; he examined the instrument and said 'Was the maker an Irishman', 'He was', 'I thought so' exclaimed Lord K. 'Only an Irishman could have done it!'.

Lambert presided at an amnesty meeting for the release of the Fenians; now Grubb was an uncompromising Orangeman [sic],[41] and although Lambert was the best mechanic in his works, he dismissed him. Sir W. took him on at the College of Science. He worked hard in the cause of the Fenians and never took one penny. He told Sir William that he himself it was who made the keys that opened the prison doors when James Stephens escaped.

THURSDAY 22 JANUARY 1914

A meeting at Mrs Connolly Norman's[42] house on the Research Defence Society,[43] addressed by Mr Laurence Steele, supported by Prof. Thompson (TCD) and Dr Fitzgerald,[44] a very picturesque old man. He has a great friend, Dr. Yeo who had been a pupil of Ludwig, and told him that Ludwig wrote an atrocious bad hand, so much so that a letter he sent von Helmholtz was utterly illegible. Von H. put it into an envelope and sent it back to Ludwig who was so distressed that he got a teacher and laboured at copybook writing until he wrote a beautiful hand. He was quite old when this occurred. L. Steele gave an admirable address, ending with the remarks that the one last field to be conquered was cancer, that the research is being carried on at the moment with mice, and putting it to the other side, Mice or Men? The meeting listened with breathless interest to the snake-bite poison experiments, begun by L.B. and Sir Joseph Fayrer, and delayed on the point of completion, for nearly 20 years by the anti-vivisection agitation, Sir J. Fayrer dying in the meantime, the experiments were finished by L.B. and Dr. Leonard Rogers.

FRIDAY 23 JANUARY 1914

Dined with Lady Ardilaun[45] at the Hibernian Hotel – 20 present including Dr and Mrs Douglas Hyde, Colonel and Mrs Guinness, Mr (Mrs and Miss) Napoleon Wyse [sic],[46] Mr Headlam, etc. Afterwards to Alexandra College to hear Cannon [sic] Hannay ('George Bermingham')[47] on 'American women' and mighty complimentary he was to them, comparing their easy and on-coming good manners to the gauche shyness of women on this side. Miss Pim who knows America well, said she could picture the scene repeated at each feminine interview 'Why Cannon Hannay, how quite too luvly [sic] yew [sic] are'!

A series of charming tableaux taken from Hugh Thomson's *Pride and Prejudice*, and acted with great charm and vivacity by the girls of the College, might almost have been taken as the 'retort courteous'.

SUNDAY 25 JANUARY 1914

To Croydon Park to see Captain White drill: a good display of 70 men, drilling with sticks. Captain White has had as many as 600 out, but this was only the picked ones for a slow drill, as he is trying to get money for boots for the men. What is it among so many? 15,000 men out on strike.

MONDAY 26 JANUARY 1914

Aunt Angel [Bickerdike] was talking of her family and youth. She was called Angel after one of the beautiful Misses Wray, who had been called after Angelica Kauffmann. There were seven sisters Wray of Ards near

Letterkenny. They all married into the best families in Ireland, and two of them married Stopfords, and Anne was the mother of the [blank] Stopford who became Archdeacon of Armagh and afterwards Bishop of Meath. After they were married they began life at Killybegs in a white house and all his children were born there and afterwards moved to Armagh. Their son Edward Adderly Stopford was an inseparable friend to his father, and was rector of Caledon only twelve miles from his father. He married Ann Duke, whose mother was a Park.

Their eldest son John George Stopford was called after his father's greatest friend, the Primate, John George Beresford.

Angel, and when she was christened, her grandfather sent a car 12 miles to say 'Her name is to be Angel'.

Robert, who was called the 'lily of the north', having red hair.

Edward Adderly Stopford.

When she was four years old her grandfather was made Bishop of Meath, and insisted on E.A. Stopford accompanying him. But E.A.S. was broken-hearted at leaving his parish in the north and Aunt Angel says he never ceased to regret his northern parish, and the parishioners so sad at his going, they turned out in full force and followed his carriage out of the parish, as though it had been his funeral. They had a wing of a house at Ardbracken, and they were there one year during which was born

Elizabeth

(Aunt Angel says that one year was the happiest of her own life.) Then E.A.S. was made Archdeacon, and they all moved to Kells where were born

Jemmett

Alice

Louisa Jane

James, who died at 8 months

James T.A.

They left Kells in 1881. E.A. Stopford resigned from ill-health.

Aunt Angel's first dinner party was in London at the Primate's (J.G. Beresford). She was 17 and wore a white muslin dress and was delighted! She had strawberries at dessert, and the butler poured champagne and then handed round ice to put in it, but the ice bewildered Angel who put it among her strawberries and then realized that wasn't the place for it from the look on the face of the butler.

The Archdeacon introduced weaving into Kells when he first went there, gave them looms and teachers, but it all fell through because they wouldn't take any interest.

WEDNESDAY 28 JANUARY 1914

Sir Roger Casement came. Very pleased with the progress of the National Volunteers, after a very representative meeting in Limerick. Very full of the German Steamship Co. and their failure to call at Queenstown,[48] the last excuse given being that there were not sufficient bookings beforehand. He says they have been distinctly told by the Foreign Office that they are not to come; and that if Sir Roger published the whole facts of the case from the beginning, he would raise such a storm of indignation both here and in America, that he would wreck the 'Anglo-Saxon Alliance' Great Britain is so anxious to work up with America.

THURSDAY 29 JANUARY 1914

Aunt Elizabeth[49] came. She tells a story of Aunt Angel when they were at Kells. Angel visited among the poor, and one old woman bewailed that she had no faith, for she read in the Bible that the hairs of the head are numbered – and she was quite bald. Angel wrote to her aunts, Alicia and Anne, and asked if they could find any wig of their mothers, and send it to her. They [found] an old wig; and Angel took it to the old woman whose faith was enabled to grow again.

Letter from Lauder Brunton in London to Elsie, 25 January 1914 –
He is 'arranging all mother's letters to me and mine to her ... a somewhat
sad occupation yet ... it brings back to me the pleasures of the past.'

[TUESDAY 3 FEBRUARY 1914]
Lecture by Mr Alec Wilson son of one of the first four partners [of
Harland and Wolff] on Belfast ship-building at the RDS [Royal Dublin
Society]. Really magnificent slides by Mr Welsh. To tea afterwards at
the Cafe Cairo with Mr and Mrs Ll. Praeger,[50] Mr A. Wilson, Dr Scharf
[*sic*][51] and Prof. Wilson.[52]

MONDAY 16 FEBRUARY 1914
The White Star Line *Arabic* came into Queenstown Harbour about 2 on
Sunday 15th; berthed the harbour, took up passengers and sailed out.
The Cunard liner *Carminia* came half an hour later and sat outside the
harbour in a choppy sea; the tender with all the English and Irish mails
and passengers on board waited for nearly four hours, at the end of
which time it suddenly sailed away to America, leaving them all sitting.

The German Hamburg Amerika line did <u>not</u> call on Feb.12th, owing
to their representative having been sent for to Berlin, and subsequent to
this they briefly stated that they could have nothing further to do with
the project of calling at Queenstown! The *Irish Times* contains three
columns from Sir R. Casement giving a résumé of the whole from the
beginning.

1.p.m. Sir R.C. to lunch, having come straight from London where he
left Aunt Alice 'beautifully dressed' going to lunch with Lord Haldane,[53]
who had sent for her specifically to pick her brains about Ireland and
the Home Rule Bill. Sir R.C. full of the Queenstown business, he says he
is going to America to make things hum; that England is giving Home
Rule to Ireland largely on account of the Irish-American majority on

the other side, and to draw their vote in favour of the Anglo-Saxon alliance. They are now shaving the Bill of any of its value, and if it is proved to the Irish-Americans what is going on, and the treatment of Ireland as per the Cunard Co., the Irish-American majority will wreck the Anglo-Saxon alliance on the other side, which is a matter of vital interest to both Government <u>and</u> Opposition as it is a policy of Empire.

TUESDAY 17 FEBRUARY 1914
Augustine went to Belfast to give a lecture to the Field Club, on the 'History of Woods and Trees in Ireland'.

FRIDAY 20 FEBRUARY 1914
Lunched at the Homestead office. AE has re-painted the walls with glorious figures in blue and gold and silver garments, with gold flames and gold torches and a tropical wood behind. The Temple of the crocodile is faintly discernible through the forest foliage, where the tiny boy erstwhile rode the crocodile across the top of the cupboard which has since been transformed into the Homestead Larder. AE is absent with a bad cold in his chest.

Letter from AE, from 17 Rathgar Ave to Elsie [n.d.], apologising for missing the lunch engagement and to thank her for the pineapple.

SATURDAY 21 FEBRUARY 1914
To dinner Sir Roger [Casement], Mr and Mrs Praeger, Mrs. Dobele, Uncle Ned, and Susan Mitchell afterwards, also Prof. Macalister.[54]

Mrs Praeger was telling Miss Mitchell that she and the Creightons (friends) took a house one summer at Glenade, Leitrim, that had formerly belonged to Miss Mitchell's mother's family. They had left it because it was 'full of ghosts'. Mrs Praeger was telling her that her party had found it very ghosty and full of noises and she added, 'one of them saw a white bird fly out of the window'. Susan gave a gasp. 'That is our family ghost', she said.

SUNDAY 22 FEBRUARY 1914
Augustine, I and Praegers out by train to Tallaght, and along the Dodder, it was in spate, and the weather was wild, a hurricane of wind, rain and later snow.

MONDAY 23 FEBRUARY 1914
Exhibition of pictures by Jack Yeats[55] in Merrion Hall – Sea-scapes, and landscapes in Kerry. Miss Purser introduced us to Jane Barlow – of the Irish [Idylls], a sweet fragile lady in black, with a gentle face and large gentle blue eyes. Miss Purser met Mother years ago at Mrs. Merrit's house, and Mother said to her 'I am so glad to meet you as myself, not as my husband's wife or my sister's sister'.

The barometer went down yesterday further than has been recorded before, and in one case ran clean down beyond the recording figures altogether. The Wexford lifeboat was lost on Friday going out to the wreck of the French ship; the lifeboatmen were on a tiny island with nothing to eat but cockles, and had to keep walking day and night to keep alive, but were rescued on Sunday.

TUESDAY 24 FEBRUARY 1914
Sir Roger came in after attending the All-Ireland meeting of protest at the Mansion House. He saw Baron von Horst in London and the Hamburg-Amerika line are taking up the line that they are greatly disappointed but still hope to come, when they can get over objections raised by the White Star and Cunard Lines, thus putting it on purely commercial grounds, although the representative of the H-A line was

sent for to Berlin and told by the Kaiser that England had intimated that their coming would be regarded as an Unfriendly Act!!

The Foreign Office has been openly accused of direct intervention, in the American papers, but has not denied it, although it is a deadly accusation in the face of the Anglo-Saxon Alliance they are working for. Sir R. talked of his mission to Delagosa Bay during the Boer War, while Lord Salisbury was Prime Minister, of what it was wished he would say, of what he really did say, and how only Lord S. in the whole Home Government would agree with him when he came home and told them he had really saved them from making fools of themselves and the country.

He spoke of the Congo and Putomayo, and how he had taken up the question of the Congo natives on his own initiative, with no instructions, and how Mr. (now Lord) Emmott[56] and Herbert Samuel[57] had backed him up to begin with, Lord E. to the end, H.S. only as long as he could figure as the pioneer of a righteous cause; then he dropped it. Sir R. has never put faith in H.S. and now he has justified it by his parting thrust on the Cunard business, just as he was retiring.

The cyclone indicated by Sunday's barometer was in Switzerland, the wind blowing 140 miles per hour.

WEDNESDAY 25 FEBRUARY 1914

With Kitty McCormack to Bray to see St John Whitty's[58] furniture factory, now running about 10 yrs. Mr Wilson in his lecture on Feb. 4th [sic] said he looked forward to the time when Irish people would be sending in Irish designs for interior decoration of the Harland and Wolff's boats. Kitty was keen when she heard, and the Dun Eamer guild have rugs, curtains, tapestries and stools; and now St John is keen, and she can do panelling, carving, furniture. She and Kitty are to work out designs together and see what can be done.

She has done the organ woodwork and iron railing work for Bray church, and [a] very good woodwork screen in the chancel of Christchurch.

In the morning to Glasnevin Bot. Gardens, for photographing the original golden yew from which have been taken all other golden yews. Sir Frederick Moore[59] said his father, Dr. Moore could remember it and that it probably dates from about 1800, the founding of the Garden.

SUNDAY 1 MARCH 1914

Walked from Tallaght to Enniskerry over the Feather-bed Pass and by Glencree reformatory. Took 5 hours. A brilliant glowing day, with strong wind behind us, and occasional hail storms, vivid colours. A view right over Dublin Bay and [Harbour], and across the plains N.[North] to the Mourne mountains, all at once ... Coming round on Glencree there rush into view Kippure (hidden in hail), Maulin, the Duffs, Slieve Cullen (the Sugar-loaf) and Bray, the sea sparkling and opalescent. The pool of sea under Bray Head is always more opalescent than anywhere else.

Postcard of Poulaphuca from [Douglas Hyde] to Elsie, 1 March 1914 – 'A great many thanks for the brochure on the [Cunarders] and their fellows. Its a pity that the "German Boar-hound" has been warned off. I wonder who wrote the pamphlet – was it really an American?'.

FRIDAY 6 MARCH 1914

St John Whitty came and stayed to dinner to meet Mr Forbes[60] and discuss possibilities of procuring timber, Irish, from the Department [forest] stations, etc. for her.

Sunday 8 March 1914

Mr Phillips here for the week-end. He and I and Augustine to Bray. Rattled to and fro and up and down the shingly beach between Bray and Woodbrook, in search of the submerged forest. But the tide was not really a spring tide, and though armed with two maps, and written instructions, no forest appeared for to be dug up with the garden trowel, brought for the purpose. And the tide that was not a spring tide came up and covered our labours, so we hied ourselves to Dundrum to see the Crosbies[61] and discuss the crossing of trees with Miss Crosbie ...

Saturday 14 March 1914

Father's 70th birthday. Family dinner in the evening. Col. Stopford,[62] Mrs. Green, Mrs Jemmett Stopford,[63] Robert, Jim Blaikie, Betty Blaikie, Top, Ted, Nance, I and A. [Augustine], and Harriet [Jaffé]. Edie[64] and Dorothy[65] afterwards. Family bowl presented. Uncle Jack came in like heavy artillery with the news that George had been given 3 weeks to make up his mind whether he would fight against Ulster or send in his resignation from the army.[66]

Father ... Talking about quinine he remembered the time when the Spaniards cut down all the cinchona trees in Mexico and sent up the price of quinine in Europe to 16/- an ounce, about 1880; and Perkins, whom he knew, set about to work to try and make it synthetically, and failed, but came upon the discovery of aniline dyes. He could not get enough money to work them, so it was Germany who stepped in there.

Tuesday 17 March 1914

St Patrick's Day. Wedding [anniversary] day. Sybil here, pedestrian celebration over Bray Head.

FRIDAY 27 MARCH 1914

To Kingstown with Sybil to see Aunt Lily who goes to Derry tomorrow to stay with Hugh, and hopes she may get there and back alive. Kingstown harbour very lively; two men of war just outside. We walked to the end of the jetty and watched busy motor launches full of officials whizzing to land from the ships; but no one could tell us the names of the ships, or give any information.

SATURDAY 28 MARCH 1914

One hour after we left Kingstown in came the *Firefly* and the *Pathfinder* with Sybil's friend Capt. Martin [Leake] in command![67]

30 MARCH 1914

Sir Roger Casement came in about 11 and sat conversing till 3; he had just come back from Belfast, and had found there 54 war correspondents of foreign journals – a greater number than had assembled anywhere since the Boer War. He of the *Vossische Zeitung* had left Berlin at 20 minutes notice. He had said can I not go home for my toothbrush (?). The *Vossische Zeitung* replied 'If you do not catch this very next train you will be too late to get into Belfast before the siege begins'. So there they are all arrived, and there was 'Nothing doing'. Unto [sic] them Sir Roger and they, panting for copy, interviewed him in turn, and he gave them the proper Home Rule views and was thus able to communicate them to every country in Europe through its most respected organ.

Lady Shaw of Bushey Park has a cousin in command of a regiment, who declared he would never go against Ulster. She opened her paper one morning and saw he was stationed in Belfast; so she wrote and reproached him. He replied that no one was so surprised as himself to find himself there. He had been ordered to embark his regiment at Kingstown, and they had sailed under sealed orders. Night fell, and when daylight disclosed the scene, they were in Belfast! This is what the *Pathfinder* and *Firefly* were doing.

Letter from Alice Stopford Green from London to Elsie, 31 March 1914 –

'I was in the House yesterday at that extraordinary scene of Seely[68] resigning and Asquith[69] leaving the House. The situation looks to me graver every day and I should not wonder if the Tories succeeded in driving out the Liberals. However, the Liberal benches are crammed and are very enthusiastic, and the Tories are I am told uneasy at their own position and are afraid of an appeal to the country. Nobody can look forward for a few hours as things are now ... My love to Augustine, and I am, Your very affectionate and devoted ASG'

Top and I went down to his [Hubert von Herkomer] studio at Bushey Park at Xmas to see his portrait of Father. He had not been well, but was in very good spirits ... He did not want to alter a stroke in the painting saying that the personality and the portrait had interested him very much, and he considered the result very good; but he said as Father really wished it, he would re-model the hands, and Father must give him another sitting. But Father's health prevented it while Herkomer was still able.

SATURDAY 11 APRIL – SATURDAY 18 APRIL 1914

To Sea View, Glencormac, Bray (Mrs Heatley). When we left there were 10 people including old Mr. and Mrs. Nicholls. He said he had met us at the O'Farrelly's, and fell upon us warmly. He presently complained about a lady who had our room the year before – 'an English lady, who having married a colonel, thought nobody was good enough for her'.

SATURDAY 18 APRIL 1914
Crossed to London.

SUNDAY 19 APRIL 1914
At home Father, Nance, Aunt Helen and Ellie.

MONDAY 20 APRIL 1914
To Harriet's week-end cottage by motor (Chipsted), stopping at the James Allen School, Dulwich, for Nance to direct gardeners.

WEDNESDAY 22 APRIL 1914
Father and Aunt Helen to the Private View of the Academy. Quite pleased with the appearance of portrait. Aunt Helen came home with the remark 'There were no two people in the whole place I admired more than ourselves'.

FRIDAY 24 APRIL 1914
Aunt Alice arrived to breakfast. To the 'Homestead' office. AE out being sculped [sic], but Susan, Lord Selbourne and Sir Horace [Plunkett] buzzing round a portrait of Sir H. which AE is painting. AE and Miss O'Farrelly[70] in this evening. Very dismal talk on the Situation.

Letter from Augustine Henry in Dublin to Elsie, 3 May 1914 –
'I was glad to get your letter, and am now writing after all sorts of excitements – Aunt Alice spoke at her meeting [of Irish Women's Council], newspaper account enclosed. I went to the Abbey Theatre Ulster play ... Susan Mitchell has been in with her new poem in *Statesman*[71] ... she sang it to Sir Roger C. and to me a few minutes ago.'

WEDNESDAY 24 [JUNE] 1914

Alice and May Wordsworth[72] are staying with the Stopfords. May is 3½. She was asked where Uncle Ned was one day; she replied joyfully 'Uncle Ned is at the public house' (Uncle Ned spends his days at the Plunkett House).

FRIDAY 26 [JUNE] 1914

Augustine to Scotland, to Capt. Stirling [for the Royal Scottish Aboricultural Society diamond jubilee excursion].

Letter from Augustine Henry from Scotland to Elsie, 29 June 1914 –
'We heard this morning about the shocking assassinations at Sarajevo, which may have bad effects for European peace …'.

SATURDAY 4 JULY 1914

Aunt Alice arrived 11pm.

Sir Roger has gone on the 'long journey'.[73]

SUNDAY 5 JULY 1914

Dillon[74] told Eoin MacNeil [sic] lately that a charge had been made against an organizer of the N. [National] Volunteers that he had spoken against England i.e. Empire. MacNeil [sic] answered, 'As far as the charge of speaking in this manner goes, this is the charge that has been and is being made against you by all the Tories in England, and in the second place we have no organizer'. With that the conversation dropped.

MacNeil [sic] told the party[75] months ago that Dillon wd. be the steadfast opposer of the Volunteers and told them to watch his movements. Dillon has already broken everything wh. he did not control. He broke the financial movement of 1896 the most promising movement that ever arose, in uniting Unionists and Nationalists. He drove Hely [Healy][76] out of the party. He drove O'Brien[77] out of the party. He fought the co-operative movement, and now he is fighting the Volunteer movement. He has now no hold on Ireland except through London and the party.

Redmond[78] is not the real leader of the party. He has probably the best brains, but he has not the willing power and he is simply driven where Dillon and Devlin[79] wish. If he had kept in touch with Ireland and the party had known the people and had faith in them, they wd. never have made the concessions of exclusion [of Ulster from Home Rule] of March 9th. The Volunteers were well in existence, the country was alive and the party knew nothing of it. Redmond wd. have been safe then if he had announced that he would consider any amendments within Home Rule, but nothing whatever outside it. He should never for one instant, if he had believed in the country, have accepted Exclusion.

He [Redmond] came over for a fortnight at Whitsuntide, hid himself in his Wicklow place, went to a dinner at Clongoes [sic] College[80] and to one other similar function, but did not venture on a meeting with his fellow-countrymen, and he wd. not dare to do so now, he has his party behind him, but he and they know that the country is not behind them.

The attempt is being now made to bring the Irish Volunteers under the same wooden discipline under which the party has been so long drilled; it will be interesting to see how far the non-democratic methods which have succeeded in a small organization, will succeed with a body of men who have for the first time brought forward the idea of the People of Ireland. One of the extreme party describes it as the 'lady who went out to ride on the tiger'. It will be a conflict between the double powers of organization represented by the financial system of the party and the Hibernian system of Devlin set against the new popular and democratic spirit of Ireland.

Much hostility has been awakened in America by Redmond's request for funds to be collected on the old party system and paid through the old party Treasurer. How will these funds be used? How can Redmond, head of the Constitutional Party, having violently seized the headship of the Volunteers supply them with rifles contrary to the Proclamation? How can he account for the money if he does not give rifles? His aim will doubtless be to pay a host of organizers and in this way seek to attach a party in the Volunteers, to himself.

He objected to the old Provisional Committee [of the Irish Volunteers] on the ground that it had too many residents in Dublin, not representative of the country, eleven of the twenty-five he adds are resident in Dublin mostly quite unknown. Half of the whole number are unknown to Irishmen generally, of the other half that might be taken to be more or less representative, four are Archbishops and clergy, and three are M.P.s. The additional twenty-five that he proposes are a tri-partite body elected by himself, Devlin and Dillon, in equal parts, but in no conceivable way representative of the country. (There has been considerable rivalry between the Foresters and the Hibernians;[81] it will be well to watch the Foresters in future developments.)

WEDNESDAY 8 JULY 1914

Mrs. Green is very anxious, expecting news that doesn't come. Monday night at 1a.m. a terrific knocking at the front door, and a postman with a telegram from the G.P.O. for Mrs. Green. The telegram was given in at 7p.m. in England and delivered here at 1.a.m. The delay en route can be ominously accounted for, knowing the system of post office espionage. The yacht is expected at Cowes and is two days late and there is no news.

AE came in the evening and talked till 11.30. He wrote out this poem for Mrs. Green; he says 'The Catholic clergy oppress the laity and the Protestant laity oppress the clergy.' He rolled out the story of the Mahabaratta with enthusiasm, saying that only in Judaism and

Celtic mythology did you find the same 'enobling' ideas, the individual with the sense of being part of a majestic Whole; as opposed to the Greek individualistic idealism … he longs to write a treatise on the Gods of Poets and has parodied the poems on God of Yeats,[82] Francis Thompson,[83] and James Stephens – the latter beginning 'Hi, God, get off that throne', James Stephens was shocked, but AE said laughing, that each poet after hearing the parodies, left off writing poems on God.

THURSDAY 9 JULY 1914

Aunt Alice left for Belfast. An hour before she went a telegram came to say that all was well. Mr. de Montmorency came in this morning and he and Aunt Alice confabbed anxiously. He was asked to resign from the Naval and Military Club[84] on account of being a Nationalist. He refused, whereupon he was told that if he did not resign, his name would be struck off the list. He wrote to the King, as being the most important member of the Club, and pointed out the flagrant injustice. Nothing more has been said to him about resigning, and three weeks has elapsed so he is 'waiting to see'.

SUNDAY 12 JULY 1914

Augustine returned from Scotland.

MONDAY 13 JULY 1914

Mr Robinson, New Zealand representative to the Scottish Arboratorial trip came. He is head of the Forestry in New Zealand.

Letter from Elsie's cousin Dorothy Stopford, written from Ardrie, Antrim Rd., Belfast [city home of F.J. Bigger] to Elsie, 14 July 1914 –
'My dear Elsie.

I write to save Aunt Alice. It is so interesting here – on Sat we saw the colours presented to the Belfast Regiment of the Irish Volunteers – a fine regiment who did wonders after only 2 months drill – on Sun we motored to Ardglass – and saw the castle and all there; I now realize how lucky it was I did not follow my telegram there! It is about 40 miles away from here! The 12th was kept on the 13th and so we motor [*sic*] down yest. [yesterday] and saw the procession go by – Most orderly and the big drums were grand – and you could see the effect drilling has had on the populace to a marked degree, the difference between a layman's walk and the military tramp and carriage of those who were [Ulster] volunteers. Don't believe the accounts in the papers of the dangerous state of the city – we can see no difference, the 12th celebrations seem to have passed off very quietly and except for the crowds yest. there has been no sign of unrest as far as one can see. Everything seems exactly as usual and the Volcanoe [*sic*] on which we are told we are sitting at present shows no sign of itself. The order and quiet are amazing. Aunt Alice heard from Cowes – all well so far, but not since. If you are in touch with Nance (I believe you are in London) tell her that John [Bigger?] ran away 10 days ago, and has married a girl from the Slade school – Nance will be interested, I believe his family are very much distressed.

With love to Nance and yourself and many thanks for your kind hospitality which I fear I used rather cavalierly – but enjoyed never the less very much,

Your loving Dorothy.

Buy a *Daily News* tomorrow for article which Aunt A[Alice] is now writing in her shirtsleeves. P.S. I left some books at your house which I will pick up on my way back.'

TUESDAY 15 [14] JULY 1914

Dined with Miss Pim and Miss Constance Pim[85] to meet Mr. and Mrs. Standish O'Grady.[86] He very keen on Fourrier's Socialism.[87] He thinks as far as the present moment goes, that the time of Parliaments is over. He says only certain conditions in the world history can ever be governed by parliaments, then come vital crises when Force is the only referendum and the Army becomes all powerful and you get a Dictatorship. Probably with the termination of the lifetime of the strong man, events have settled down again to a condition to be governed by committee, i.e. parliament. Standish O'Grady thinks the moment for this is again approaching. We have no very strong man except Kitchener[88] – we may have him as Dictator yet!

WEDNESDAY 15 JULY 1914
Crossed to London.

Letter from Paul Heger[89], at Ixelles, Rue Des Drapiers 23, Brussels to Elsie, 14 juillet 1914 –
'I'm following what's happening in Ireland in the papers as fervently as Mr. Carlson [Carson][90] himself, and I see you have time to arrive before the revolution erupts. I'm going to do my best to make sure that events oblige you to stay in Brussels!'

THURSDAY 16 JULY 1914
Dr John Mitchell, son of Weir Mitchell[91] and his daughter May came to lunch. Owen Wister[92] is Dr. Mitchell's first cousin and his wife having died six months ago, they are travelling together in Europe.

FRIDAY 17 JULY 1914
Professor Ker[93] came to tea and repeated with gusto the Glasgow toast 'Here's to us, Whae's like us? Damned few!' Father recounted to Mrs. Mitchell his case of a Glasgow stockbroker who fell from his horse, and lost seven years of memory.

SATURDAY 18 JULY 1914

Arrived in Brussells [*sic*] 9.10 a.m. Professor Heger at the station to meet us, and his two daughters Madame Péchère and Madame Beckers received us at his house … after lunch M. Péchère and his two little boys came in. M. Péchère was asking Augustine about the state of Ireland and Augustine was replying, 'It appears very calm on the surface, but there is a volcano underneath' … Has turned out of his own suite, bedroom, bathroom and study, for us, he is never tired of arranging something interesting for us, and is the very kindest and most charming host ever born.

SUNDAY 19 JULY 1914

Motored out to Groenendaal[94] in the morning … we all met for lunch under the trees … Such a gay, cheery lunch, and so pretty under the trees … After lunch we drove again and visited the Musée Colonial, i.e. Congo, and returned home in the evening about 6.

MONDAY 20 JULY 1914

Prof. Heger took Augustine to the Solway Scientific Institute of which he is Director, and Augustine then went to the Natural History Museum … Madame Péchère took me to the Picture Gallery and was most interesting … Brussells [*sic*] is being completely changed and very beautifully laid out, and Prof. Heger attributes all the improvements to King Leopold, who was especially fond of parks, and doing landscape gardening.

TUESDAY 21 JULY 1914

This is the Fête Nationale,[95] and everybody was out in the streets enjoying themselves. We saw the King [Albert I] with his two boys pass on his way to a distribution of prizes … At Court St. Etienne, the

Comte Goblet d'Alviella[96] met us and took us to his Chateau de Court St. Etienne. Mde. la Comtesse is American, they have a son married, and a young daughter about 6 ft 4 or 5 with dark hair and very blue eyes, a markedly Irish type, quite unlike either father or mother. In the course of conversation it came out that she had a great admiration for Irish writers, especially Synge's *Playboy of the Western World*.[97] The Comte is professor of comparative religions (Principes de l'Evolution réligieuse) at the University, and is also a keen archaeologist … Augustine has had a huge success since [we] arrived … At 4 they sent us to the station. Prof. Heger accompanied us all the way to Brussels, drove us to the Gare du Nord and let us in a back way, so that we escaped collision with the London Lord Mayor who arrived just as we left.

WEDNESDAY 22 JULY 1914

Arrived at Stratford Place 8 a.m. After tea called at the Phillimores, Carn House, Campden Hill. Lord Justice Phillimore[98] gave Aug. 2 seedlings of cork oak from about 18 which he raised himself from seed brought from Rhonda, Spain.

The Conference called by the King [George V] at Buckingham Palace to consider the Irish situation and a rapprochement, has failed.[99]

Letter from Augustine on RMS Leinster [on his way to Leeds] to Elsie, 'Monday morning' [27 July 1914], RMS Leinster and annotated 'Private' in the margin –

'Dearest Elsie.

I wrote you last night and doubtless the papers will have given you an account of the gun-running business and the subsequent massacre in the streets.[100]

Aunt Alice arrived about 7.00 pm, preceded by a telegram, that I found on my return from Dalkey with Mr. O'Beirne about 6pm. Immediately after Miss Spring Rice[101] came in, seeking Aunt Alice and she stayed on here for supper and for the night. She was very tired – as she apparently was the lady who steered the yacht that brought the guns. Dorothy Stopford doubtless knows all about it and she will tell you of the incidents precedent.

I left this morning before either Aunt Alice or the other lady were awake. Aunt Alice will remain in Dublin till at any rate I return on Friday … It is better for you to follow our programme: go to Birds and return to Dublin in week following. I go to Muckross this day week and stay possibly till Wednesday evening in that week or till Thursday evening in that week …

I gave you last night my opinion on the crisis: it cannot go on as Asquith can't yield permission to Nat. Volunteers to arm and Redmond will be called on now to leave him, if he doesn't let the Volunteers arm.

In view of the fact that the police will probably not interfere with the Volunteers – and that there is dissension in the ranks of the soldiers: it is possible that pressure will be put by King on Redmond and Carson to agree to something – and that might end the situation: but it is unlikely. On the whole however the betting is that Asquith will dissolve parliament inside a fortnight. Carson has all the cards, as his people are disciplined: and he may refuse even to give in in the slightest to Bonar Law[102] and company.

What is very sad is the stupidity of the people on the Nat. [Nationalist] side who did not recognise the force of Ulster and tried to arrange something. Biggar is now writing letters that he should have written two years ago [In margin: letters of friendship to Ulster]. The Nationalists have no statesmen whatever – no person to look ahead – no one to lead. Asquith and Co are of the same calibre and are not up to Carson's 'form', in the language of the ring.

It will be nice to see you again. If O'Beirne hadn't come in just before lunch, I was on the point of going out to the offices and would have seen

45

the whole gun-running business … Aunt Alice missed the landing of the guns, owing to being misinformed – the fact is it was well managed: only it was made too "melodramatic" the landing ought to have been done in the evening, at night and all encounter with soldiers might have been avoided. There are very prominent people [involved] in the affair; but I don't care to give any information in a letter, which is of course likely to be seen – not that I know much more than I have told you.

I will send you the Irish papers of this morning from Leeds to Stratford Place. Good-bye. I love you very much and <u>miss you</u>. The key of the cellar is unknown to Annie or Mary, but I dare say Aunt Alice will find it out. I was able to produce a bottle of white wine and there was quite a nice supper for <u>three</u>, although neither they nor I expected any one … There was beef (cold), [beautiful] salad … and a bottle of graves! The poor lady who had been on the yacht appeared at dinner in a smart red petticoat, as evidently she was soaked through. Good-bye again.

Kindest regards to your father, who evidently need not be told everything …

Augustine'

Note from J.G.B. [James] Stopford to Elsie, 27 July 1914 –
It thanks her for a present and commented, 'I see I see the govt. has managed at last to get some blood in Ireland but it is not the kind they wanted. Protestant blood was what they were after'.

Postcard from Alice Stopford Green to Elsie, [27 July 1914] –
'Mary Spring Rice spent last night here [the Henry home in Ranelagh]. <u>Very</u> well and extremely sorry not to see you – admired house and garden much. "It's an honourable thing to be a hayro [*sic*]", said the cook as she got the hot bath. All going well I stay here till Saturday morning. Then away on a Barrow train with Mr. Bigger. We are not uneasy about the situation. Volunteers are getting in good discipline. A.S.G.'

MONDAY AND TUESDAY 27–28 JULY 1914

Stayed at Wire Mill, Stewart, May, Agnes and John at home.[103] Agnes and John on the lake among the water lilies and swans and grebes; and singing and playing delightedly at the piano. Stewart spraying infant apple trees. What a peaceful contrast.

Letter from Paul Heger in Brussels to Elsie and Augustine Henry, 27 July 1914 –

'How can I avoid discussing our new worries with you? It is the immediate prospect of war; I've just read that our soldiers are being called up. Will your great country, so recently peaceful, be able to use its influence to stop a European war? I really fear that the folly of the people will bring us to the abyss once more. If this must happen, the days spent with you walking through the forests around us will have been the last weeks of our peaceful dream and of our illusion. They would close an era of our lives very poetically.'

WEDNESDAY 29 JULY 1914

To Amersham to visit Dr Bastien[104] and Sybil.

THURSDAY 30 JULY 1914

On the brink of war. Every European country mobilizing.

FRIDAY 31 JULY 1914

Bath. Edith and Arthur and May Bird. Edith and I went to Cheltenham in a motor char-a-banc after a servant. Via Painswick and Stroud, and back by the Seven Springs where the Thames rises, Cirencester, Malmsesbury, where they are now reviving the pillow lace industry when it had fallen to seven last old women lacemakers.

3

A World at War:

The Diaries August – December 1914[1]

Elsie was in London visiting her father when Britain declared war on Germany. The impact of war was immediate. Germany had invaded neutral Belgium on 4 August 1914 and by the end of the year the British Expeditionary Force (BEF) had been in battle at Mons and Ypres and only a frantic effort had saved Paris from the German advance. Any hope that the war would be over by Christmas soon vanished and both German and Allied forces began digging the defensive trenches which were to be the dominant feature of the First World War in Europe.

In Ireland the threat of a civil war over the introduction of Home Rule vanished, overshadowed by the wider global conflict. Civilian life also changed dramatically and swiftly and before the end of the year Elsie was enrolled in a first aid course and joined the Voluntary Aid Detachment (VAD) at the Royal College of Science for Ireland (RCScI) in Dublin.

Elsie's diaries for August–December 1914 contain a large number of newspaper cuttings on the progress of the war in France and Belgium and at sea, together with personal diary entries about events in Ireland and about her family involved in the war.

❋

SATURDAY 1 AUGUST 1914

Drove up to Highgate with Father ... Father very depressed by the situation ... .

SUNDAY 2 AUGUST 1914

Very quiet in London. Father sorted books and I read to him. He went over old books of photographs ... Father and I were together in the study when the paper was brought in with the declaration of war. Father read it out, and then said 'It has come at last: well I have done what I could.' It is fifteen years or more since he foresaw it and began preaching it in the *Manchester Guardian* first and forming the National League for Physical Education[2] to try and prepare the nation for it.

MONDAY 3 AUGUST 1914

Returned to Dublin. Traffic very congested with special trains full of soldiers.

WEDNESDAY 5 AUGUST 1914

Germany declared war against Belgium and England.

Letter from 'Bet' [Elsie's sister Nance] in London to 'Gab' [Elsie], 3 August 1914 –

'Dearest Gab.

I am glad you got home safely and found Aunt Alice there. Events have moved on terrifically and now England is embroiled and the hounds are loose. The great question all the week-end was supplies. The papers beg one not to help to raise prices artificially, never the less, I bought a tin of biscuits to-day and a tin of dried milk. The stores were full of people with terrific long lists. What will the poor do? I'd have got tea and biscuits anyhow, but the milk was extra, It may come in useful for Barbara.

The streets here flame with placards; otherwise everything is quiet. There is a sprinkling of khaki with bulging bags and knots of men in front of volunteer notices and proclamations and a general feeling between woe and depression. I wish the trams would stop; they are incessant I don't think I can stay here for good. It is like a work house and a barrack in one, quite detestable!

Ted writes that they are pulling down a pier and a hotel at Portsmouth which are right in the line of fire. What is it like in Ireland? It was acknowledged as the one bright spot in the morning's *Times*.[3] My weekend was lovely. I slept out of doors in the hammock last night … It was a glorious night with a moon and I heard sheepbells in the bushes most lovely. Will anyone buy pictures now think you? How long will Aunt Alice be with you and how is she? Do tell me when you write. Give her my best love. With love to yourself, From Bet.'

THURSDAY 6 AUGUST 1914
Miraculous conversions all over Ireland, people from the opposite camp <u>pouring</u> over to the I.N.V.s [Irish National Volunteers].

FRIDAY 7 AUGUST 1914
Sir John Ross's[4] resignation as Chief Commissioner of Police has been accepted.

SUNDAY 9 AUGUST 1914
Erskine Childers[5] came to see Mrs. Green about the position of the National Volunteers. He stayed to lunch, a lean bronzed man with strong and sensitive features and the kindest eye. Very direct and quiet. It <u>was</u> his, the 'White Yacht' (see July 8th) that landed the guns at Howth, with Mrs. Childers and Mary Spring Rice on board.

When they got to sea again a cruiser came prowling round them and they politely invited all the officers to 'come on board'!

Connor [*sic*] O'Brien's[6] expedition landed the guns in Wicklow, at Kilcool [*sic*], on the *Kelpie* his own boat. One of these boats was in Kingstown harbour when a customs official's head appeared just over the edge and he said 'You will please all report that I have carefully searched this vessel', and vanished!

Bulmer Hobson[7] came to tea, Horas Kennedy and Susan Mitchell to supper.

MONDAY 10 AUGUST 1914

France declared war on Austria. (contradicted later)

What is obviously a later note is included here –
July 1922. Mrs Verney, the Garter, Fleet [London] told me that for the first three days and three nights of the war the troop-trains roared through Fleet from Waterloo to Southampton at intervals of <u>2 minutes</u> without a break during those 72 hours. She said the sound was like no other train, because each train was packed full and weighted equally from end to end. She herself timed them, having been told it was occurring but not wholly crediting it. She checked them by a watch and they were exact to the two minutes. No single hitch occurred.

WEDNESDAY 12 AUGUST 1914

Augustine came in at 10 a.m. to wish me many happy returns: then he said reflectively 'Curious old birthday!'

Aunt Alice is very worried over the Home Rule business. Carson has told his men that none are to volunteer for active service until they know what the Government is going to do in regard to the bill. The National Volunteers are under the command of Col. Moore[8] and Col. Cotter,[9] and have their War Office in Dawson street, but the organisation is still very chaotic – in fact there are too many people organising; and there is no definite clear policy at all.

Three women's societies are starting work, ambulance chiefly; the Cumman-na-bMan [*sic*] [Cumann na mBan], who formed themselves in Nov., contemporary with the N.I. Volunteers, to assist them; the Nat. Volunteer Aid Association formed last month, for the same purpose, but to attract into it all those who would jib at the Cumman-na-bMan, and the United Irishwomen are also forming detachments. Semi-official recognition seems to have been given to the C.n.bM and to the N.V.A.A. by the Volunteer head quarters, which they now wish to deny. For the moment there is great confusion. Lady Aberdeen is organizing Red Cross work, and may jump the whole thing.

Uncle Jack writes from Dover, where he has recently taken rooms, because he wanted 'a nice quiet place'!, that 3 detachments of soldiers left on Sat. under sealed orders. Their wives, and they themselves thought for Belgium, but 2 days later the wives had letters from them saying they had been landed at Cromer. It is thought that raids along the east coast are expected.

Erskine Childers has been working hard over here in connection with the I.V.s, since the gun-running, but the Admiralty wired for him and he was to cross yesterday. It is years since he wrote *The Riddle of the Sands*[10] and it <u>was</u> he himself who actually did explore. His friends pressed him to publish it, and he said he could not 'write', all he could do was to put down exactly day by day what happened. He knows more than any man in the British Empire about the coast of Friesland, and the Admiralty summons at this moment may be the sequel to that book.

George is at Farnborough (Uncle Jack writes), organizing the aero-corps, too busy to write, but Uncle Jack thinks some are being sent to Belgium. Nance and Harriet [Jaffé] go to Dr. Cantlie's[11] lectures at the Polytechnic, and father is preparing to turn Stratford Place into a hospital. Ted is to take a week's holiday, and go on duty at Barts [St. Bartholomew's Hospital, London] for so many are rushing abroad he will be more use at home.

Gerty Keily[12] [*sic*] writes from St. Thomas' Hospital that they are giving 500 beds, and preparing to build a pier into the Thames for landing. Queenstown is being fortified, and the steeple of the Cathedral hastily taken down. Built with money collected from all over the world, it was within a few weeks of completion, but it was beautiful, white and tall, and would be too good a landmark.

THURSDAY 13 AUGUST 1914
England declared war against Austria.
The College of Science started its Women's Branch (ambulance) of the Defence scheme. They are prepared to turn the College of Science into an emergency hospital at 12 hrs notice, commandeering beds, sheets, etc. from the Merrion Square district.

SATURDAY 15 AUGUST 1914
Augustine left for Co. Clare to meet Mr. Phillips and map out the geographical flora of district north of Ennis. He ran over all his last directions driving to the station, 'Don't unlock the roller top desk, keep all newspapers, – go through all letters – and be sure to change all the specimens, etc., etc.; and don't worry about England, America will see to it.'

SUNDAY 16 AUGUST 1914
With Aunt Alice to Foxrock to see the Stopfords. Mrs. Kennedy was there, Horas has just volunteered.

To AE's in the evening, Mr. and Mrs. James Stephens there. He has just finished a new book and AE returned him the MSS. after reading it, last night saying it was the best he had written yet. AE said the *Crock of Gold* had great charm, without any guiding purpose, but this book has both. *The Demigods* it is called. There were four heavy females from a 'Civic' camp in the Dundrum mountains, and talk flagged.

MONDAY 17 AUGUST 1914

Still no news of any sort in the papers. Kitchener takes a dark view and demands 100,000 more men. But <u>not a word</u> of official news filters through to the papers about our fleet or the German fleet, or our own troops.

Aunt Alice took Erskine Childers out to lunch in town. He had returned again from London, but the Admiralty telegraphed for him today again and he went over this afternoon. He <u>is</u> to pilot them in the waters of 'the Riddle of the Sands'. He told Aunt Alice he used to know them well and hoped he hadn't forgotten them. He is very sad for he is so immensely needed over here with the Volunteers, and that is the work he would like to be doing. The troop ships blow awful sirens every evening at 5 and 8; they sometimes sound like wailing banshees, and sometimes they roar and bellow like some devouring beast of the Apocalypse.

There is something haunting in the number 44, it pursues us with curious doggedness. The War Office of the N.I.Vs is 44 Dawson Street, Col. Moore lives at 44 Fitzwilliam Place. Mary Spring Rice stays at the Arts Club, 44 St. Stephens Green.

Miss Bloxham,[13] clever and courageous, the only Protestant home ruler in [blank], and waging an open fight for free opinions, so that she has only one house left where they will take her in and let her a room, – she is at 44 Haddington Road. And our ambulance class has overflowed its limits of 40, to the fatally attractive 44, thus causing much communication with the Department [Department of Agcriculture and Technical Instruction (DATI)].

Letter from J.C.B. Stopford [Uncle Jack], from Dover to Lauder Brunton, Monday [n.d.] –

'This letter is only gossip and does not require an answer. 3 regiments left here on Saturday night. Ladies who saw their husbands off did not know their destination. Letters that come since simply show that they have been landed, not in Belgium but in Cromer. My car and chauffeur arrived at Farnborough Sat. night and found G.B.S. [George Stopford] also under orders for Scotland; on Sunday morning his orders were changed and on Sunday night he started by train with 20 mechanics and packed aeroplanes for someplace in Yorkshire. I believe he must have been sent to start a new station there. There was a great hurry and fuss and the car I sent was rushed about looking for men, tools and lorries; A lot of officers seen him off but he went alone. I expect there must be some fear of raids on the East Coast. The torpedo boats here have rounded in a lot of German trading ships, and the crews to the number of 200 have been sent to Horsham to be imprisoned. There was considerble fear of a ship being sunk in the opening of the harbour. The car arrived back this afternoon,

Yours, etc.

The chauffeur say [*sic*] the aeroplanes were flying at Farnborough but George didn't fly; he seemed to have been employed in directing matters. He was too busy to write.'

WEDNESDAY 19 AUGUST 1914

Lord Macdonnell[14] came to see Aunt Alice this morning. He is very optimistic about the war and says it will be over almost immediately and that the Home Rule Bill will be on the Statute Book next month.

He was in the House on Aug. 3rd when Redmond made his speech: he says they were not cheers that went up but yells. Yell after yell, and the men jumping on their seats and waving their arms for victory. No one knew how anxious England had been over the Irish Question. A friend of Lord Macdonnell's was sitting near Prince Lichnowsky (German ambassador) told Lord Macdonnell that he turned quite white and nearly fainted as Redmond made his speech. Germany had counted heavily on the Irish split.

Kitchener is now raising his new army of 100,000 men, and 'supposes' Ireland will supply its quota, i.e. 10,000. Subject to this, Kitchener will drill and arm the rest of the Irish Volunteers for home defence. The situation is now critical. Devlin had Prof. MacNeil [*sic*], Bulmer Hobson and one or two others to meet Redmond at dinner last night. This is the first time that Redmond has met the Provisional Committee since he 'jumped' the N.I.V.s.[15] Mrs. Green hears that Eoin MacNeil [*sic*] is satisfied with Redmond's plans, whatever they may be is still unknown.

This evening came AE and Mrs. Russell, Dr. Bergin[16] and Miss Bloxham ... [AE gave an account of an alarming evening meeting with Fitzpatrick, an eccentric mystical poet who believed that Shakespeare was the second coming of Christ] ... AE related the encounter to W.B. Yeats, who envied AE his meetings with strange peoples. Some time afterwards Yeats was addressing a small audience in London – some society searching after truth, – and he related the story. 'And if', said Yeats 'such a man exists he ought to be among us tonight.' In the shadows of the rear a dim form rose up, 'I am he'.

He had gathered unto himself one more disciple, and together they ran a paper called 'Bethlehem' (?) [*sic*] of which four copies reached AE; and after that no more.

The Irish Volunteers are in a very critical condition; Kitchener is waiting to see can he get the 10,000 men to join the British Army; if so he will <u>arm</u> and drill the remainder for home defence. <u>But</u> the Irish Volunteers have offered for home defence only, and even Redmond did not offer more. They cannot get guns on their own account; from America they are contraband of war, in England there is an embargo on them; the Gov. want them for Kitchener's new army. Redmond, with the money collected in America bought 10,000 in Antwerp, and foolishly had them embarked from the place they were bought. As soon as they started, the authorities in Antwerp, with a view to future favours, telegraphed to Sir Edward Grey.[17] Sir E. Grey telegraphed all round the coast of Ireland; when the ship arrived, it found every point guarded. It put out to sea again – probably went back to Antwerp where the guns have been seized. But it was known to have only 3 days water on board, and another ship was sent after it, but no word has since been heard of either ship; and the money and guns are gone.

THURSDAY 20 AUGUST 1914

Erskine Childers has left on active service. He is to pilot the British Fleet in the North Sea, and all the intricate waters of the *Riddle of the Sands*. He has been given the rank of lieutenant, so that in case of capture during the war, he shall not be shot.

FRIDAY 21 AUGUST 1914

I dreamt last night we said a heart-rending good-bye to Heger and his family. Today there is the announcement of the German occupation of Brussels. The Government moved to Antwerp early this week.

Letter from Augustine in Lisdoonvarna to Elsie, 21 August 1914 –
'A policeman came after us out on the [illegible] and <u>very politely</u> told us, that he was obliged to ask our names, which we gave. The <u>spy</u> mania is a little in vogue – with the police – who have <u>absolutely</u> nothing to do

in this part of the county, but eat and drink. The hotel is in full swing, dances etc. at night and a bar full of drinking men till 1 a.m. Card playing and pitch and toss all over the place – all gay and very innocent. I have seen no trace of any book being used in this centre by man, woman or child (The schools are shut up at the moment)... I am pleased that you are liking the class at the R. College Science and that all is getting on well there. I am sure that Mr. Dowling[18] and the others are very polite and that they are certainly full of admiration for your practical good sense. It is worth so much in Ireland, getting things done, making a success, not merely a success: but the best possible in any scheme.'

Letter from Augustine in Lisdoonvarna to Elsie, 22 August 1914 –
'I am glad that all is gone on successfully at the college. I daresay the [*illegible*] will be all right; but people must have patience at times like these. It appeared from yesterday's papers that the Germans have arrived in Brussels, where no resistance would be offered. I suppose people will be quite safe; but uncomfortable with the Germans billeted on them.'

SUNDAY 23 AUGUST 1914
To lunch with the Praegers. Mr Praeger was telling of his sister Rosemary[19] getting an order to do an advertisement poster for a hardware firm.

Letter from [Harriet Jaffé] in London, to Elsie, 17 August 1914 –
'Dear Elsie,
With us all is well. Sir Lauder has not been so placid for weeks. He is quite gentle and peaceable now, and likes his 'living arrangements' very well. His car has been laid up and Sir Lauder said one morning 'I would like to practice revolver shooting'. 'Oh' said I 'There is a range about 5 minutes from here. We went that morning – walked. Sir Lauder had his shots and we walked home again. As a matter of fact the range is very near Oxford Circus, and he walks now every morning to Oxford Circus,

practices his shooting and comes home again. This morning we had a lot of shopping to do and we went out at 9.30 and did not get back till 11.10 ... Nance and I go to 1st aid classes each night so she comes here to lunch and supper each day but I am always here also so there has been no friction ... Mrs Amy (Nurse Fulton) has been in to lunch every day. Capt. Amy has gone to the Front and she wants to do something so Sir Lauder is trying to get her made a matron of a temporary hospital, as she is too good to waste as an ordinary nurse ... In London we have no difficulty with food or prices.'

MONDAY 24 AUGUST 1914
Namur has fallen.

[28 AUGUST 1914]
Dublin Bay is studded with twelve great boats, among them Cunard liners. They are for transport purposes. They have a desolating effect on this corner of the world.

SATURDAY 29 AUGUST 1914
Russian troops have been landed at Aberdeen, the transport was from Archangel through the White Sea round the North Cape, through the British Fleet along the east coast of Scotland and landed at Aberdeen. They were entrained for the south and are supposed to be crossing from Dover, or else to Cherbourg via Southampton.

MONDAY 31 AUGUST 1914
Mr Phillips here the weekend, left this morning. James Stephens brought the two children to lunch. They played round the garden, and were so happy. Aunt Alice chased round with them, and James Stephens said 'They haven't been so happy for ages; they have never been in a private

garden. They have known the flowers in the Luxemburg [Gardens], but never as their own to touch.'

The Czar [Nicholas II] has changed the name 'St. Petersburg' to 'Petrograd'.[20]

THURSDAY 3 SEPTEMBER 1914

Bea came to lunch. Hugh Hartford's wife and child are staying with them. Hugh went to Boulogne to join his regiment, the Cheshires. News comes today that 18 of the officers of the Cheshires, out of 22 are 'missing'.[21] Hugh and 3 others are safe. They think Hugh hadn't time to reach the front, and now there is no regiment to join.

[N.D. POSSIBLY 3 SEPTEMBER 1914]

AE came in the afternoon. He and A. [Augustine] and Prof. Somerville[22] discussed the war. AE came to cheer A. up and 'lure him back to Chinese philosophy', knowing how gloomy he was feeling. He said that I reminded him of a picture by Mde. Vigée Lebrun,[23] and that I was a civilizing influence giving them tea, and cakes on plates amid their discussions of war.

Letter from Lauder Brunton in London to Elsie, 8 September 1914 –
Dearest Elsie
Things are quite quiet here. Cloudless skies such as I never remember to have seen for so many consecutive days in England – cool breezes – weather perfect. It is hard to realise that Armageddon is going on now and that later we may suffer from its effects ... George is at Aldershot. You will see from the enclosed cutting[24] that he is now Captain and is one of 4 flying instructors.'

[He also tells Elsie of his correspondence with Sir William Leishmann[25] regarding troop inoculation, and with Sir R. Baden Powell[26] regarding the use of Boy Scout troops in the war effort, working with the Coast Guard and with the Territorials.]

FRIDAY 11 SEPTEMBER 1914

Letter from Aunt Elizabeth giving news of Bob and Juliette. Bob is shut up in a German fortress (unknown) and Juliette and the children are with her mother in Baden. The Grand Duchess of Baden, cousin of the Kayser [*sic*], is Mde. de Geymüller's friend, and is doing what she can to get him released. They were in Mulhouse the first time the French captured it at the beginning of the war, and Juliette and the children took refuge in the cellar all during the night of the bombardment. The last Juliette saw of Bob was being taken to the railway station with Mr. von Glehn and about 60 others, as prisoners, Bob carrying a basket of provisions prepared by Juliette and Mr. von Glehn having only a hunk of black bread. The destination is unknown.

SATURDAY 12 SEPTEMBER 1914

Sir John and Lady Ross came to tea. He has resigned his Commissionership of the D.M.P. [Dublin Metropolitan Police] and they are shortly going to Rostrevor[27] for good. They were talking of the reprisals the Indian troops are likely to take on the Germans, in revenge for the German insults to Indians before Pekin. Sir John Ross said Sir Pertab Singh had told him the Germans called them coolies and were generally offensive, and that the Indians would never forget it. Aug. said the dislike of the Germans before Pekin was general, nor were they so very efficient. As a matter of fact, the Americans and Japanese got in first (into the town). The Japanese marched up to the main gate, and took it by storm at a tremendous loss of life to their side. The Americans discovered the main sewer and dashed up that! The Japs and the Americans arrived at the same moment; the Americans marched to the Embassy, but the Japs marched to the Bank and occupied it!

Augustine was in [blank] doing Customs duty when a Chinese official told him a telegram had arrived from the Empress saying that all foreigners were to be slain. 'What do you think of that?' asked the official. 'Obviously it is a forgery!' Said A. [Augustine] cheerfully, 'otherwise we would all be dead by now'. Nevertheless he telegraphed to Sir Robert Harte, who answered more diplomatically than assuringly 'Put no trust in the Chinese'. Whereupon A. sought out his Chinese official friend and regretted that he had to change his mind since the day before, but times were troubled, and the British authorities thought it not fair to embarrass the Chinese with his presence and would therefore remove it. He packed seventy-three boxes that night and travelled.

The Empress had issued an order commanding all foreigners to be slain, and it was accepted in the first Province and passed on to the Province adjoining. But that Governor, finding himself at close quarters with the British despatched a repliqua [sic] of the telegram with the following comment – 'This telegram has been received, but we have no doubt whatever it is a forgery'. No further action was taken by the rest of the Governors of the provinces of China.

The Press Bureau declares the rumours, great and small, of Russian troops in England, is an empty bubble. A. is now in the proud position of being the only man in Great Britain, who never believed it for a moment. Everybody else 'knows someone who met a man who had seen the 129 trains conveying them etc. etc.', and is prepared to stake their immortal soul on its truth.

WEDNESDAY 16 SEPTEMBER 1914
First Aid exams at the R.C.S. [Royal College of Science for Ireland]. 38 went in and 30 passed.

THURSDAY 17 SEPTEMBER 1914

Lunched with the de Montmorencys. He is leaving his work as county inspector of the N.I.V.s [National Irish Volunteers] and has got a commission in the Dublin Fusiliers. He invented a shell for firing at aeroplanes, and sent up the idea to the War Office yesterday. It is a shell and chain for shooting over the aeroplane, on the same principle as the rocket across a ship.

FRIDAY 18 SEPTEMBER 1914

Came to Tankardstown [Co. Meath] to stay with Mr. and Mrs. Blackbourne ... Mr Blackbourne belongs to Co. Meath, and his aunt Mrs Blackbourne owned Rathfarnham Castle until her death and this time last year it was bought by the Jesuits for a training school ... The Home Rule Bill received the King's assent, but the working of it is put off till after the war.[28]

SATURDAY 19 SEPTEMBER 1914

A lovely walk over the fields above the house with a view of the sea, and south to the Dublin mountains. After lunch to Randalstown, 7 miles away, to call on Sir Nugent and Lady Everard. They started Irish tobacco growing, and having bred cattle on Mendelian principles, applied them to tobacco with very successful results ... Lady Everard was busy rolling masses of bandages.

SUNDAY 20 SEPTEMBER 1914

Were motored into Slane and A. and I walked along the banks of the Boyne while Mr and Mrs. B. were at church. After lunch came Dr Rose, their doctor, who lives in Navan, a young man, very nice. He has experimented with alcohol as the antidote for carbolic acid poisons with great success ... It has been taken up and is now gradually filtering into the last editions of First Aid books. Dr Mather Thomson[29] being a Meath Hosp. man, we have it in our notes as <u>the</u> antidote for c.a. poisoning, par excellence.

22 SEPTEMBER 1914

It is exactly 2 months since we left Brussels. We have written to the Hegers offering to take any of them in, and sending it to Count Goblet in Antwerp, but it is so unlikely to reach them.

Letter from Lauder Brunton to Elsie, 20 September 1914 –
'I am glad your nursing classes are all doing so well and that you have passed your exams with flying colours, I never doubted that you would. I wrote to Sir. R. Baden Powell asking him whether it would be possible or advisable for him to raise a troop of Scout Cadets by [illegible] senior scouts. I have not heard from him but in the *Daily Mail* yesterday I see. A scheme is under consideration by the War Office to give authority to Lieut. Gen. Sir R. Baden-Powell to raise a battalion (probably a cyclist battalion) of Old Scouts and Scout Masters ... Possibly' Sir R. Baden-Powell may extend his scheme to include Boy Scouts of 14–15 years of age as I suggested. How is Aunt Alice? Or where is she?

   With kindest regards to Augustine

   I remain your loving father,

   Lauder Brunton'

Letter from Alice Stopford Green in Dublin to Elsie,
20 September 1914 –
'You are a dear sweet patient devoted sympathetic hostess. I give you all my love and thanks. I have done no garden [*sic*] today, I think I was too tired. Col. Moore brought back such bad news. Lord Roberts[30] is only out for enlisting. Redmond the same. The Volunteers to be squeezed out. The Prov. Comm. [Provisional Committee of the National Volunteers]

worse than I told you – None of us know what to do. I go [to Leitrim and then to London] with regret, but if any need I'll be called back by telegram ... Saturday was a busy day, and I had no heart left today. I did mean to mow your grass and do a lot of things in the garden. Confound their English tricks – they interfere even with that.

Your grateful and loving ASG'

WEDNESDAY 23 SEPTEMBER 1914
Evelyn Gleeson, Mr. and Mrs. Wright,[31] and James Stephens and Mrs. came to dinner. Augustine raised the question of 'La Foule' just written by Le Bon.[32] James Stephens said 'All crowds are vermin. I was once by the pond in St. Stephen's Green, and there were three little fluffy ducklings on the water. I said "They are lovely" and I began to throw them some crumbs of bread. In a moment there were a hundred, and they were <u>vermin</u>. There was a picture in the salon, of an eastern harem, full of beautiful women, all naked. When you looked at one, any one, she was beautiful; when you looked at the mass of them they were <u>vermin</u>. I saw a great procession in Dublin, it marched down Westmoreland Street, carrying banners, it marched in detachments, in great order and with dignity. At O'Connell Bridge it suddenly dispersed and scattered up and down the streets; it was <u>vermin</u>. Human dignity is swallowed up by crowds.'

Letter from Elsie's brother Ted at The Royal Portsmouth Hospital to Elsie, 24 September 1914 –
'Dear Else,
We have been pretty busy this last week for Martin has gone over to Belfast for his holiday and left Elliott and me to push the hospital along together. I am leaving on Monday DV [Deo Volente] and WP [weather permitting] and Tuesday anyhow so I can get 24 hours sleep before going to Barts on Thursday. I shall be in residence straight away there

as they have made me full HP [house physician] on account of their shortness [*sic*] of men. I expect there will be even more work there than there is here with only two of us. I wish more and more I had never said I would do their job but had just volunteered but there will probably still be time at the end of my appointment. I got news of George from Uncle Jack when I was at Dover. When he resigned from the flying corps, they kept him in the artillery for about a couple of months and then gave him the aerial coast defence of the East coast from Montrose to the mouth of the Humber. That was taken over by the naval airmen so they made George instructor to the Flying School which is a permanent post with about £700 a year. There are four such instructors. So now he is at Farnborough with rank of Captain. Uncle Jack says he may be called off to the Front at any time.

I had a postcard from Dobie[33] who is in the London Scottish,[34] about a week ago. "We start for Armageddon tomorrow by the 8.40 from Watford. I believe Paris is our immediate goal." I hope he gets through all right.

Yours Ted'

SATURDAY 26 SEPTEMBER 1914

We walked back from Dundrum to Terenure to see Susan and Jenny Mitchell in their new house, 12 Wesley Road. They were having a species of house warming on top of sundry boxes, etc. but generally in elegant order. A Miss Hogg, Mr. Norman and AE were sitting busily painting the tiles surrounding the sitting room mantelpiece. They were of a scarlet be-streaked marbly hue, which AE said was delirium tremens and he was adding delicious blobs of blues and purples until he attained the effect of a very rare, gorgeous and costly marble. Then he [AE] read us his last poem, on the gods of the war, – a grand poem, and every single sonorous syllable vibrated.

SUNDAY 27 SEPTEMBER 1914

John Simon[35] came in for a flying visit this morning. He came over with Mr. Asquith for the Asquith-Redmond Volunteer meeting on Friday. [Augustine] believes that 99% of the National Volunteers are prepared to back Asquith. On the other hand we heard from Miss Harrison[36] that the meeting did not in the least re-present [sic] Irish feeling. Colonel Moore stays on, backing Redmond. The I.V.s [Irish Volunteers] throughout the country want to be <u>doing</u> and before all things to be armed and equipped. They are dying of [inaction] from the incompetence of the Provisional Committee. The £1500 privately subscribed for gun-running, was to be recovered by the sale of the guns, and re-invested for further work, but the guns were never called in and sold, they are scattered about anywhere now, and no money was got in. The only hope of the I.V.s lies in strong discipline and reorganization. The Prov. Com. failed, Redmond might succeed. John Simon says General French[37] is an extraordinarily capable <u>practical</u> man, and has the complete confidence of his army.

Letter from Lauder Brunton in London to Elsie, 27 September 1914 –
'Ted comes tomorrow and begins his work at Barts on Oct. 1st. He is rather keen to go to the front but must do the work at Barts unless he gets a substitute ... while I was at Dover a doctor, one of my old students, called one day in a state of great excitement. His son is in the [Hon.] Artillery coy. And they had to leave for the front on such short notice that they were unable to get inoculated against typhoid.'

TUESDAY 29 SEPTEMBER 1914

The greengrocer's youth came round this morning full of excitement at the recruiting sergeant having tried to make him enlist, and related it all to Mary.[45] 'Is it wanting to make a soldier of you they are? Deed and that's the worst news I've heard yet! Is it so rejooced [*sic*] they are in the army that they'd be wanting <u>you</u> in it? God help you. And indeed ma'am he had to admit it!'. I said I thought she had been too sweeping to the poor youth, 'And would <u>you</u> be wasting good powder on <u>him</u> ma'am?'

THURSDAY 1 OCTOBER 1914

Mrs Hartford and Hermione, Aunt Lily and Bea, to tea, games and they left at 5.15. At 5.30 arrived James Stephens, Iris and Seamus![38] ... Aunt Alice came in having interviewed Devlin. He gives her confidence as he really seems to want the Irish Volunteers to do well under Redmond. Redmond is curt, domineering and yet aloof from it all, but Devlin wants it to be worked by anyone willing to work it and a little business inspired into it. They are taking a good line in that they are not going in for disputes against the Eoin MacNeil [*sic*] minority, either on finance or any other question. Devlin wants now a forward policy, but Redmond suggests nothing, and Devlin himself is up to his eyes in work, with his A.O.H. [Ancient Order of Hibernians] among other things. Aunt Alice suggested to him to get drilling at various centres giving the men as much practical work along with their study as the winter would allow and then with the Spring they would all have equally reached a point where they could go out training together. She gave him <u>much</u> practical advice, especially that the members of the A.O.H. should volunteer if they wished but that the A.O.H. and Volunteer movement should in no way get mixed up or that the I.V.s should in no way become associated with any political side, this took a great rise out of Devlin – 'because', she said, 'the A.O.H. is a civil movement and the I.V.s is a military one'.

Augustine has finished his paper on the 'Artificial Production of Vigorous Trees' embodying his Mendelian experiments of the last two years, at Cambridge, Kew, and Glasnevin ... Augustine has named the cross 'Populus generosa', i.e. 'of noble birth'.

FRIDAY 2 OCTOBER 1914

Aunt Alice went north to meet Mr. Bigger and do a historical trip of south Leitrim. After dinner came Colonel Moore, Captain White, Logi Wilson,[39] Susan and Jenny Mitchell, and AE. Colonel Moore is full of anxiety to have a really serious organ for the I.V.s, nothing that shall degenerate like the 'Freeman' [the *Freeman's Journal*] has done. His whole idea is to get Aunt Alice, if not as editor, anyhow as sub-editor. He says there is no one else can do it. Captain White was very low in his mind. He will wait a little longer and see what they evolve, but he says he is worn out with the deadening incompetence of leaders and has almost decided to volunteer. AE says that the much abused British Empire has groped hold of an eternal principle that the others haven't grasped. It has realized that there is such a thing as <u>individual freedom</u>, and starting with Magna Carta it has striven after it, and now when the British Empire is threatened, it is <u>that</u> that the individual is individually moved to stand up and fight for.

SATURDAY 3 OCTOBER 1914

Augustine and I to Belcamp, Mr Harry Geoghan's [Geoghegan] place near Malahide. He has rescued a derelict 80 acres and turned them into fruit, vegetables, and flowers for the Dublin market. Jammet's restaurant gets its supplies from him. A quaint old house where Swift lived and Grattan visited. Mr. G. has only been there 3 years and worked wonders. Miss Purser, her niece from California and Miss Gertrude Pim also there.

Letter from [Mary Crum[46]], Wire Mill, Lingfield, Surrey to Elsie, 2 October 1914 –

'My Dear Elsie,

Mlle. S. seems to have got over her horror of remaining within reach of the Germans. [portion illegible] … to help place a mother and daughter but I did not know their class or anything of them. There's a jeweller's family from Louvain in a cottage near Lingfield being entirely supported by Admiral and Lady [Foote] ... East Grinstead is going to fill one or two empty houses with them next week. I have been staying for a few days with Lady [Keogh] and dashing over here. Now she has gone up to London with her husband for a week or ten days before he returns to the Hospital work in France. I had a most interesting talk with him about the Mon's affair. We were deserted by the French Territorials on the left – and the Gen. on the right did not support us and when asked for an explanation afterwards said his horses were too tired. Whereupon Gen. Joffre hit him across the face with his own sword – but whether he shot himself afterwards – as report has it I don't know. Except for that terrible cutting up we have done extremely well – and one of our men is worth 10 of any of the others. We keep very cheerful and whistle and sing and cheer – and no other shooting compares with ours. But the German artillery is deadly and frightfully accurate. Sir Alfred [Keogh] saw the aeroplane dropping bombs on Paris from an enormous height. He was in the St. James Hotel, Rue de Rivoli. Paris was deserted and left open for the Germans – to try to trap them inside. Sir Alfred thinks we are turning them and routing them all right now – slowly but steadily – but that the war only begins when they're on the Rhine.'

[Elsie added on same page] – When Gen. French found that he was deserted he gave the order to certain regiments to cover the retreat, the Cheshires, Hugh's regiment among them, and the Cheshires simply dashed themselves bodily on to the German front and were cut to pieces. (See Sept. 3). Their heroism was magnificent. The retreat was effected in some cases by the soldiers running for 15 miles without a break. After that came the fearfully critical week when Germany threatened the northern coasts of France and made entrainment impossible from Havre northwards. John Simon told Uncle Ned last Sunday that the men together with London motor omnibuses had been shipped over from England to La Rochelle and the busses had then conveyed them to the front.

SATURDAY 10 OCTOBER 1914
Antwerp has fallen.

Cutting from the Irish Times, 12 October 1914 – 'Parnell Day. Dublin celebration. Ugly conflict averted'. [The article was about three simultaneous demonstrations marking Parnell Day at Glasnevin Cemetery. Elsie underlined 'Dublin Volunteers had been ordered by Mr. John McNeill, chairman of the original Provisional Committee' and then, 'Citizen Army headed by James Larkin' and finally, 'Volunteers supporters of Mr. Redmond's section of the committee.' In the margin she noted – 'The Three Irish Armies'.]

SATURDAY 10 TO MONDAY 12 OCTOBER 1914
To visit the Wrights at Glenmullen Cottage, Castlecomer, Co. Kilkenny. A charming little cottage at the opening of a glen. He is the head of the geological survey and they are working the country of that district. Horas Kennedy and Mr Valentine and one other from the outdoor survey are under him. Their posts will be kept open till the end of the war.[40] The coalpits are owned by Mr Warnisford [*sic*] and the manager is Mr Maher, who married Mr Fletcher's[41] (of the Department) daughter.

Letter from Lauder Brunton in London to Elsie, 11 October 1914 –
'I shall be delighted to see you over here if it should be advisable for you to come but the fall of Antwerp seems to me to be the beginning of a serious campaign against England and the seas may no longer be safe from German ships nor London from Zeppelins. Aunt Alice is coming

here today to tea and Ted to supper. Robert Stopford has just returned from Paris and is very anxious to go out and do Red Cross work. Uncle Jack is better. I have not heard any more news of George but I believe he is very hard at work training aviators.'

SATURDAY 17 OCTOBER 1914
Laid out the Mitchells garden at 12 Wesley Road, Terenure. Plan of garden as conceived by AE. Garden measurements 20 feet x 19 1/2 feet.

Letter from M. [Fleury] in Paris to Elsie, 17 October 1914 –
'the English have rented the Trianon Palace, the grand hotel, to accommodate their wounded ... Mr Dobie guarded the [Complans] bridge with his territorials. He spent two days and two nights in the trenches, but the Germans did not attack his [position].'

MONDAY 19 OCTOBER 1914
To see James Stephens at 2, Leinster Square. The *Demigods* is coming out. J.S. showed us the first copy:- he said 'I have the loveliest donkey and the loveliest tramp that were ever brought together in fiction – besides a regular duck of an Archangel!'

Postcard from James Stephens in Dublin to the Henrys,
24 October 1914 –
'We are off at short notice to Paris and have not time to go bid you adieu. Thanks for the cushions which are here returned. Good luck to yourself and your husband from myself and my wife. James Stephens.' [Comment by Elsie] 'They fled back to Paris without any warning on Monday 26th with the children.'

Letter from Aunt Alice, at 36, Grosvenor Road, Westminster to Elsie, 29 October 1914 –

'Dearest Elsie.

Here is a story. There were 10,000 Russian Reservists in the States and Canada. They returned to England at the beginning of the war expecting to go to Russia by Archangel. Transports failed and the journey could not be done, so they crossed to France and were fighting there. People in England knew them whether they came from Russia or Canada by the snow on their boots and in the carriages. Those that came from Russia were reported to be so savage that they gnawed the wood of the carriages. They blocked also the penny in the slots with kopecks. Now since the Reservists did come and did go to France have you and I or Augustine the best of it? Are we to give him a blank cheque of confidence for the future? It is very interesting to watch legend in the making and the public is not such entire fools as is supposed.

I am having not a gentle pressure but a very stout controversy with Mr Redmond and Mr Devlin on the National Volunteers and his odious vituperation. Unless the next number is much abated I will write publicly. Those who have seen the correspondence think the next number will tone down. I am extremely unhappy over the whole affair. In my heart I think the right lies with Eoin MacNeill and my political instinct guides me to side with Redmond. I do it without either joy or confidence and if he goes on with this cursing I will break off.

You ought to be making great use of your horse radish. I cannot have horse radish because it comes from abroad.

I am yours affectionately, A.S.Green.

P.S. I have met a Belgian refugee here whose family knows the Hegers. He will try to find out for me where they are and he thinks they are still in Brussels. He tells me that my friend M. Pirenne has remained at Gard. I will let you know as soon as I hear anything.'

SATURDAY 31 OCTOBER TO TUESDAY 3 NOVEMBER 1914

Edie and Nance here. Nance to interview Professor Campbell[42] for work during winter. Both left for Mount Trenchard[43] on Tuesday morning.

SATURDAY 7 NOVEMBER 1914

Letter at last from Prof. Heger. Mr. and Dr. Webb, Prof. and Mrs. Cole[44] came to dinner. Mary rebuked us on the matter of consuming so much food 'We ought all to be on our knees with a cold collation – thinking of the soldiers.'

Letter from Paul Heger in La Haye, 3 November 1914 –

'since the German occupation we have pieces of communication – by post, telephone or telegraph.'

SUNDAY 8 NOVEMBER 1914

The Japanese have taken Tsing Tau and will administer it till 'the end of the war' (Perhaps till the end of all things).

TUESDAY 10 NOVEMBER 1914

Madame de Kisch came to tea. She is the daughter of the Governor of Namur who is now interned, niece of General le Boulanger, and her husband is an officer at the front now fighting at the French Rosendal. She is a doctor (mouth, teeth and throat specialist) and has offered her services at the front in France, she is waiting to hear. She did not leave Brussels until Sept. 28th and then her husband insisted, and she came to England, Dublin, Gorey and finally found refuge with Dr McGuire in Dublin. She knows the Hegers slightly; chiefly through Hospital work, and she said 'Do not be alarmed for Dr Heger's safety, the Germans will not touch him; first he is respected by the Germans as also by the Belgians, and besides he is the most beloved man in Brussels, if they laid a finger on "Heger", il y aurait une révolution' (Alas, poor people, much use that would be!).

They were <u>all</u> turned out the hospitals, from the least to the greatest. Madame de Kisch went one morning to do her usual rounds of the wards, accompanied by her cook and maid, all carrying 'porte-mangers' of stew made of their pigeons which they had been forced to kill (by order). Mme. was told the Director wanted to see her. When she went to his room she found him with his head buried in his hands. 'Ma chère enfant' he said ' on nous ôte nos malades'.

She went sadly to her wards and began her rounds. An orderly came up and said the German officer wanted to see her. She replied 'Dîtes lui que je n'y vais pas. S-il désire me voir qu'il vienne ici'. Before long the officer came fuming into the ward and ordered her out. She pointed to the Red X on her arm, and she said ' Je suis une femme, je travail pour la Croix Rouge, vous devez me respecter'. He continued to be very abusive, so Mme de Kisch replied 'Eh bien je pars, mais le Géneral von der Golz eu entendra'. Immediately he changed his manner and said there was no need for her to leave, that he would see about a special permit for her. The patients wept, and she said bravely 'Mais je reviendrai, n'est-ce-pas que je reviendrai demain?', turning to the secretary 'Mais certainement vous reviendrai' he said. 'Mais je savais que c'etait fini. On nous a plus permis de revenir'.

WEDNESDAY 11 NOVEMBER 1914
Crossed to London arriving Thursday Nov. 12.

London is more than half empty ... There is a large camp and horses feeding in the Green Park. To reach Aunt Alice in the evening one groped one's way and tore blindly and hopefully across abysmally black crossings. Only a few street lamps are lit and the great arc lamps of Oxford Street have shades above them. All down Bond Street the shop windows have either blinds drawn half down or their lights veiled with blue. Piccadilly was pitchly dark; a very small number of motor buses hurtle headlong down the emptier streets and every taxi is placarded with an exhortation to enlist. The embankment was black and deserted, and two great eyes of light peered restless and squinting, through the cloudy skies, sometimes flashing down to earth, from the great searchlights at Westminster.

Robert Stopford left Charing X [Cross] at 7.50p.m. with the First Anglo Belgian Ambulance; eleven men and Miss Noel. Robert looking fine, in uniform. Aunt Connie, Dorothy, Aunt Alice, Lady Young seeing him off and Mrs Cobden Sanderson seeing off Miss Noel. Their destination is Dunkirk. The dark station and the crowds in uniform with Red X, the kit and stretchers was like the dim confusion of a dream. The train drew out and the whole platform <u>cleared</u>. And then they crept away and melted so thinly and sadly.

Dr. Clemceau came in to see Father; they had 3 days to leave Constantinople. He has left his house and books and furniture and hardly expects to see them again. He is prepared to go as a doctor to the front, if possible to a point where his knowledge of Russian and Turkish will be useful. He says that for some years past, the Russians have spoken of Constantinople as 'Czargrad', and look forward to it as the future capital of Russia.

He thinks the Russian régime will be more progressive, for he thinks Turkey has been ruined by its Young Turk Govenment which has fallen entirely into the German meshes.

13 NOVEMBER 1914

Ted came in the afternoon and the silver was sorted.

SATURDAY 14 NOVEMBER 1914

Mary Crum came to lunch; she is Lady Superintendent of a hospital (Red X) in a private house at East Grinstead; Stewart has been made Major.

Went to say goodbye to Emily Kemp and May McDougall leaving shortly for the front with a St John's Ambulance corps, eleven nurses, Emily as cook and May as orderly. Emily heard from a man in the Fleet that the suspense was terrible. They are kept moving at tight tension night and day. In his ships <u>all</u> glass has been removed so as to obviate glass splinters when in action. All paint has been scraped off the outside and inside of the cruiser, and all furniture and paraphernalia has been removed into one store-room so that the cabins are bare and dreary, and as they cannot be quite without light, the portholes have been boarded up and everything made light-proof with the result that the atmosphere of the ship is appalling. He told her the 'midnight watch is enough to break a man', for although they go in complete darkness, they are going at full speed all the time.

2 field postcards from soldiers of British Expeditionary Force in France thanking for presents, e.g. tobacco.

Copy of letter from Robert J. Stopford with the 1st Anglo Belgian Ambulance, Hotel de Kursaal, Dunkirk to Lauder Brunton, 15 November 1914 –

'My dear uncle Lauder,

I thought it might interest you to hear how things are going here, so I am seizing the opportunity of being on guard alone in the lower regions of the hotel to write this letter.

We got here without any excitements except a rather rough passage, and came up to the hotel for lunch. We are about a mile outside the town of Dunkirk and about 2 miles from the railway sheds where the hospital is, and the docks. The work is extremely well organized, except that the tendency is for the English parties to do the larger share of the dressings, while the French doctors and orderlies look on and smoke ... our party is now divided. We have established field dressing stations near [Fumes], and about 15 or 20 of our men are working there just at the back of the firing line. The rest of us, another 40 or 50, are here mostly doing orderly work in the sheds, though of couse some are motor and ambulance drivers ... Long trains of cattle trucks come in with the wounded on stretchers in the straw. The men are carried in to an enormous shed which holds 700 or 800 (there are 2 sheds). They have rough beds of planks on stands with a straw mattress and rug. The men are put on these and gradually the dressers work around reporting the worst cases to the doctor who decides whether they shall be taken to a permanent hospital in Dunkirk or out on a hospital ship as soon as possible. Sometimes the sheds are filled and emptied twice in an evening.

The number of gangrenous wounds is terrible, but as far as one can see, the pain from such a wound seems to be greatly numbed. There are a great many cases of wounds to the brain ... Their sufferings must be simply too awful, but they bear it with an heroic fortitude which is really marvellous. They hardly make a sound, with the exception of a few of the French Colonial troops, who begin to yell as soon as you look at them.

The wounded here are almost all French with one or two stray Belgians and English. There have also been a good many German prisoners wounded here. One night last week, two Turkos [sic], who were very badly wounded, crawled to the far end of the shed and tried to cut the throat of a wounded German. They were only stopped by the arrival of the curé, such a nice old man, who goes about cheering them up and getting them drinks.

The arrangements, as far as they go, are good, and we have plenty of dressings and the ordinary necessities, and we send all the very bad cases to one of the permanent hospitals.

I must stop know, as I have to wake up the next guard and get a few hours sleep ... I'll write again when I have seen some more.

P.S. There are several other English parties here, including the Duchess of Sutherland's.

16th – Since writing, this work has started again at the station in 6 hour shifts, and plans are being prepared for our own hospital and for 2 dressing stations at the front.'

SUNDAY 23 NOVEMBER 1914

The Praegers are just back from Belfast. The 'queer naval doings' is the manufacture of dummy dreadnoughts. Mr P. says it is such an undertaking that it can't be concealed from anybody. Craft of a suitable size and any sort of age, go in at one end of the docks and come out at the other in about a fortnight full-blown battle ships, with four funnels, conning towers, and all complete and painted a dull grey colour. Their purpose is unknown.

SATURDAY 29 NOVEMBER 1914

An order has been issued in Ireland forbidding further rifle practice throughout the country.

Letter from Stopford Brunton [Elsie's brother] from Montreal to Elsie, 1 December 1914 –

'Dear little sister,

I wrote you a manuscript letter a day or two ago in answer to your long one, but I have been very bad about writing any way ... My dear Mr Morkill, whom I believe you know, is already one of the overseas forces, and is going to England with the second contingent.

I have been put in charge of a platoon of the McGill regiment and am running around and outpost duties and generally playing at soldiers with great energy. In addition I have got a course of lectures, of which you have probably heard from Father, and they have been increased so much that they take up the greater part of my time ... The McGill regiment is a very weird and wonderful machine comprising about twelve hunded men who are all drilling furiously, but of whom only 5% have any intention whatever of ever going to the front. However the enthusiasm is enormous, and it will do these fellows good to get some drilling of some sort and teach them that there is such a thing as obedience to orders.

I wonder if the Spring-Rices with whom Nancy stayed are any relations of the British Ambassador in New York. The name seems to be the same, but I do not know if they are any relations.

I am spending much time yelling 'hay leg, straw leg' to a bunch of doctors and although I have not had the joy and pleasure of witnessing the performance I am told that Dr. Adami[53] is drilling manfully in the regiment. I believe you know Dr. Adami and will appreciate when I tell you that he pants and ramps round and round the campus and mountain in a most wonderful manner. I believe it is really quite a sight for the blind to see the old gentleman tearing around'.

Cutting from Letters to the Editor, Irish Times, 2 December 1914 –
'as one of the invalids landed there [Dublin] from Boulogne,to say that nothing could have exceeded the kindness accorded to us. For myself, I was one of a number taken in a private motor to 34, Eccles Street, where everything that care or skill and money could be done for us by the Sisters there, and by Sir Arthur Chance.'[47]

3 DECEMBER 1914

Dublin Castle has been taken over as a hospital for soldiers, Miss Macdonnel as matron; Lady Aberdeen bossing it all. Had an interview with Dr Lumsden re R.C.S. V.A. detachment. Men are urgently needed to meet hospital ships and transport wounded to motors, but women there are enough already [*sic*]. Mrs Praeger came to tea, she is going around collecting from all native Germans in Dublin, for German wounded prisoners in Templemore. They have no occupation whatsoever, and she wants to supply something. The German pork butchers in Dublin are a large and strong guild, and in the course of collecting from them, a wife of one of them told her they all 'belong to a church called the "Mormon church"'! The Dublin pork butchers are all naturalized Germans and are a staunch Mormon community. She also went to General Friend to get permission to visit the German prisoners, but hasn't obtained it so far.

Mary sighs for the calm and peaceful days when she was in Oxford 'with the beautiful poplin [*sic*] trees all along the river banks, and the boats floating down from Cambridge'.

7 DECEMBER 1914

AE, Susan and Jenny Mitchell and Professor Cole after dinner. Much talk till midnight.

9 DECEMBER 1914

Aunt Alice arrived.

10 DECEMBER 1914

Mr Barton[48] came in at 5.30 before crossing to London. Annie flew over to Stopfords to fetch her [Alice Stopford Green] back, and just as his patience was exhausted and he fled, she dashed up the doorsteps on top of him. His brother is a lieutenant and expecting every moment his captaincy. He is in charge of the garrison at Orlock Hill, and he also reports the dummy battleships (see Nov. 23rd). He says he sees them go in liners at one end, and come out battleships at the other. They have cargoes of cement to make them sink in the water to the level of a battleship, and are perfect imitations. Lieutenant Barton knows some of the men who are to man them: they are called 'the Suicide Brigade'. All they knew (or will tell) is that the dummies are to be accompanied by destroyers, which are to pick off the crew all but one man to each dummy, who is to remain on it till the last instant, and then throw himself into the water.

Lieut. Barton's main work is stopping the light signals that [are] being sent over Lough Swilly. When he first arrived they went on every evening, and he arrested 3 or 4 suspected people, and now there is very little of it, but the German torpedoes continue to lurk around, and he keeps on receiving orders as 'Stop trawler 74, black funnel, white diamond' etc., as these are the means of supply of petrol, etc. for the submarines. But so far he has not seen one of these trawlers.

The mystery of the *Audacious*[49] he explains as follows – the *Audacious* <u>was</u> torpedoed and the crew <u>were</u> taken off by the *Olympic*; the general rumour then was that the *Audacious* had sunk, and that the Admiralty kept it a secret. AE knew, but was forbidden to publish, so also Brayden of the *Freeman*.[50] But Lieut. Barton says she did not sink but that they managed to tow her over to Glasgow, and when the water was pumped out, there was very little real damage; she is now nearly fully repaired. That it was because she was saved and not lost that the Admiralty kept it all so dark.

His brother had a yarn that three German transports had landed in Lough Swilly and landed their men, but that the transports were all sunk and the men killed to one man, and a man who was fighting them in the trenches himself told the Captain of Lieut. Barton's regiment!!!

Erskine Childers is still safe, but it is not known what he is doing; his work is connected with the naval-aero department. Mrs Childers hears from him.

11 DECEMBER 1914

A stormy wet day. Mrs. Green having been offered a 'cosy motor' by Mr. Devlin for the day, she and I careered round Dublin and the ordinary storm rain was converted into a severe needle bath by the rents in the motor hood. The chauffeur let us in and out with a stout twig off a tree, by which he worked the door catch, otherwise unresponsive. Lunched at Jammet's with Sir Matthew Nathan,[51] newly arrived as permanent Under-secretary. He regards the Sinn Fein movement as serious, and spoke earnestly to Mrs. Green to throw her influence pro-British: 'You have power, use your influence for your country's good'.

He was governor of Hong-Kong, and left China in 1907, and has come here to adjust the finance of the Home Rule Bill (Greater powers and less money).

The Department [DATI] have started cutting down expenses at every tail-end. The retrenchments are going to be severe.

Friday afternoon – Still stormier, but the Marquis and Madame the Marquise McSweeney [*sic*][52] de Macshanaglass turned up on the 'Clonskea tram'. Presently came Colonel Moore, and last Mr. Lysaght. The Marquis' mother, whom he took us to see in June [?] year, at Versailles, could not make up her mind to leave her horses, so she would not come to England. Then, just when the Germans were marching towards Paris, the Government said her chateau was in the firing way, and she must go, so she had to leave her beautiful chateau with all the collection of stained glass, and medieval statuary, and her superb horses, and wander among friends in the S. of France.

Macshanaglass is a ruin, so they are looking for a habitable house at Killarney. They are very agreeable. 'Our friend Lord Ashbourne' as the Marquis affectonately calls him, shakes his head gloomily over the Marquis' past, but it also seems unfathomable. He was 14 years master of ceremonies at the Papal Court, and much beloved in spite of the shattering blow he dealt them all by marrying a Protestant, the daughter of the Grand Duke of Hesse. They all rejoiced to meet Mrs. Green.

Friday evening – AE came in.

SATURDAY 12 DECEMBER 1914
Sir Matthew Nathan came, his one great puzzle-query is 'Who is going to be the ruling class in Ireland?' under Home Rule.

Letter from Lauder Brunton in London to Elsie, 13 December 1914 –
[He is vacating the family home in Stratford Place, London and moving to an apartment] –'We are clearing out very quickly and next Tuesday the house will be empty of all the things we do not take to the flat.'

MONDAY 14 DECEMBER 1914
Aunt Alice left for London. She is very distressed at the pro-German tendency. Her line is perfectly clear, she has always worked for Home Rule in Ireland, but from the very first she has said that 'foreign intervention would be disastrous'. In Nov. she told John MacNeil [*sic*] quite definitely, and she has told Roger Casement the same thing, ever since he went to America. Now there seems to be a great danger in America of a big division over the war. President Wilson is for the Allies, but there is a vast American-German faction, they have now the Hurst newspapers, 600 in all, under the editorship of Arthur [Brisbane], all working a pro-German campaign and likely to be headed by Roosevelt.

According to the *Daily News* and *Leader,* Dec. 10, Robert Stopford's Red X detachment is at Woeston, about 5 miles behind Ypres, fetching wounded from the fighting line, and spoken of as 'working magnificently and fearlessly under perilous conditions'.

Letter from Alice Stopford Green to Elsie, 18 December 1914 –
'George arrived late last night with sudden orders to fly to the front Saturday morning. Jack had a great shock and a bad night ... Mr Barton wants to go to you often – do ask him. I want to hear how Nancy is fixed up, and if she cannot leave Dublin.'

25 DECEMBER 1914

Nance and May K. [Kerley] with us; to the Edward Stopfords in the afternoon and supper in the evening at home, ourselves, Evelyn [Gleeson], Mrs. MacCormack, Dorothy Strick, Kitty; Susan and Jenny Mitchell.

Copy of letter from Robert Stopford to his mother from the Friends Ambulance Corps, British Field Post Office, Dunkirk, France, 26 December 1914 –
'There has been a lot of work for our cars lately – and the need to evacuate one of our stations in a hurry. However, all our people got safely away, tho' in the French part of the building they were not so fortunate. Do you read the French official communique ever? If so, did you see last Tues (I think) 'The enemy bombarded the Hospital at Ypres' – well, as they say, we had a very busy Xmas, I am assistant adjutant here, which means a lot of work. We are the central distribution station for all our stations (7), that is, that all stores, etc. come to us from Dunkirk, and have to be sorted out and sent on to the various stations, and as everyone had abt [about] 30 Xmas parcels it meant some work. Then on Xmas Eve, 3 of us went to the Midnight Mass in the nuns chapel. It was most impressive, with the officers in uniform, and the nuns, with the thundering of the guns outside. Xmas Day we had all our ordinary stores work to do, and as well to prepare for dinner, to which we had invited the other stations. At 5.30 we sat down to dinner in our room, 30 in all, to a Royal feast. The room was decorated with holly, and

we had 2 long tables on different sides of the store, loaded with fruit, chocolates, preserved fruit, etc., we had an enormous amount. We had 2 huge turkeys roasted in the nuns kitchen and 8 or 10 plum puddings with 200 bottles of beer, 2 of wine, 1 of port and 1 of whiskey – so we did ourselves well. After that we had songs, recitations and violin. We kept it up till 11 when we retired to sleep the sleep of the just till 6.30, our hour for rising. It was an extraodinary sight and great fun – and all your Xmas presents were lovely. I can down any amount of chocs, and the socks and hanks [handkerchiefs] are splendid. Will you thank D. [Dorothy] for hers very much. I'll write to her later. Oh yesterday, there turned up the 2 long lost parcels of yours and a tin of things from Miss Jaffé, after 6 weeks, and a sort of apology from the G.P.O. They were very welcome. [Illegible] has sent me a jolly little plum pudding, amongst other things. Your mittens I love and wear all day long, they alone save me from frost bite this bitter cold weather. It is really bitterly cold specially in our office, wh. is a long stoned [sic] flagged room downstairs. It is also our store, and we are working there till any time from 11 p.m. to 2.a.m. Mr Nevinson[54] was out here a few days ago and promised to go and see you. Also Miss Slade, the Matron of St. [Mels] Hosp. would like to meet you when she returns in the New Year. She is so nice ...

There is some arrangement being made, by which we shall all get leave, between now and March. We would have 8 days off. What time would you prefer. I thought of applying for the middle or end of Jan. What do you think? It will be fun to get over for a week. It was 6 weeks last Thursday that we left. The time has gone like lightening. I have just burnt the elbow out of my tunic, on the stove, in an attempt to get out a grease spot, which is rather a nuisance. Desmond MacCarthy is out here, such a nice man. He came out separately, and joined on to us, as a sort of convoy leader – you see I stay mostly at home, but the cars spend all day going out to the Aids posts to collect wounded who are brought in there on stretchers. Sometimes they work all night too. We had to evacuate our Hospital Station suddenly the other day, as the enemy started shelling it. I missed it all being here. The other day Col. Seely[55] and Ramsey MacDonald[56] turned up to lunch – of course I was out, just my luck. I don't know how long I shall be out here. I may go back quite soon or I may stay out a bit longer as the powers direct. You know the man I persuaded to have his arm amputated – we had quite a touching scene afterwards. He would never let his arm be dressed unless I was there holding it and he absolutely refuses to let me come up here. It was very touching. Here we keep a sort of general store. All the French army come in and beg cigs and chocolate, and to get joyrides to Dunkirk. Yest. [Yesterday] a man came in and asked for a pair of military trousers, and we have a lot of sick men who come in to be dosed. MacCarthy and I generally see them and dose them with chlorodyne or quinine. I have to do a good deal of interpreting as I am one of the <u>few</u> people generally out here who can speak French. Consequently I have good practice in it. I had to go and interview an old Dr. Colonel the other day, and get a letter of thanks out of him – a very tactful piece of work. Our chief excitement is watching [planes] which come often over here till there [sic] driven off by shrapnel fire. The other day one dropped 3 bombs, but did no damage. We have a most ingenious gong here, composed of 3 empty shell cases which ring beautifully just outside the kitchen … We have also a gramophone, a great delight, especially to the nuns. Everyone is decidedly slack today: Xmas dinner is the cause. I fear that we have a long day – 6.45, Breakfast, 12, lunch, 4, tea, 6.30 Supper, bed. Of course in the office we are later at night. Last night at the end, we all sang 'Auld Lang Syne' and then we had 3 cheers for Geoff as Commandant, and 'for he's a jolly good fellow' – very striking – the 30 men in uniform dancing round the decorated table, in the bare room, in the glare of 2 acetylene lamps. Your letters come in 2 or 3 days, and are a great joy. If any of the family, or connections, care to write, they will be sure of much gratitude, even if not of an immediate answer. Yours, Robert J. Stopford. Address is Friends Ambulance Corps, British Field Post Office, Dunkirk, France, Postage 1d'.

26 December 1914
To London, 36 Grosvenor Road [Alice Stopford Green's home].

28 December 1914
Father Jose ? [*sic*] came to dinner, a Capuchin monk from the Basque country close to St. Jean Pied de Port. He is very keen on the nationality of small countries.

Letter from [James Stopford], 28 December 1914 –
'GBS [George Stopford] started last Wed. to fly to the front in France on a machine he had not seen before but which he reported as a good one. He was to report himself at Dover. He only got as far as [Redhik?] where owing to repeated snow-storms he gave up the journey and flew back to Farnborough where I think he is still detained by heavy fog. On Xmas day he was warned by wire and spent the day hunting in the sky but without result. He was after a German on a [Junker] who did not get so far west.

I think this was the same man that dropped a Bomb on Dover and then flew to the Thames. He was chased by two naval aeroplanes at Sheerness but got away and flew to Woolwich, there he was tackled by an airman on a fast machine armed with a Maxim who had been warned by wire. He overtook the German and fired at him at 400 yards and thinks he got him but the Maxim jammed.

He stuck to the German and escorted him down the Thames and saw him take the sea at the [coast] with 150 miles of water between him and home so perhaps he never got there. The Guildford man was fired at on his way home by every detachment of soldiers he flew over and George fears he may be fired at when he reaches Dover. Ever yours.']

29 DECEMBER 1914
George Wakeling[57] up from Oxford for two nights. Lord MacDonnell and Colonel Moore to tea.

30 DECEMBER 1914
All of us to the 'Palace' in the evening.

31 DECEMBER 1914
Father moving into the flat. Aunt Alice took us to [the comedy] *Potash and Perlmutter* in the afternoon.

4

A Year of War Work and Personal Loss:

The Diaries 1915[1]

INTRODUCTION

1915 was a year of setbacks and stalemates for the Allied forces. In Europe the battle of Neuve Chapelle, the second battle of Ypres and the battle of Loos resulted in great loss of life and inconclusive results, and a new weapon, poison gas, was used for the first time. The Gallipoli campaign was a disaster. On the home front, 1915 saw the first Zeppelin raids on Britain and a submarine blockade, restricting import of essential materials and consequent shortages. In her diaries for 1915 Elsie includes a vast quantity of cuttings from various newspapers about the events of the war, tracing the campaign in the Dardanelles, the battle of Neuve Chapelle, battles of Ypres, an air raid on London (2 June 1915), Gallipoli, the war on the Russian front and battle of Loos. Interspersed with these and the diary entries are letters from her relations and friends serving in France and Belgium, photographs and a pamphlet for a 'war club for women' in London.

The death of a friend, Madame DePage of the Belgian Red Cross, in the sinking of the *Lusitania* in May 1915, is noted. Elsie's younger brother, Ted, was killed in 1915 during the battle of Loos whilst serving with the Royal Army Medical Corps (RAMC). He was 25 and had been in France for just two months.

In Ireland Augustine, who was 58 in 1915, did not join any of the armies but continued with his own research work and advised on forestry policies. Elsie became more involved in her work as a member of the Voluntary Aid Detachment (VAD) at the Royal College of Science for Ireland (RCScI). With the u-boat blockade of the British Isles and Ireland, imported materials like cotton wool for surgical dressings became scarce and the possibility of using a native material, sphagnum moss, was investigated. By the end of 1915 the RCScI had become a War Supply Depot for the collection and processing of this moss for medical use, which then dispatched to hospitals in the various theatres of war. Elsie served as Quarter-Master of the committee which managed this sub-depot. Elsie's sister, Nance, moved to Ireland in 1915 and began working in Mount Trenchard, prompting their cousin, George Stopford, to ask, 'Why has the whole family suddenly gone to live in Ireland?'

❀

1 JANUARY 1915

George [Wakeling] returned to Oxford. Juliette, and the five children are staying in a boarding house near to them, and Ethel, Mary and Evelyn are to go to school together. George is 'in loco parentis' and very good to Juliette. Bob is safe but most uncomfortable in the [blank] camp, near Potsdam. They had a card from him on Xmas morning, printed in English and distributed to English prisoners to send to their friends wishing them 'a happy Xmas and a brighter new year'.

Robert [Stopford] has been hit by a shell at Dunkirk but luckily unhurt.

2 January 1915

The *Formidable* was sunk in the Channel by a mine. The storm is appalling. The waves at Bognor are house-high, and the floods between B. and Pulborough extend for miles along the railway as far as the eye can see on either side.

The Harrison children growing up fast. Ned says it has been a good year and the farmers are in no way anxious about food supply, but horses and labourers are being swept from them.

Letter from Robert Stopford, serving with the Friends Anbulance Service in Belgium, to Elsie, 2 January 1915, with covering note 'The officers and committee of the Friends Ambulance Unit earnestly request in the interests of the Unit that no portion of this letter shall be published in any journal whatsoever' –

I do love to get letters from home! However, I hope that before very long I shall be over for a week in London to see everyone. I wish that you could be there but I suppose that that is past praying for.

I am sort of adjutant to our party and secretary to the hospital all rolled up into one and am consequently pretty busy. In fact if it wasn't for the nuns I'm afraid that we should have queer meals sometimes. My duties extend from haggling in the town to get oranges down from 2d. to 1½d. each to ordering a motor lorry full of supplies from Dunkirk, or from dressing up as a young lady (as I did last night, to the intense enjoyment of the nuns and some 20 refugees who live in the cellars here), to arranging with the Abbé for the baptism of a new-born baby in a cottage near by.

The town is fairly quiet now but they lob a few shells in every day and our ward of 'blessés' is generally pretty full. We had a visit from a General Melis the other day: he is Inspector General of the Belgian medical service. All the Drs were out and I had to show him round. Fortunately the orderlies were engaged in pouring Jeyes fluid on the floor of the ward so he remarked on the cleanliness and freshness of the typhoid ward!

We are extraordinarily comfortable for a 'bombarded' city. We live in a huge lunatic asylum (fortunately empty of its former inmates) and in what is really clover with beds and stoves and meat to eat and if, for instance, we find a shrapnel bullet in a rather tough piece of 'beef', we say 'ce n'est pas magnifique, mais c'est la guerre' and feel very virtuous!

I must now close what is, I fear, rather a drivelling letter, with my love to Nance and Augustine. Will you tell Nance I love her waistcoat and how beautiful it is and that I hope to write to her very soon. But tonight from 11.30–12 is, I think the first day that I have had to write anything except hasty notes to my Mamma, since I first came here a fortnight ago. Yours affectionately,

Robert J. Stopford'

6 JANUARY 1915

Returned to Dublin. There were 4 soldiers in our carriage and one said he saw himself the *Audacious* blow up in Lough Swilly. He said he was on sentry duty above the Lough and he saw a column of fire go up from the Lough. The next day he saw the funeral of the only man who was killed and he was not on the *Audacious* but on a boat near by and was hit by some flying fragment. The soldier would not tell us any more, because A. [Augustine] was sceptical, but this was the first <u>first-hand</u> evidence we have had of any of these mysteries.

SUNDAY 10 JANUARY 1915

Aunt Angel[2] died about 8 p.m. She took ill quite suddenly ill about 7, then rallied. Nance and I went at 9 p.m. but they were unable to send in time ... She was like a beautiful abbess of the Crusader times, just as they lie in marble in the cathedrals in France.

WEDNESDAY 13 JANUARY 1915

Burial in Mount Jerome cemetery at 9.30 a.m.

Postcard from C.S. [Constance Stopford] to Elsie, [no date] –
'Robert has been transferred to [Ypres] where the Friends Unit has a civilians hotel and he has been made adjutant ... Geoffrey Young was home for 2 days and gave a capital account of Robert. He has very big staff, there is, 3 or 4 drivers, 2 dressers, 2 ambulance drivers, Robert and about 10 nuns. The nuns look after the food and it is very good, about 70 patients. Robert <u>was</u> hit by shrapnel from a bomb – but not wounded, only bruised. C.S.'

Letter from Marryat Dobie to Elsie and her sister Nance, 13 January 1915 –
'this is the first opportunity I have had for thanking you. At first our letter-writing was officially limited out of consideration for the hard-worked censors; then for 3 weeks I was in the firing line and couldn't write at all ... while we were on the firing line we got our letters regularly; but our parcels collected in thousands at a town ... I wish I could write brilliant or vividly describing accounts of the trenches – I really don't know how I can describe them. Dig a ditch about 4 feet deep and 2 wide in your garden and go and stand in it and then you'll know what one is like. We have had fairly beastly weather but the trenches didn't get very wet and we worked in short shifts, resting in various ruined buildings, so that on the whole we had quite a good time. And things

of that sort always seem far worse than they actually are ... We are now having a short rest in a town. The children are an awful curse, always begging for "souvenirs" – i.e. food, cigs, etc. ... a box of 'comforts' came to our company from a small town in Fife. I got a pair of mittens and some cigarettes with a little note written in a child's hand "Dear Soldier, Hope you will enjoy the cigarettes and soon be home again." I shall send her a post-card to delight her.'

21 JANUARY 1915

AE is worried about America; he fears they will go to war on the American Note and the *Dacia* test case.[3] He had an amazing story of Professor [Macan] and Sir R.C. [Roger Casement] in Berlin.[4]

The old poet Lysaght[5] went to see him last Sunday evening, and bewailed the modern methods of warfare.

TUESDAY 26 JANUARY 1915

Augustine took the Marquis MacSwiney to dine at the Scientific Club and the Marchioness asked me to dinner at the Shelbourne. She is a most handsome and charming person ... After dinner the Marquis, Augustine and Mr Praeger came in and we had a festive evening.

[WEDNESDAY] 27 JANUARY 1915

The <u>true</u> story of what happened in Lough Swilly, vouched for by the son of Col. Thornton who was there.

Four British battleships were <u>resting</u> in Lough Swilly, when suddenly a German submarine appeared. The British battleships got up full steam and went tearing round and round Lough Swilly not daring to slacken for an instant – with the submarine at their heels.

At last they sent up a hydroplane, and it located the submarine when it in its turn was having a rest.

The British sent down divers with entanglements for the propeller, and they pinned the submarine to the bottom of Lough Swilly.

The British are now raising the German submarine.

1 FEBRUARY 1915

George Stopford, though still a Captain in rank, has been made Chief of Staff to receive wireless messages on his aeroplane. It is a new appointment carrying responsibility and great honour.

Letter from Alice Stopford Green in London to Elsie [no date] –
'Your Lough Swilly story beats the Russians [story] out and out. It's a gem. I am sure Augustine believes this time.'

3 FEBRUARY 1915

The Marquis and Marchioness MacSwiney came to dine, and afterwards Miss Purser, the Praegers, Mrs Hutton and Margaret, Mrs Hutton bringing her beautiful illuminations from the Gaelic Psalter at Compostella. They stayed till 12.15 ... The Marquis met Mrs. Hutton for the first time and they were delighted with each other. The Marquis told her he had resigned his post in Rome to do that which Daniel O'Connell had done once (fight a duel).

4 FEBRUARY 1915

The Northern India Forestry authorities read a review of Augustine's article on poplars in the *Irish Homestead* (Nov. 14th) and wrote back from India to the London agent of I.H. to send out a copy of the Department's Journal. They referred it to AE, so it came back to Aug.

Professor Houston[6] lectured to the Forestry Society, we dined at the Shelbourne with the Marquis and Marchioness and all went on to the lecture together, Mr Forbes came back for the night.

The story of the Russians (see Oct. 29 [1914]):

At the outbreak of war the Postmaster General thought it would be as well to have a reserve supply of telegraph poles, so an order was sent to Russia for 10,000 Norway spruce. These were out of stock so the reply came back 'Sending via Portugal 10,000 Russian poles, tall and straight, suitable for maintaining long lines of communication'.

Susan [Mitchell] says of Professor Cole, 'If you meet him on a wet day and he stops to speak to you, it illuminates the whole street'. She wondered why this belongs to a few people, and she thought 'perhaps because in the minds of some people there is room for winged things'.

Susan went house hunting with Seamus O'Sullivan[7] to help her. They looked at a house in Leinster Square, and there was a dark room under the stairs with ivy growing in at the window, it was gloomy and forboding and Seamus O'Sullivan suddenly broke a sepulchral silence saying 'There's more come through that window than ivy!'.

18 FEBRUARY 1915

Mr Elwes here. He rushed off again as usual at 6 a.m. ... Mr Elwes is supplying charcoal to the War Office; they wanted 1 ton of charcoal per week for fuel and for lining the trenches. Mr. E. interviewed all the principal timber merchants in the City [London], but they could not together have supplied as much as a cwt. So he cut down 25 acres of his own timber, and he tried for English, Scotch, French and Belgian charcoal burners, with very little success. Then he asked the Gov. for German charcoal burners, and a guard, [who would] be responsible for them. However, it appeared to be against the Hague Convention, as it would mean the prisoners being employed in the manufacture of war material. So he had to manage as best he could, and after very expensive experiments, he is now able to turn out the charcoal.

19 FEBRUARY 1915

A lecture at the R.D.S. [Royal Dublin Society] on Cancer by Prof. MacWeeny, [8] [*sic*] to which Aug. went. He is interested in the point they have reached in the investigation of cancer, as it coincides with the point they are now at regarding hybrids. Cancer is apparently a continuous growth of cells, which growing too fast for normal nourishment, invade all of the rest of the cells in search of it. The established fact so far is that you must kill it, either by surgery or by radium, as it can be killed but cannot be checked.

The point in hybrids, i.e. first crosses, is that with them the limit to growth is very much less than in normal trees, that is the cells go on reproducing very much more rapidly, as the tree growth is all a question of cell-reproduction.

Aug. thinks that if investigations could show what constituted the <u>check</u> to growth, and consequently what factors removed that check, that then results could be obtained as to what cancer really is, and what constitutes the vigour of the first-crosses.

All grants for libraries over here have been stopped on account of the war, but the National Library has had the straight tip from Lloyd George that if they raise a big enough petition and do it quickly, they will get theirs again. The Librarians, Praeger and Best are starting on a great campaign.

Mr Praeger gave me tea in town and we went to the 'movies', very American and uninspiring, and nothing of the dash of *Under Sealed Orders* and *The Fatal Prediction* at Rathmines.

The sun has shone for the first time and the first crocuses blazed open today.

Mr Wright went to lecture in Belfast and Mr. Praeger went with him. They saw the dummy battleships (v. Nov. 22nd) and say there were four in dock, beautiful imitations, quite complete with turrets and wireless apparatus, but the upper part of the outer shell only canvas painted, and the wooden guns not even rounded, but square blocks painted black. No one knows their use. Aug. believes them to be inwardly fitted with one real gun and torpedo, and that they are really merchant ships in wolf's clothing.

They are also fitting to two of the real dreadnoughts steel crinolines, i.e. cases of steel 10 feet outside the real body of the ship, with the space between filled with water. It is supposed they can swim through mine belts and explode the mines, clearing a passage for ordinary battleships.

THURSDAY 25 FEBRUARY 1915

Research Defence Society meeting at the R.D.S., lecture by Professor MacWeeney [sic] at very short notice, on 'Preventative medicine during the war', giving tables of statistics for the Franco-Prussian, American-Spanish, Boer, and Russo-Japanese wars, showing the amazing effects of inoculation for enteric [fever] on the reduction of the death rate. He dealt with typhoid, tetanus, and threw in meningitis.

The definition of cancer cells in last week's R.D.S. lecture was 'Cancer cells are cells which have lost their sense of responsibility to a corporate body'.

On Friday Professor Starling lectured on 'the Heart' and we dined with Prof. and Mrs. Francis Thomson to meet him; prof. of physiology at University College.

Wild storms go on every day; only some yellow crocuses are out, and a white daphne, very small, and a beautiful iris.

I am translating *Patsche in Boton: Jahrbuch* A. Engler, vol. 48 Leipzig 1913, for A.'s use in writing up a description of his new species Larix Olgensis, which he has just established, from the specimens sent by Captain Baker from Olga Bay, Siberia ... Mary gazing admiringly at A. striding off to the College, 'Oh, Mam, isn't the Master beautiful! Isn't he like a bee. Sure isn't his skin like an egg? And all that has gone through his brain, God bless him.'

Copy of letter from R.J. Stopford in Ypres [to his mother, Constance Stopford], 1 March 1915 –

'We are having a busy time. This place is still more or less an evacuating Hosp. but I have very little to do with it. We searchers are still quartered in this building, but we are under our own O.C. Allen Baker. There are 3 of us and 1 nursing orderly, that go out every day with one or the other of the doctors.

2/3/15 – There was so much [censored] last night that I gave up the attempt to write and went to bed. Tonight is quieter but I have just had a bath and am very sleepy. We each go out with a nun (as Interpreter) and go from house to house and find out about them, and whether they are suitable for billets, and if there are any sick, we have them out. I am sort of second in command of it, under Baker, and as he is away most of the time I have a good deal to do. I am armed with written authority from the Belgian Gov. and the British Army to remove all 'sick' people in this town to Hosp. Also I have passes for all 3 Armies!! We have however hardly ever had to use force. I loathe doing so, and have only let it happen in one of my cases ... of course nothing but the greatest urgency and the fact that it is all for the best for these sick people to come to Hosp. would make it defensible. We are working quite far from the town sometimes now. Yest. [Yesterday] I visited on my rounds, the people in the cellar of what was before, the Museum here. Only the walls now stand, 20 minutes afterwards one wall fell down in the gale and an old woman was killed a little farther along the cellar where I had been. Also the (censored) artillery has been busy, generally near where we have been. It is rather exciting as long as it keeps to a respectable distance.

Robert J. Stopford.

Note from Mrs Stopford –

The 'sick' mean the typhoids and they are working away to get it out of the place. Most successfully. About 7,000 have been inoculated, and in 4 days work 400 houses were disinfected and only 3 new cases found. They want to have it safe for billeting our soldiers there.

FRIDAY 12 MARCH 1915

Captain Gibbon[9] gave an exceedingly interesting lecture, very badly reported. He explained how the R.A.M.C. [Royal Army Medical Corps] had altered its organisation to suit necessity. There are 3 lines of trenches, firing line, supporting trenches, reserve trenches, then a blank ground, so that it is fairly free from fire. The wounded can be recovered from the firing line, i.e. the trenches, till nightfall, and then they are brought to the blank ground in front of the artillery line, where the doctors and field ambulance do what they can for them, and send them on to the field hospitals. These are behind the artillery and right out of range of the enemy's fire, and here the wounded are fed as well as cared for. Then they are sent to the rail-heads (clearing stations). Some men are sick from shock and fatigue, and require only a bath and rest; some require several days and are sent to convalescing houses in the neighbourhood, and both of these can return to the trenches in a few days. Some have to be sent to the 'base' hospitals which are always at a port town, of which we have 3 at present, Boulogne, Rouen and Le Havre. They are only kept there as long as absolutely necessary and are removed in hospital ships to England. The organisation is so good that a sick man can be got from the firing line to a London Hospital in 36 hours.

Sick and wounded are however a secondary consideration in war. The first consideration is to get fighters to the front, their supplies, and their ammunition, and sick and wounded men must wait their turn for transport.

Captain Gibbon was out in the early days, September when the medical officer was sent forward. He was attending to two wounded men when he was shot in the leg, and a bone broken. He continued to inject morphia into the two patients, he hove the bodies on to his horse, and he led the horse between 3 and 4 miles to hospital with his own bone broken. Heroic. It is doubtful if the leg will ever recover.

19–21 MARCH 1915

To Avondale to stay with Mr. and Mrs. Forbes for the week-end. Mr. Black has just got his commission in the Army Service Corps and Professor Campbell has come down to see about arrangements here, bringing Mrs Campbell. A fire on Sunday and a very dry gusty March day. The fire spread up from the river. Campbell, Forbes, Henry Black, and over 100 helpers from Rathdrum fought it from 1 till 4.30, and got it out just in time. Had it jumped a narrow neck it would have roared up the plantations perhaps swallowing the house.

Letters from Rfm. Quinn, of RIR [Royal Irish Rifles] regiment, from Wellington Barracks[10] Dublin, 20 March and 25 March 1915 –

'Dear Miss,

In answer to your requesting me to send for any little article I should need. I shall kindly ask you if it be in your power to forward on at any convenient time some woollen socks.

I am thankful for the care you and your Partner took of me while on furlow [*sic*], and am glad to say my feet are in splendid condition excepting that they are always cold.

I am,

Yours Truly,

Rfm. Quinn.'

Rfm Quinn to Elsie, 25 March 1915 –
'Dear Miss Henry,

I am very thankful to both you and St John's Ambulance Core [*sic*] of being able to send me those socks and am hoping you and your partner are in the best of health as I am myself, thank God.

I shall be going back to France next week and I am no [not] very much upset about it because one must take things as they [*sic*]. I will now close my short letter hoping you are feeling the best. I am,

Yours truly,

Rfm. Quinn'

20 MARCH 1915
Loss of the *Bouvet*, the *Irresistable* and the *Ocean* in the Dardanelles.

Letter from George Stopford [in France] to Elsie, 24 March 1915 –
'Dear Elsie,

It was awfully good of you to send me the shortbread. Most excellent stuff thank you ever so much for it and also for the socks which are perfect. Thank you so much. I am so glad to hear you are all well.

I am very fit but in rather an unhealthy place as most of the time other fellows seem a bit seedy. Why has the whole family suddenly gone to live in Ireland? Awful place I think except for the hunting! Well we are not having too bad a time out here as our present billets are in a pretty big town. The weather has been very bad for flying but shows signs of improving soon. The worst of it is that when it is fine you have to fly yourself silly – so many hours in the air. I am flying a Bleriot Monoplane single seater, its rather nice and being small it is rather small for the gunners to see. However they manage to spot it alright.

I hope to have some leave as I have had none for over a year now, but its all stopped for the moment. I wish K's [Kitchener's] army would hurry up over. There won't be anyone left in the old army if they don't! I hope you are both very fit.

Best love to everyone.

Love, George'

Postcards from Marryat Dobie [in France], 20 and 23 March 1915 –
'Don't write until I tell you my new address! I am taking a commission as censor – at least have applied for one. Thank you awfully for your last parcel and letters. I'll write as soon as I get settled. Will you send Nance and Ted a p.c. [post card] too, about not writing. Marryat Dobie'

Pamphlet for 'A war club for women is open at Ye Spotted Dog, Harrow Road' [London]:
This club is for the wives and dependents of Soldiers and Sailors, all of whom are heartily welcomed ... membership fee, halfpenny a week [The organizer was Harriet Jaffé]; also included is home-made badge – 'service duty'.]

SATURDAY 3 APRIL 1915
Came to Aughrim, Miss Cowle's Hotel.

SUNDAY 4 APRIL 1915
Cold winds, brilliant sun, cloudy intervals. Walked to Mucklagh, Pierce O'Mahony's place, through a cirque of mountains and round into a valley, high up ... He is still in Bulgaria where he spends a great deal of his time, this year on account of the war he has wintered there.

MONDAY 5 APRIL 1915
Took a little train to Shillelagh.
To Coolatin, Lord Fitzwilliam's place ... The great Stafford had a residence here, he thought it the most beautiful place in the world and called it Fair Wood.

FRIDAY 9 APRIL 1915

Left Dublin for Bushmills 9 a.m. 3 hours in Belfast so walked to Norman and Clark's[11] docks. Three armoured cruisers are there in repair, the *Magnificent*, the *Mars* and one other. The ferry took us close up under them, very forlorn they looked, dirty grey and rusty, as though they were centuries old. Enormous skeleton of ships coming into existence loomed up in amazing size and quantity.

Arrived 5.40 at Port Rush [*sic*]. Miss MacNaghten meeting us, it is about 8 miles out to Runkerry. The house stands plump on the Atlantic, all by its isolated lone. A big storm raged on Wednesday and the sea is still rolling in very rough.

SATURDAY 10 APRIL 1915

Very wet. Went up to the school which the Miss MacNaghtens are building in memory of Lord MacNaghten and which will be finished and opened in August. In the afternoon to Dundrave which belonged to the grandfather and till this year to the Miss Mac.N.'s brother. He died in the new year and it belongs to his eldest son who is only 19. He is Lieutenant in the Ulster Division.

SUNDAY 11 APRIL 1915

Another grey day. Aug. went off along the shore to where the River Bush runs into the sea. It is a great place for kitchen middens. Mr. [Young] did some clearing in ab. 1908. The sand had blown off one of the cleared bottoms, and A. found a fine 'scraper' (used for scraping hides etc.).

There was a parade service at Bushmills church packed with Ulster regulars, U.V.F. [Ulster Volunteer Force], Boy Scouts. The officers think there is little chance of getting to the Front. The Ulster Volunteers insist on sticking together as a body, and Kitchener will allow no terms of that sort. He will not spare them arms and ammunition to practice with, and they are not practiced enough to be of any use unless drafted into ordinary regiments for military training.

Letter from Lauder Brunton in London to Elsie, 25 April 1915 –
'I shall be delighted to see you when you come but it will be a Painful pleasure so long as there are submarines about because I shall worry badly before you come and I shall worry still more if you get across safely until you are back in Dublin. Please wait until things are safe. You are too dear to me for any risk to be run.'

FRIDAY 23 APRIL 1915 TO SUNDAY 25 APRIL 1915
To Kilkenny to stay with Capt. [Hervey] and Mrs de Montmorency at Troyswood. Arrived on Friday evening.

Sat. A wet morning, and the most amazing great hay market going on in Kilkenny, hay being bought by the Gov. Afternoon fine, and we all went to Major Humphries, agent to Dow. [Dowager] Lady Dysart ... She runs a big woollen factory and owns the Kilkenny Woodworkers ... .

29 APRIL 1915
Top's wedding day.

Letter from Top [Stopford] in Montreal to Elsie, 9 April 1915 –
'Dearest little sister,
I wrote to you to tell you about the marriage and I cabled father ... I have leave from Major Anderson from April 30th to May 16th which is a Sunday and we are going off to Guysboro for our wedding trip. I have a steady job now and I'm in the throes of reading examination papers for men who are qualifying as officers ... I am procuring a new uniform for the occasion and shall be beautiful to behold but Betty I understand is to be a dream of fair [woman] and trailing clouds of glory rolled into one with two little bridesmaids to hold her up on either side ... the

robins are arriving back here once again and the spring is coming. It is curious how remote the war seems to be here and how much we lead our ordinary lives but it must seem much nearer to you all over there and I do hope it will stop soon. Give me some news of Ted will you if you have any. I am now on the permanent force of Canada and am instructing in military engineering and map reading.'

Letter from Betty Brunton (née Porter) to Elsie, [May 1915] –
'We had a fairly agitating time of it before the wedding although the Porter preparations were completed almost a week beforehand. So many presents arrived every day, and Top had to work up to the last minute ... Top was not sure until two days before the wedding whether Frank Morkill, who is his greatest friend, could get leave or not, for his regiment expected to get ordered away at any moment. However, fate was kind and Frank came, and was a most sympathetic efficient best man. It made all the difference in the world to Top, for the two are absolutely devoted to each other, and Top was beginning to feel a little solitary, as I was in the midst of all my family, and he had nobody of his very own.'

SATURDAY 1 MAY 1915
Prof. and Mrs Phillips to lunch, also the Praegers. In the afternoon Mr Sheridan, Minister for Finance in South Africa. He says S. Afr. presented the same difficulties as to government as present day Ireland, Natal being their Ulster. They solved it by granting concessions about education.

SUNDAY 2 MAY 1915
Spent the morning at Glasnevin, among the poplars. Walked down the Tolka to the sea and took tram to St. Anne's, where we wandered round

the gardens with Mr Campbell, the head gardener, he has been there 38 years and is a great man.

THURSDAY 6 MAY 1915
The Marquis and Marquise MacSwiney, Mr Sheridan, Mr Kelly and Col. Moore to lunch and afterwards to the Botanic Gardens, looking their best ... Mr Sheridan was best man to Sir Percy and Given Gironard in S. Africa; Given has just re-married – a Mr Oppenheimer at the Cape.

FRIDAY 7 MAY 1915
Rostrevor – looking quite wonderful, half Irish spring with soft blue mist over the Carlingford Lough and Mts and half sub-tropical ... Sir John and Lady Ross and Mrs Lawrie, a niece of Lady Ross, whose husband Colonel Lawrie was killed at Neuve Chapelle.

SATURDAY 8 MAY 1915
News that the *Lusitania* has been torpedoed off Kinsale.[12]

Telegram from Lauder Brunton in London to Elsie, 11 May 1915 –
'Madame de Pages[13] drowned in *Lusitania*. Professor Heger here Savoy Hotel. Awaiting de Page return with body from Queenstown'.

Letter from Harriet Jaffé in London to Elsie, 13 May 1915 –
'My dearest Elsie,
My last letter told you Prof. Heger had just been in. Next morning Sir Lauder and I went to the Savoy Hotel to see if we could help him but there was nothing to be done. When Prof. Heger arrived in Dover however our Douane took all his Belgian money from him (to stop speculation in Belgian notes) they said, so Sir Lauder hurled a pocket full of notes and money at him – so that he has plenty of money while he is here, and then on his return, his Belgian notes will be reimbursed to him, I expect

... Prof. Heger has first to get permission to bury Madame DePage in the little bit of Belgium that is left, and then the French have to give their consent to his returning via Dunkirk – and he has to endure all these delays ... while his soul is scorched with sorrow and sadness ... Prof. Heger told me he thought that Madame DePage had suffered very little. The morning was beautiful – the passengers had seen the coast of Ireland and light heartedness and rejoicing timidly crept into every bosom. The passengers breakfasted – then went on deck – the morning was superb and light heartedness was giving way to conscious joy when a hideous snake like movement seemed to trouble the still blue waters. Another writhing in the waters and a fierce hiss and the *Lusitania* listed. Six torpedoes tore at her bowels with wild demonical rage, the waters hissed with fury and spat with hate, and the passengers were swept hither and thither like foam on a crested wave. Madame DePage had become very friendly with a surgeon on board who I think was also going to the Ambulance at [illegible]. He seized a lifebelt and put it round her, asked her if she could swim. She feared not – he assured her all was well, she was just to cling to him. Then either from the *Lusitania* herself, or from some of her boats, an object fell across his temple and he swooned. When consciousness returned, three and a half hours later, he put out his arms to shelter Madame DePage – and called her gently by her name – but alas the sea had meanwhile claimed her as its own, and the laughing ripples played with her corpse and kissed her feet. Poor Monsieur DePage!! He had to seek her amongst a wreckage too painful to imagine – too awful – to search for his loved one from their midst'.

19 MAY 1915
Crossed to London, the boat scampered over well under 3 hours ... London very noisy, fussy and jaded, and the streets full of motor

transports. Father and Harriet well. Poor Prof. Heger must have had an awful 3 days in London. The Queen of the Belgians came over incog. [incognito] at the time and sent for him. Mde. DePage was a personal friend of hers, and it was the Queen's own wish that Mde DePage should go over to America on the Red X mission. She broke down completely when Heger went to see her, saying she felt it was on her account it had happened. Poor Heger had to comfort her too.

He told Father that when Churchill sent the marines to the relief of Antwerp he gave the Belgians a solemn assurance that he would send sufficient backing to relieve the city. Heger said if they had believed him they would now not even hold the tiny corner of Belgium they have, but they did not believe him at the time and relied only on their own strength so that they still have preserved the S.W. corner of the country. There Mde DePage will be buried.

George Stopford came to tea at the flat, and a Mr Anderson from Montreal, in the Canadians, a friend of Tops. George said the bomb-dropping from aeroplanes is a frightful waste, it is just fireworks and no use at all, only the papers insist on having it done! The real value is the scouting: every morning they start out over the enemy's lines and go over every railway station to count the trains. All transport and movement is carried on at night so that the actual moves cannot be seen, but the trains etc. at the railway stations indicate where the troops are massing and the reports are brought back to the British. That and the focussing for artillery are the real uses. George says you can direct gunfire from an aeroplane better than from the battery itself even when you can see the object aimed at. Generally the airman has an observer, but sometimes he has to do it all alone. He works it by maps divided into minute squares, he hits upon what he believes to be enemy guns, but it is even difficult to tell what are the guns from at that height, then he signals to his own battery, 'and then you STARE, presently there comes a puff of smoke and then you STARE --- again, and then you signal corrections.' George says no wind now deters the airmen, they fly in a gale, and that one day was so rough, he was frightfully sea-sick, and he said it was no joke being sick in the middle of a wild storm and having to manage the machine at the same time.

FRIDAY 21 MAY – SUNDAY 23 MAY 1915
With Aunt Alice to Bexhill for her deafness.
Ted came over on Sat. from the R.A.M.C. training camp at Eastbourne, looking simply splendid. Aunt Alice and I enjoyed unalloyed glory marching him up and down the front and sharing a ceaseless volley of salutes. They saw from their camp a destroyer out at sea, and suddenly a little white puff; whereupon the destroyer whipped round and let off four gun shots, regardless of the fishing boats in the vicinity, so they think there must have been a submarine.

Ted says their only occupation is 'shingle shifting', i.e. carrying buckets of shingle from the beach up Beachy Head by way of solidifying the swampy paths in camp. But the officers may not lay a finger to it and would apparently joyfully lend a hand to break the monotony. Ted says you must have a religion in the army; one man, being asked what was his replied 'Christianity', 'There isn't such a religion' they said, 'you must be Church of England'.

Aunt Alice went out dining last week, and sitting beside Lady Lyttleton[14] she said to her 'Perhaps it will amuse you to hear that I have just been told the outbreak of war is due to my having travelled round Ireland last summer with a German professor (Kuno Meyer[15]) and telegraphed to Germany that there would be a civil war between the North and South in Ireland!'. To her surprise Lady Lyttleton chuckled delightedly and said 'Oh yes, we've known that all along'. Mrs Green said 'Well perhaps you would like to know what really did happen'. 'Oh no,' said Lady Lyttleton, 'we like to have confirmation of what we've all known'. So the hostess interposed and insisted on Mrs Green telling what really happened. She had travelled in Ireland last May and she had written to Kuno Meyer that there would <u>not</u> be civil war in Ireland. This letter had been communicated to Schiemann, the personal friend of the Emperor's and had appeared in print in the *Kölnische Zeitung*.

We spent Sunday morning on the sand, we spoke of her will and the disposition of her library. Ted came to lunch. I returned in the evening to London and Augustine and I went to see Mrs Rogers who sails to rejoin her husband next week. Ted and Aunt Alice saw me off at Bexhill Station. London looks unspeakably beautiful with a clear east wind blowing all the time, but at night like nothing on any planet, being chiefly illuminated by tiny red lamps to show where the road is up. However, as from time immemorial all London roadways come up in May you get along fairly well. The sky is beautifully lit by search-lights, but the intermediate space is turgid as no buildings or vehicles have lights, they are mainly distinguishable from each other by the buildings standing still, and the vehicles moving five times as fast as when there was light. They also scream five times as loud, and the police I think take cover in the innumerable trenches which run parallel to the red lights and lie under the road. You scream loudly, run fast, and escape with your life, 'Everybody's doing it'. Once in comparative safety, London can be really appreciated, because it stands up against the summer sky with no dazzle of light to blind. Westminster and the Houses of Parliament looked really magnificent, so stately and dignified with a stream of agitated humanity tearing round their feet, and the restless searchlights peering above them for the sinister perils threatening from an unknown where and when.

MONDAY 24 MAY 1915

Italy has declared war on Germany.

Cutting from Dublin Evening Mail, 26 May 1915, with report of new Coalition Cabinet –

'Sir E. Carson accepts office: Mr Redmond refuses: Mr Balfour succeeds Mr Churchill at Admiralty' with note on the side in Elsie's writing – 'Winston must go'.

Letter from Marryat Dobie, now commissioned and on Chief Censor's staff, Boulogne, BEF, 23 May 1915 –

'My dear Mrs. Henry,

I hope that from my long silence you have not concluded that I am an ingrate or a Partaker of Glory (as Uriah Heep described his defunct father). But the last weeks have been a bit of a rush and, even in calmer moments, of mental confusion. I was suddenly called up from the trenches to General Headquarters to see about taking a commission on the censor's staff (on May 20) and have after many vicissitudes arrived at the above address. I had to hang around G.H.Q. for a fortnight waiting for my commission ... I got it and came and reported at the office here. That evening I noticed what a lovely complexion I had, and next morning discovered that it reached half way down my chest, so I went to the hospital at [Wimereux] with measles ... After an uneventful fortnight there ... I was shipped home on leave, and to my joy they gave me 3 weeks! I went to have lunch at the flat and Mrs. Green took me to tea at her house. We had expected Ted from Eastbourne, but he didn't turn up.

I am at last at work ... and very busy indeed. The time I had in the trenches seems incredibly far away. In some ways I regret them, especially now that the weather is better but I don't think I should ever care to return to the rather monotonous life of a private, with its utter lack of initiative or responsibility. Also one sees far more of what I consider the interesting part of war here – the organization and the variety of it all – stores, trains, ambulances and all the rest of it.

I spent a good part of my time in London, but really enjoyed myself more in the country, where my mother and I could loaf about together ... I have still a pair of socks which Nance sent me – one of the few survivors of the old muddy days. You two were simply ripping in writing to me and feeding me and clothing me and brushing my teeth. Out there a parcel has all the spiritual interest and excitingness which it has to a child, quite irrespective of the material pleasure to be got from its contents ... Goodbye for the present. Please remember me to Dr. Henry; also to Nance when you write.

Yours sincerely,

Marryat R. Dobie'

3–7 JUNE 1915

To stay with Colonel Tottenham at Ballycurry (Ashford, Co. Wicklow) a lovely spot ... Mr Watson, director of the Dublin Steamship Co. staying also the week-end.

9 JUNE 1915

RCS [Royal College of Science]Women's V.A.D. [Voluntary Aid Detachment] drill meeting here, a good muster, all 5 officers and 18 members; Mr Haigh to drill us, Dr Winter, Commandant, and Dr Lumsden here. Everyone in clean white aprons, some in uniform. Great effort at 'form fours'. Drill from 4.30 – 6, in the garden and afterwards Dr Lumsden vaccinated an eager volunteer (for hospital work), and they all dispersed 7 p.m.

Letter from Marryat Dobie at Boulogne to Elsie, 12 June 1915 –
'I have been busier than I have ever been in my life ... Our chief allows us to take a half-holidays (or rather quarter-holidays) on condition that we spend them taking exercise, not for our own pleasure, but to make us more efficient servants of the State. Once when we had just come out of the trenches in the L. Scottish [London Scottish] I was eating some very good stew and enjoying it visibly, and a man with me said "You know the government isn't giving you that stew out of kindness to you. It isn't giving it to you at all. It's giving it to your rifle. Without your rifle they don't care 2d. about you" ... I shall tell you if I come across a lonely soldier in any letter ... I have in the past come across genuine cases of men who have been very sad because they have had no parcels themselves and have therefore felt ashamed of sharing in their pals parcels. An aunt of mine has about half a dozen lonely soldiers. She writes them what my relations tell me are the most rotten letters. She also sends them novels, after carefully reading them to see if they are suitable for the young British soldier.'

26 JUNE 1915
Came to Mullaghmore, Co. Sligo ... a lovely peninsula on the south side of Donegal Bay ... Mr O'Byrne spending 2 days here, we drove on a car to Lyssadel [*sic*] and spent the whole day going through the woods, later meeting Sir Jocelyn Gore Booth[16] who showed us rock plants and a general view of the gardens.

MONDAY 5 JULY 1915
Came to Bundoran ... A watering place where it is almost impossible, short of risking your life, to get into the water at any point.

Tuesday 6 July 1915

Took train to Ballyshannon and crossed the town to the narrow gauge railway which runs to Derry. An hour or so brings one to Donegal. From Donegal walked 3 miles to Lough Eske Castle belonging to Major White who called one day at Cambridge. He is now in E. Africa. He is interested in planting and has done a good deal in his demesne ... it has a deserted forlorn appearance, nearly all the men of the estate having gone to the war.

Friday [9 July] 1915

Took train to Beleek and walked back ... the police inspector 6 ft. 6 1/2 in. arrived in the evening in pursuit of inquiries after Mr. O'Byrne. He left us at Lissadel to return home, and we gather that in taking in Dromahair on his way home he couldn't resist the chance of exercising his German on the German hotel-keeper (one of the institutions in that town), and greatly excited local suspicion!

Saturday [10 July] 1915

Arrived at Mrs Armstrong's Commercial Hotel Lisnaskea. The whole world is travelling today, as the '12th' is to be celebrated tomorrow. Orange flags are flying from Church steeples and orange lilies are in full bloom in the gardens. The train was packed with soldiers on a week-end leave ... Most people have drink taken anticipating doing honour to the 12th.

Sunday [11 July] 1915

To Crum Castle on Lough Erne starting at 9.45. 15 miles there and back and 2 hours walking in the demesne. Lord Erne has been missing since Mons and no news of him ... Mr Reid the gardener took us round and pointed out where he himself saw the light of Lough Erne ... it has been seen by many people, by Lady Erne frequently, and on all parts of the lake ... a similar light appears on the loch at Inverary.

Letter to Lauder Brunton from Hugh Robert Mill [?] of Hill Crest Surrey, 21 July 1915 –

'I am pretty sure that no suspicious lights have been seen at Inverary as we are in constant communication and every bit of warlike news or gossip is reported (the last was a report by a wounded Inverary Argyll and Sutherland Highlander that the Germans in the trenches opposite his company let them know that they knew the regiment by singing 'Bonnie Mary of Argyll'!). I have long known of the lights on Lough Erne and have heard many explanations long before the days of the German spies and radio-activity. Some light was undoubtedly seen and the bulk of the evidence which was very contradictory, seemed to be against an artificial origin. Whether it was a Will of the Wisp or an electrical discharge seems doubtful; but I am pretty certain it is not a case of signalling. I am very sorry to hear so poor an account of your health. If you had not done so much for the health of others you would have been better yourself no doubt, but I hope the gratitude of thousands is some consolation.'

24–27 JULY 1915

To stay with at Mount Trenchard, Foynes with Lord Monteagle[17] and Mary Spring Rice. Mr and Mrs Percival and the baby were there, and Lord Ashbourne, very full of Paris War anecdotes.

[NO DATE, AUGUST 1915]

Professor Heger trying to get back to Brussels; the Germans have interned his son-in-law, M. Beckers, because he refused to allow the dynamo at his factory to be used for making barbed wire for the German trenches.

FRIDAY 5 AUGUST 1915
Warsaw has fallen.

1–8 AUGUST 1915
Nance and Dorothy here, 6th and 7th Dr and Mrs Stapf.
Mrs Stapf very lively, Dr.S. very large; Mary remarked 'Sure didn't I have the cleaning of his boots, and wouldn't four of them have flagged the kitchen floor'.

Letter from Lauder Brunton in London, to Elsie 11 August 1915 –
'Ted came to town yesterday to get one or two small things he needed. He looked in at tea time and then returned and had supper with me at 7, leaving for Marlow at 8. He expects to leave for the front today or tomorrow. On Saturday last Ted, Aunt Alice and I went to see some experiments of Mrs Ayrton[18] on the repulsion of poisonous gases by [fans]. The results were so extraordinary that on Sunday I wrote to Sir Alfred Keogh[19] and Sir Douglas Haig.'[20]

Letter from Lauder Brunton in London, to Elsie 22 August 1915 –
'I had a letter from Ted last night. He is now located somewhere in France about 30 miles from the front ... Uncle Jack is at Hastings. He wrote to [call] my attention to the papers of the 20th containing the note which appeared in the gazette of the 19th: 'Special appointment Royal Flying Corps; Central Flying School. Officer in charge of Experimental Flight (graded for pay as a squad. Com.) – Captain G.B. Stopford, R.A. Flight Com. Military Wing, Aug. 6th'. I heard from Col. Shirley who said he could do nothing for Top but advised him to apply to the Canadian Government to be sent to the front for purposes [of] instruction. Top writes that he has had a conversation with Col. Hughes, brother of Gen. [John] Hughes who has lately been at the front from Canada. It is hopeful.'

Birthday card from Ted in France to Elsie, 23 August 1915 –
'I'm sorry it has come too late but surely it was worth waiting for! Will write to you properly soon.'

24 AUGUST 1915
Lunched with AE and Susan at the 'Homestead' today. AE is busy writing a terrific poem on the beasts of the apocalypse.

Letter from J. Lumsden,[21] M.D., St John's Ambulance Brigade to Elsie, 5 September 1915 –
'Many thanks for your letter and for the arrangements you have made for your Detachment for the 11th. I am [delighted] to know you will be represented ... I feel I must thank you for all the help you have given us. Personally I have much valued your advice and I feel you have a knowledge of people and things – there are so many talkers but so few real helpers!'

MONDAY 21 SEPTEMBER 1915
[*This entry a mixture of pieces by Elsie with other contributions from Dorothy Stopford and Alice Stopford Green*]
  Dined with Sir Matthew Nathan at the Under-Secretary's lodge. Sir Matthew, Aunt Alice, Leonard Knox, Mr Kerlin the Secretary, and us; also Dorothy. We had not then begun buttonholes in public.

[Added by Dorothy Stopford:]
'Sir Matthew took Elsie down, and had her most of the evening. In fact when I asked the Sec. next day how he liked her he said "Well the fact is I only spoke to her for 2 minutes!" They spent most of the time in the ogre's den sharpening pencils. D.S.'
  Leonard Knox arrived in the middle of dinner his motor bicycle having broken down. He had to sit next nobody as Dorothy had spent

16 hours in the motor in scouring Dublin for a girl for Mr Kerlin. Then when Leonard was late Mr Kerlin took me in and so to pay him out I talked across him to Leonard Knox, which made him go to sleep. Next day I sent him a chaste buttonhole (in contra-distinction to Dorothy's scarlet gladiolus) with the poem –

Books in running brooks

Sermons in stoles

Manners in cigarettes

And FEELINGS in buttonholes

He wore the buttonhole deaded [*sic*] at dinner and revived the next morning after careful tending. It and the poem accompanied him to the office.

Added by D.S.:

'On the way down through the Park I tackled him on the subject ... A few days later after the weekend at Elsie's I took him a large michaelmas daisy as a buttonhole. He came down the next morning and suddenly in the middle of breakfast jumped up and went to fetch it. He returned with it looking very spruce and alive and said "What would Ms Henry say if she knew I forgot it?" So I exclaimed that it wasn't given to him by Mrs Henry at all but by me, though of course if he had known that he wouldn't have rushed off to fetch it. So he said very neatly "In that case I shouldn't have forgotten it!"

Leaving the heroine(s) to her happy reflections we close this wonderful human document (Editor [Dorothy Stopford?]).'

Every morning the 'Interned' Aunt Alice and Sir Matthew used to start five minutes after breakfast and walk together to the park gates, receiving the salutes together of the POLICE; wearing the Rose he brought her from the garden for breakfast, and munching his apple, and <u>not</u> talking about Ireland.

[*Added by Alice Stopford Green:*] 'Aunt Alice choked under an oppressive atmosphere for many days, but after a Bigger bracing at Belfast returned to use the last day for a thrust of the thin end of the wedge. (ASG)'.

Letter from Dorothy Stopford, from the Under-secretary's Lodge in the Phoenix Park to Elsie, 29 September 1915 –

'Dear Elsie,

In contradiction to my post card since we got your letter, we won't arrive in time for dinner so don't hurry back. I pen this in a privy councillor's coat, a Lieutenant Colonel's trousers, an insignia and cloak around my neck of the Grand Cross of St. Michael and St. George. I will explain this folly tomorrow. I am masquerading in Sir Matthew's best clothes,

Your loving

Dorothy'

2 OCTOBER 1915

Crossed to London with Aunt Alice, Dorothy and Edie. Stayed at Grosvenor Road.[22] Visited Devonshire House and St John's Gate for information re staffing of hospitals over Great Britain with women clerks, cooks and typists.

TUESDAY [6 OCTOBER 1915]

Mrs Ayrton to dinner, bringing photographs of her 'fan' and the experiments showing its use for blowing back the poison gases from the trenches and clearing the trenches when they are already full. Each fan weighs a little over 1 lb. She has great difficulties in getting her experiments shown, but has now received an admirable report which has been sent in to the War Office.

Wednesday [7 October 1915]

Came to de Walden Court[23] and have been put to bed for treatment under Pa's own eye.

London's a perfect turmoil of agitation and <u>sooty</u> black at night. There are constantly accidents of people killed by motors, crossing the road, at night. An awful restlessness pervades everything.

Thursday [8 October 1915]

She [Hertha Ayrton] telephones that Mr Greenslade her assistant has orders to hold himself in readiness to proceed at any moment to the front with fans.

Postcard from Hertha Ayrton to Elsie, 10 October 1915 –

'I am so sorry to hear your heart is not strong, but I hope it is only a temporary weakness which the rest will cure. Please thank your father for his kind message and for writing to your brother about the report. I am afraid your brother must have had an arduous time since Loos.'

13 October 1915

A Zepplin [*sic*] raid 9.30 tonight. A furious scurrying and hissing of taxis, everyone hurrying to their posts. Only one Zep. visible to us, travelling eastwards, very fast, and looking like a streak of light. <u>Very</u> high. Too high for our aircraft to get level with. The pong! pong! of the anti-aircraft guns going all the time and the shells bursting everywhere like rockets at a fireworks show. Everyone rushes into the street to gaze. Harriet was out watching a public house for the 'Watch Committee' when a man came up – said 'You'd oughter be at home, missis, taking care of the Kids, this isn't safe'. Then she saw the Zepplin [*sic*] streaking along.

OCTOBER 1915

[The diary includes a number of letters, newspaper articles and obituaries (including copy of the corps diary from Wed. 22 to Thursday 30 September 1915) for Edward 'Ted' Brunton (1890–1915), Elsie's brother, who was killed at the battle of Loos while serving as a lieutenant in the RAMC.]

They include one from the family friend, Marryat Dobie from Farnham, Surrey to Elsie, 27 October 1915 –

'Dear Mrs Henry,

Some chance made me look today at the casualty list for the first time in months and I saw Edward's name on it. I feel my own loss is so great that there is nothing [which] I can say about it, and he would have hated much talk about it. I have read enough of men of great promise being killed, and though I know how dear and how unlike anyone else they must have seemed to their own relatives and friends, yet I could never really [appreciate] properly the waste of this war until it was brought home to me this morning. [Please tell] Nance how sorry I am.

I am glad at least that his death, if it had to come, came at a time of victory; the saddest thing is when precious lives are thrown away in an unsuccessful, foolish enterprise, or by some wretched piece of bungling.

I am afraid that this letter is full of complaints for my own sorrow rather than consolation for yours – but I could not hope to give you any consolation, and this will at least show you my sympathy.

Yours very sincerely,

Marryat R. Dobie.

I dislocated my elbow (motor bicycle fall) on my way to a new job at Béthune, and am getting it massaged. I should be able to return to France in a week.'

3 November 1915

Small dinner to discuss draft scheme for introduction of Physical Training into Universities as a sine qua non. Sir Donald Macalister[24] took me in and they were all depressed having come from the General Medical Council where they had been forced to agree to medical students up to 3 yrs training being taken as unstarred men. Sir Donald seemed to think the two most pressing problems from his point of view were how to supply the future medical men, and how to hand on the 'traditions' of the Universities. Oxford and Cambridge are practically empty except for some coloured men, and Glasgow being open to men and women has now become almost entirely women.

He is somewhat bothered by the workings of the Insurance Act in his district as he is responsible for it. At one place he had a very capable young man, who was however 'seconded' by the Commissioners, for an elaboration of reasons. A young woman doctor took his place and worked on well. Then after the war came, volunteers were established there for training purposes. They had no medical man, and the Government said the care of their health must be undertaken by the local medical practitioner! who accordingly was quite willing for the job, but a little puzzled as to regulations, etc. and wrote to Sir Donald. Sir Donald was also responsible for the island of St. Kilda, but as it was so small and inaccessible they decided a nurse would be more useful. So a nurse was sent out. After a while however she was so smitten with homesickness that she abandoned herself to grief and wireless telegraphed that she must be removed and would not stay. No boat could get there, and Sir Donald appealed to the Admiralty and finally a battleship was sent out and escorted the home-sick nurse back to the mainland.

4 NOVEMBER 1915

They have appealed against the taking of medical students for fighting, and Sir Thomas Fraser came in more depressed than ever, for Lord Derby[25] replied that if the war wasn't won in two years, there wouldn't be a country to consider here at all.

6 NOVEMBER 1915

This evening William Logan of the Grenadier Guards came to see Father. He was Ted's servant, with him at Loos. They went together to look for Major Ponsonby, missing. They did not find him, but very nearly got into the German trenches. That was on the Monday or Tuesday, for Logan was wounded on the Tuesday and removed and did not see Ted again. Logan was sent back to hospital in London and only discharged today to the Chelsea barracks where he heard for the first time, and so came direct to Father at 7 p.m. He said Ted was absolutely fearless, and that he worked incessantly, over and above what was expected, and that he was at one time 36 hours on end bandaging and dressing. He said Ted had a beautiful horse of which he was very fond. They did not find Major Ponsonby; he was only found after being missing 18 hours, dead.

9 NOVEMBER 1915

Augustine arrived from Dublin. Mr M.H. Spielmann came. He hears from the Heger family through his brother the banker and D. Weiner. Prof. Heger did get back to Brussels safely. Mr S. says Prof. Heger took an almost keener interest in Miss Cavell's work than even Dr. Depage [sic], and said that Miss Cavell[26] was a paragon of virtues, but in dealing with the authorities, of very determined and uncompromising opinions, and that he had sometimes had considerable difficulty in smoothing things over, and they had foreseen trouble, but the shock [of her execution] had been terrible.

Mr S. says things have settled into a sort of working plan and the Bruxellois (Belgians) retain their indomitable courage and hope. The Germans organized a great concert at the Théatre de la Monnaie in the summer and had some famous musicians up from Berlin, in order to try and get on a friendly footing with the Bruxellois. When the performance took place there were 3 Bruxellois in all present, and one of these was a Professor of the University, with a German wife. The following day Professor Heger, as Rector of the University, sent for him and reproved him, saying that Belgium was not a conquered country although it was invaded by the enemy, and that as unconquered people it behoved the Belgians to hold out together against friendly advances of any kind, and he requested him to resign. This the Professor did, and went home. Prof. Heger had been given a pass to go to Berne and left the next morning, but hardly had he gone than the Germans arrested the Rector pro-tem of the University! Prof. [Heger] worried constantly about this during his absence and it made him immoveable in his determination to get back into Brussels.

A further concert was got up 2 or 3 months later. This time every seat was booked beforehand by Belgians. The Germans were quite pleased and encouraged. When the hour came however the players were confronted by such a total vacuum as even Nature abhors. Not one single soul was in the building.

Letter from Blanche [Cole, wife of Professor Granville A.J. Cole,] in Dublin to Elsie, 5 November 1915 –
Describes the establishment of the War Supply Depot 'in a small way, at the College of Science' and the appointment of the committee, with Blanche being appointed as treasurer – 'I am not a blooming book of minutes, but an Impressionist on the art of writing history.'

NOVEMBER 1915

Mrs Wright and I went to see Mr Fletcher [secretary of technical instruction at DATI] and get the Department's permission to become the Sphagnum centre for all Ireland. Mr Fletcher said 'Where do you get your supplies of sphagnum?' and Mrs Wright, looking young and lovely and innocent replied 'I have turned on the Geological Survey of Ireland to collect it all over the country'. The Secretary for Technical Instruction gave a little gasp and then winked at me 'Even the meanest things have their uses'.

27 NOVEMBER 1915

George Stopford is in the 19 General Hospital, Alexandria, with typhoid.

Letter from Harriet [Jaffé] in London to Elsie, 4 December 1915 –
'I expect Sir Lauder will write to you. Capt Picton Phillips called on him today. He was the last to see Ted alive. He said Ted absolutely knew no fear and was bright and cheerful. Then the shell burst came and caught him just behind the ear – he fell and died instantaneously. The officer did not actually see Ted fall because the shell, in bursting, threw up such a cloud and a neighbouring house interfered with his line of vision. He went at once to the spot where Ted stood – and Ted was already wrapped in that infinite peace and forgetfulness of all earthly troubles and lay in calm and heavenly quiet ... Capt Phillips was Ajt [Adjutant] to1st battn Welsh Guards.'

7 DECEMBER 1915

Robert Stopford has arrived safely at Salonica.

[21 December 1915]

Annie Carroll, one of the 'supernumeraries'[27] who was taken on as cook at 'Kingstown' Brighton, wrote 'I am quite able for the cooking but it is very hard to make meat stretch on all of them, they give very small alounce [*sic*] and when it is fat or bony it does not go very far, however cournall [*sic*] and capton [*sic*] and ackting sergent [*sic*] or Meager[*sic*] was in today and they told me he would see and help me.'

1. Elsie Henry as an infant (Courtesy of James Brunton and Nancy Willson)

This diary was written by Alice Helen, elder daughter of Sir Lauder Brunton and wife of Augustine Henry. It was begun in the first year of their residence in Ireland; it was continued as a war record, showing the information received daily by the ordinary citizen; and it was kept up later until the end of the war, for the sake of Edward Lauder

2. Elsie Henry's introduction to her diaries (Courtesy of the National Library of Ireland).

Garden at 5 Sandford Terrace
E.H. Nance. Dorothy, Kathleen Dickinson in wheelbarrow

3. Elsie Henry, Nance Brunton, Dorothy Stopford and Kathleen Dickinson in the garden of 5, Sandford Terrace Ranelagh, c.1913 (Courtesy of the National Library of Ireland).

4. Castle Shane, Ardglass 1913, Elsie Henry's diary, September 1913 (Courtesy of the National Library of Ireland).

5. Letter from Roger Casement to Elsie Henry, 26 October 1913 (Courtesy of the National Library of Ireland).

6. Letter from Eoin MacNeill to Elsie Henry, 15 December 1913 (Courtesy of the National Library of Ireland).

7. Letter from Alice Stopford Green to Elsie Henry, 31 March 1914 (Courtesy of the National Library of Ireland).

Artist and Ecclesiastic

You tell us you black coated clergymen
You have gone up unto the Holy Hill,
are the interpreters of that high will
which is the ridgepole of the heavens. Then
I charge you to make answer. Tell us when
your faces glowed with light ineffable
like his who turned from Sinai. If you still
enter the Holy of Holies, speak again
as those who come forth dark . blind into glory
wrapping the heavens about them as a cloth.
Are these dull admonitions from that sphere?
Nay, nay, you shall not rule us with that story
until the words you cry even in wrath
Break in a foam of beauty on the ear.

George Russell
A.E.

8. 'Artists and ecclesiastics' by AE, Elsie Henry's diary 8 July 1914 (Courtesy of the National Library of Ireland).

Saturday July 4th
Aunt Aline arrived 11 p.m.
Sir Roger has gone on the 'long journey'.

Wednesday July 8th.

Mrs. Green is very anxious, expecting news
that doesn't come. Monday night at 1 a.m. a
terrific knocking at the front door, + a postman
with a telegram from the G.P.O. for Mrs. Green
The telegram was given in at 7 p.m. in England +
delivered here at 1 a.m. The delay en route
ominously accounted for, knowing the system
... is expected at Cowes + is two days
... is no news.

9. Elsie Henry's diary, 4, 8 July 1914 (Courtesy of the National Library of Ireland).

10. (l. to r.) Paul Heger, Elsie and Augustine Henry, 20 July 1914, Oisquerque, Belgium (Courtesy of the National Library of Ireland).

11. Elsie and Augustine Henry with Sir Jocelyn Gore-Booth at Lissadell, June 1915 (Courtesy of the National Library of Ireland).

13. Reverse of Ted's birthday card to Elsie, August 1915 (Courtesy of the National Library of Ireland).

12. Birthday card from her brother Ted Brunton to Elsie, August 1915 (Courtesy of the National Library of Ireland).

Graves Registration Commission.

Photograph of the Grave of :—

Name BRUNTON

Rank and Initials LIEUT E.

Regiment R.A.M.C.

Position of Grave VERMELLES MILITARY

CEMETERY

Nearest Railway Station VERMELLES

All communications respecting this Photograph should quote the number (A C 44) and be addressed to :—
O.C.,
H.Q.,
G.R.C.,
British Expeditionary Force.

Owing to the circumstances in which the photographic work is carried on, the G.R.C. is unable at present to send any but rough Photographs.

14. Grave registration card of Ted Brunton, October 1915 (Courtesy of the National Library of Ireland).

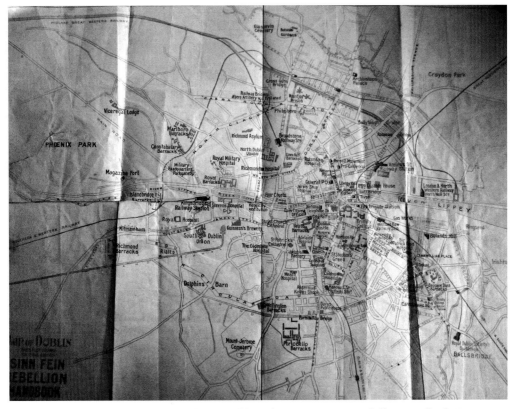

15. Dublin, Easter 1916, from Weekly Irish Times *Sinn Fein Rebellion Handbook: Easter 1916* (Dublin, 1917) (Courtesy of the National Library of Ireland and the *Irish Times*).

17. Elsie Henry diary, 30 April 1916, with Augustine Henry's travel permit into Dublin from Dun Laoghaire (Courtesy of the National Library of Ireland).

16. Elsie Henry's diary, 25-26 April 1916 (Courtesy of the National Library of Ireland).

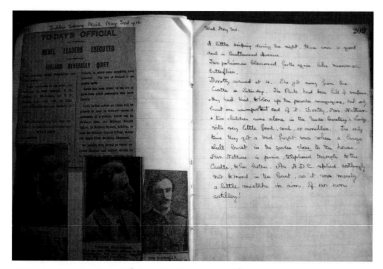

18. Elsie Henry's diary, 3 May 1916 (Courtesy of the
National Library of Ireland).

19. Elsie Henry's diary, 13 May 1916
(Courtesy of the National Library of Ireland).

20. 'Conference' by AE, Elsie Henry's diary, 26 May 1916
(Courtesy of the National Library of Ireland).

21. Elsie Henry's diary, April 1917 (Courtesy of the National Library of Ireland).

22. Some of the Committee of the Sphagnum Moss Depot at the Royal College of Science for Ireland 1918 (from *Irish Life*, July 1918) (Courtesy of the National Library of Ireland).

23. Elsie Henry's travel pass, Elsie Henry's diary, October 1918 (Courtesy of the National Library of Ireland).

HOME OFFICE,
WHITEHALL, S.W.1.

CONFIDENTIAL.

15th December, 1918.

ORDER OF THE BRITISH EMPIRE.

Madam,

I am directed by the Home Secretary to inform you that, in view of the service you have rendered on work connected with the War, it is proposed to submit your name to the King for appointment as an Officer of the Order of the British Empire.

The Home Secretary desires me to ask you to be so good as to fill up the enclosed form and return it to me in the accompanying addressed envelope at your earliest convenience.

I am,

Madam,

Your obedient Servant,

G.G. Whiskard.

Acting Secretary,
Order of the British Empire

Mrs. Alice Henry.

24. Letter to Elsie Henry regarding an OBE, Elsie Henry's diary, November 1918 (Courtesy of the National Library of Ireland).

25. Elsie Henry (left) with a friend, the great Irish gardener Fanny Geoghegan (Courtesy of the Library, National Botanic Gardens of Ireland, Glasnevin).

5

Conflict in Ireland:

The Diaries 1916[1]

INTRODUCTION

*E*arly in 1916 conscription was introduced in Britain but was not extended to Ireland. On the Western Front the year saw the battles of Verdun in February and the Somme which began in June. There were battles on the Italian front and an Allied offensive in Salonika whilst the major naval battle of the First World War, the Battle of Jutland, took place at the end of May. In Britain there were government efforts to mobilize their total manpower, either in the armed forces or in industry, and an imperial conference brought in new controls regarding food, for example meatless days, quality of bread, etc.

Elsie's diaries for 1916 contain a vast amount of newspaper cuttings following the war in the Balkans, in Macedonia, in Italy, the Battle of Verdun, the Somme and the revolution in Russia.

In Dublin Elsie focussed her efforts on the establishment of the Sphagnum Moss Depot at the Royal College of Science for Ireland (RCScI) and in getting its work recognized by the War Office in London.

Another Stopford cousin, Dorothy, moved to Ireland at the beginning of 1916 to begin her medical studies at Trinity College Dublin (TCD).

In April the Easter Rising took Elsie by surprise and in the days following Easter Monday 1916 she, together with her colleagues, was involved in getting medical supplies to the various hospitals around Dublin. Augustine was in London for Easter and, cut off from communication with Dublin, hoped that Elsie was safe in Wexford and away from the fighting in Dublin.

In common with many of her contemporaries, Elsie described the Easter Rising as a Sinn Féin insurrection.[2]

There is a gap in the 1916 diaries, from the end of May until 21 December 1916.

❋

Letter from [H. Dickinson?] at Imbros[3] to Elsie, 13 January 1916 –
'My dear Elsie,
Your very much welcome letter of 15 Dec. arrived yesterday – with its accompaniment of cigarettes. Like the Robin the brand of all brands that I love the best. I have shared them and smoked them – more I've smoked than I've shared. Decent cigarettes are very rare with us – the "Flags" and "Arf-a-mos" are easily come by.[4] If at some future time you really do remember an absent friend – and really do want to send him something – another little box would be splendid.

How very wise of Dorothy to wish to return to the land of her birth and yr. neighbourhood ... You must be most frightfully busy with yr V.A.D. and I do hope that yr dressings with the quite impossible name won't seriously increase our death rate. I think so long as the patient doesn't know what he is being tied up with he'll probably be safe won't he? The other day I bandaged a burn – not my burn – with an old coal sack and a bit of a bootlace – I hear he's doing splendidly ... After the transfer of our forces from both Anzac and Helles[5] – when I had to do – most reluctantly – the Boy stood on the burning deck[6] to each [illegible] – the place is quite peaceful not to say dull. Write again soon – with all news.'

Letter from Maud [Crawford], an Irish VAD serving at 14 General Hospital, Boulogne to Elsie, 24 January 1916 –
'Dear Elsie,

I may call you that now, mayn't I, I have always wanted to do so. Helen sent me on your letter. I only wish it was possible to accept your invitation to tea, but, as you can see, I am still in 'the pleasant land of France' ... I have been meaning to write to you for ages and ages to thank you for the parcel of things you so kindly sent me for the men and which they were ever so pleased to get. It <u>was</u> good of you and I really am more grateful than would appear from my silence.

You'll be surprised to see the above address and to know that I'm here as a patient. That deadly enemy, the 'Flue', has me in its grip for the past 10 days. I've been running a temp. [temperature] and have been pretty miserable and am now pretty weak and washed out, but on the way to convalescence. I am still in bed but hope to be allowed up tomorrow. I've only been here since yesterday morning and then arrived as a stretcher case by motor ambulance! Before then I was in the sick sister's room at the 14 Stationary [hospital base], as they weren't sure that I had not Para B., but the night before last poor old 14 Stationary was burnt to the ground. They had just time to put me into a dressing gown, wrap me in a blanket and ten of them carried me from the very tip of the building, through dense smoke, to a hotel down the road, where I remained for the night and next day was brought here – a refugee possessed of nothing save a nightie and a dressing grown, not even a pair of slippers or a hankie, to say nothing of a toothbrush! Joking apart, it is a tragedy to lose all one owns, and how am I to face the world in a dressing gown, when I'm allowed up and about. I'm hoping they'll send me home on sick leave as a stretcher case, so that I can scrape together some things. Dear old 14 Stationary, I was so happy there. I feel as if someone belonging to me had died – it's terribly sad, especially as they had a splendid Lab. and had done some wonderful work and they could not manage to save the records or a specimen. Mercifully not a soul was injured seriously, though some of the Orderlies were overcome by the smoke and every one of the patients were got out in time. It started to burn about 8 p.m. and was blazing in a very short time and it was a wonderful and terrifying sight. I believe they saw the fire from Folkestone and signalled to know what was happening, so you can imagine the glare it made. Already they have got the huts in full working order again and all the patients back again, which I think is just wonderful. Think of having to move cerebro-spinal cases! I hear they have already taken a new building which will have as many beds as the old ... Please tell Miss Reed I was so pleased to get her card and many thanks for the offer of [sphagnum moss] pads, but I don't think they'd be so much more use to us as to a surgical hospital.

Forgive the scrawl,

Love from Maud'

Letter from Robert Stopford, now serving at the 173rd Unit of Supply, British Salonika to Elsie, 26 January 1916 –
'My dear Elsie, I have to thank you and Augustine most warmly for your parcel, which was lovely. I am wearing the socks now, they are splendid and the eatables were most acceptable.

I am having a very interesting time out here as I am now running my own little depot out in the mountains. I am encamped next door to the headquarters of a division which, as you may imagine, gives good cause for trouble; but headquarters or no headquarters, I won't be squashed and now the atmosphere is much clearer.

Today, Nevinson, the war correspondent, appeared with an English Doctor in the Serbian Army and his wife, a nurse, called Beevis. They came back to tea and my tent was the scene of a tea-party. My servant, a good lad from Portadown, <u>was</u> horror-struck at the idea. 'I never thought we'd have any women here' was all he could say. The tea-party was quite a success. It seemed very strange, I must say.

It is lovely country here, but awfully cold. The day I came up here it was snowing hard and we had 8 hours in an open lorry and on arrival at 7.30 p.m. had to pitch our tents in a foot of snow. However, the weather has improved and we get bright sunshine by day tho' at night it is bitterly cold and windy. [In] fact my tent makes desperate attempts almost nightly to reach the stars. Fortunately it hasn't succeeded so far; and I have a magnificent tin brazier, originally the property of the Asiatic Petroleum Company, and converted by my servant. After the fashion of the man in *The Riddle of the Sands* he has a passion for throwing my brazier away so that he may have the pleasure of making a new one. Please excuse the paper and writing but it's rather a difficulty here.

Ever yr affectionate cousin,

Robert J. Stopford'

29 JANUARY 1916

Aug. [Augustine] thinks the Germans will make their greatest effort now, between Feb. and May, and that it will be along the Western Front, all the more so that they are proclaiming through the press, that the Western Front is a deadlock, and that they can do nothing along that line. They will try once more to break through to Paris, and <u>if</u> they can reach Paris, they can dictate peace to France. If they are beaten they will offer peace, for their financial credit abroad is so low they cannot carry on longer. But now they are at their zenith of strength, and we are in the most critical position of the whole war.

Letter from George Stopford, now convalescing in London, to Elsie, 30 January 1916 –

'Dear Elsie,

I'm afraid I have been a terrible long time in answering your nice long letter. I have also had your other letter sent back from Egypt. I am practically speaking quite well now but I shall be in hospital for about another fortnight as I am going to have one of those silly nose operations again ... I was most interested in the Sphagnum (try and say it after dinner!) ... I have seen most of the family since I have been back. I'm rather hoping to get back to Egypt but I doubt I shall be able to manage it. Love to Nance[7] if you see her.

Yours,

George Stopford'

31 JANUARY 1916

Mr Forbes came in to see A. [Augustine] last week. He was greatly excited about signalling in Wicklow. He saw a 'brilliant light', like a 'motor lamp' flashed from the top of a hill out to sea. Unable to reach it on foot, he got a friend with a motor-car to pursue it. But it had vanished, leaving no trace. The next night it came again. Clear, large, brilliant, in the crest of the hill. There could be no doubt. Mr. Forbes roused the police. All the Wicklow police were set on the hunt. Real activity prevailed, but nothing could be found.

Then Mr. Forbes poured the thrilling news into Aug's ear. A. went down town and consulted a friend who keeps a photograph shop and also dabbled in astronomy. They unearthed an astronomical chart, and A. says he proved conclusively, that the dates and movements were those selected by Venus for her most brilliant setting of the year over the crest of Cush [Bawn]. A. is busy proving it to Mr Forbes but Mr Forbes will never forgive him for evermore.

16 FEBRUARY 1916

We went to lunch with the Marquis and Marchioness [MacSwiney]. It was a 'Portuguese lunch' cooked by himself. We were asked for 1.30 but it refused to cook itself, so it was 2.30 when we began. A great festivity! Their adored Italian butler who has been with the Markiss [*sic*] 19 years and has just been extracted over from Paris after months of negotiation. He waited on us in full evening dress and white cotton gloves. He has forgotten Italian and can only understand broken French ... Our first dish had a nameless Portuguese cognomen, but it was made, the Markiss declared proudly, of eggs, fresh sausages, chopped olives, pimento and wine all beaten up together. It sounded like 'Fredgedda'. The next was liver with slices of potato stewed in tomato sauce very highly seasoned. These were the pièces de résistance by the Markiss after which the Italian butler obliged with coffee-ice, followed by gorgonzola, followed by pink meringues ... Augustine left in the middle, for an appointment; he shook us each in turn from behind by the hand, and he clung gracefully to the last hand while he made a pretty speech, when he discovered it was Mr. Kelly's second hand he was squeezing, instead of the Marchioness's! He made a final grab at hers and fled.

21–29 FEBRUARY 1916

Nance here.

23 FEBRUARY 1916

Notification from Dr. Cathcart[8] that the War Office has put Sphagnum moss on its official list of surgical dressings.

26 FEBRUARY 1916

Requests for sphagnum dressings from Addenbrookes and the 1st Eastern Hospital Cambridge; No. 9 General Hospital Rouen; No. 10

Casualty Clearing Station, B.E.F. France; Revigny Urgency cases Hosp.;
No. 17 Gen. Hospital Alexandra.

SATURDAY 27 FEBRUARY 1916

Top and Betty arrived. 'The captain is as soople [*sic*] as a deer, and isn't
Mrs Brunton beautiful?' says Mary. 'It's the grand <u>sweep</u> [*sic*] she'll
have, she'll be a great lady. But its very young to be married, there isn't
any profit out of life that way. Life is very sweet: we must enjoy it when
we can, for there'll be long enough in the bone-yard!' Top returned on
Sunday night. Nance left on Wednesday morning.

[NO DATE] 1916

Unofficial word reached us this aft. [afternoon] that the authorities are
urging economy in cotton wool at the front and the employment of
substitute – so our 'dwindling supply of cotton wool' was prophetic. B.
[Bea] shrieks with excitement and spag. [spaghnum moss] is coming
into its own.

Letter from Alice Stopford Green in London to Elsie, 12 March 1916 –
'Dearest Elsie,

Jack's life ended most peacefully today ... He left a letter to George
wishing no old or ill person, nor any occupied one, to be at the funeral
so we have decided that George and Mr Villiers and I will go, and no
one else in the family ... I may leave for Ireland in two or three days – if
so I go first to Belfast for a short motor expedition. Then to you. If I
leave later I would go first to you, if you wished it. I am glad you have
had Top and Betty with you in these days of sharp disappointment.
Dear love may all consolation come to you ...
Your constant friend,
ASG'

12 MARCH 1916

Sunday morning. Top arrived. Snow, sleet, wind and rain as usual. After lunch, in default of any picture palace being open, Betty rattled us off to visit 'Uncle Sandy' at Glenageary.

MONDAY 13 MARCH 1916

Top inspected the Depot.[9]

TUESDAY 14 MARCH 1916

The first signs of spring this year. The wind <u>at last</u> moved from N.E. We drove into the hills and round by the gamekeeper's lodge, but the snow on the hills was still lying quite low, and at the junction of the Enniskerry road, a snow-drift so deep that Betty and I had to wade, and Top and the driver half led and half carried the car over it! We were the first car for over 3 weeks across that road.

WEDNESDAY 15 MARCH 1916

Wretched again. We hugged the fire, talked and read Lucian. Top returned to London by the night mail.

SATURDAY 18 MARCH 1916

To Coolcarrigan with Mrs Wilson. Augustine planted his new cross of vaccinium from America in the Bog Garden. It came by post from America and arrived on Thursday, and was planted on Sunday. When it was unpacked, lo! It was wrapped in Sphagnum! Mrs Wilson took me to collect sphagnum and point out the best kinds for gathering, all Sunday morning, and it pouring a sleety rain.

Letter from J. Lumsden, M.D., St John's Ambulance Brigade Dublin to Elsie, 20 March 1916 –

'Dear Mrs Henry,

Many thanks for your letter and copy of your article for *The Torch*[10] which I have read with great interest.

I am sure Miss O'Brien's and Mrs Wight's visit to Scotland will be of great value; your sphagnum Depot, as I anticipated, is a huge success, and now that you have got War Office recognition, and are carrying on your researches in such a scientific fashion, yours' will be a great work.

I spoke to Mr Fannin,[11] and I think he is interested in the affair and he sees great possibilities in the undertaking, and seems to think it would be worth his while to give practical and voluntary assistance in the sublimating.

Yours, etc.'

22 MARCH 1916

Top left for France.

Opened a third day at the Depot. The War Office has today sent us word requisitioning <u>5,000</u> moss dressings per month. Mrs. Wright's report on her visit to Edinburgh, and the preparation of hard dressings, and of the sublimating process. Steam sterilization tends to harden the moss and inhibit its absorptiveness and Dr. Cathcart is now sublimating all the dressings by passing them through a solution of corrosive subliminate (1/4 per cent) and drying afterwards.

23 MARCH 1916

Letter from the War Office today asking if the College of Science wd. be prepared to become the centre for moss for Ireland, and organize, if necessary later, sub-centres. Mr Fletcher [of DATI] pleased, and all facilities are given us.

28 MARCH 1916
Aunt Alice arrived.

Letter from Lauder Brunton in London to Elsie, 28 March 1916 –
'Dearest Elsie,
I am delighted to hear that you are feeling stronger though Miss Jaffé tells me you have unexpectedly caught cold. It is so jolly that sphagnum is going so well. I send you a letter from Mrs. Amy about it in France. Dr. Dilling is pushing it at Woolwich[12] and before long it will take a great place. I wonder what is done with it after it has served its purpose as a dressing? ... I think the suggestion of Nancy's taking a room in Dublin is a very good one, and I hope the plan of growing medicinal plants will be a success.'

29 MARCH 1916
Gerty Kerley on her way back to St. Thomas Hospital.

30 MARCH 1916
Betty returned from Cahir.

31 MARCH 1916
A lovely day at last. Complete change of temperature and full sunshine. Sir Matthew came around the Depot and was interested; he motored me back here and Aunt Alice had Douglas Hyde to meet him. Great uneasiness prevails about the Tullamore incident,[13] as arms and even dynamite is scattered about the country. Funds for them are coming from America, probably from German sources.

Letter from Top in France to Elsie, 31 March 1916 –

'Dearest little sister,

The day before yesterday I flew over the lines in an aeroplane and we went in Hunland but the Huns sent some 'archie' (anti-aircraft shell) after us so we retired in good order. I don't suppose I'll ever duplicate that day. Tuesday I walked through a most impressive town and was deeply interested in the havoc which hate can create. Friday was fairly quiet so we got on well. The light is going out and it's 3 a.m. but I [can't] go to sleep as we have moved camp and some kit has been left behind including mine.

Best love from Stopford'

1 APRIL 1916

Real Spring at last, Mary waved her arms joyously at me this morning and chanted thanksgivings, at last she explained, 'The Lord has sent me a great consolation, he has crowned me altogether and all the trouble I took yesterday polishing the hall and throwing water down the steps and it after being that dirty a winter. But the lord rewarded me, isn't Sir Matthew a fine gentleman, and of the best in the land, and I afraid t'was for a little black squat of a Jew[14] I did be going to all the trouble. Isn't the Lord good Ma'am?'

Letter from Lauder Brunton in London to Elsie, 4 April 1916 –

'Aunt Alice and Betty arrived this morning about 9.30 ... Betty had breakfast and almost immediately afterwards Miss Jaffé and she went down to Castle and Co. to see about steamers to Canada.'

Letter from Top, on U.S.M.S. Philadelphia to Elsie, 12 April 1916 –

'I got home at about 7.30 Sunday night and found Betty had booked a passage on a boat sailing on Tuesday so you can imagine there was something of a wild hootoosh ... I picked up a little book in Ypres and have left it with Harriet to send to you ... which you will see was printed in 1685. It's rather extraordinary for these books to have escaped both the fire and the destruction by shells ... I met Hal Kitchener in Bailleul and he took me for a drive in an aeroplane. We went from Bailleul to Poperinghi and then to Ypres where the Huns straffed us as we were flying low but they didn't hit us ... At the last I was just behind St. Eloi when they were fighting for the craters. I was into the village and in the front line trenches a couple of hundred yards from the craters but I never reached the craters themselves. Then came an order for me to return home ... I'm awfully sorry they didn't let me go on the 1st March but held me up three weeks because it cut the time in France so excessively short.']

14 APRIL 1916
Augustine left for London.

15 APRIL 1916
Mrs Wright and I for Courtown Harbour. A lovely spot, the sandy beach running all along the demesne, which is full of ferny glens, and sheets of primroses, under beech avenues.

22 APRIL 1916
Wire from Father saying Top and Betty had arrived safe in Montreal.

23 APRIL 1916
Easter Sunday.

Letter from Alice Stopford Green in London to Elsie, 24 April 1916 –
'I am going to Darby and Joan with Augustine at Kew today – quite festive.'

25 APRIL 1916

No post by the mail and vague and alarming rumours of a Sinn Fein rising in Dublin. We got the mail train, 5.20 p.m. and met Mr Forbes in it. He knew very little, but said the Post Office and Stephen's Green is in the hands of the Sinn Feiners, and that they have shot the station master at Westland Row.[15] The train ran in to Harcourt Street[16] instead of Westland Row, and Peter met us at Ranelagh with a car. It is quite true, and everyone was unprepared. General Friend is in London, and there is only enough military to keep it 'localized'. The Sinn Feiners have the GPO and are barricaded inside. All wires have been cut and we are without communications to England or the rest of the country. They have the line from Kingstown to Westland Row, and they have Kingsbridge station, Jacob's factory, Guinness Brewery, and the quays, and the Four Courts. Annie went all over town yesterday and saw a flag flying from the top of the GPO, the republican colours, red, white and green, and on it the words 'German and American Allies Help'. A machine gun is mounted on the top of the Post Office and they were firing with it.

WEDNESDAY 26 APRIL 1916

The firing continues; they have the gas plant and the power station of the Tramway company, so no trams are running. It is a glorious warm spring day, the trees all bursting into bright green and the birds singing. It is perfectly quiet here, but cyclists bring along all sorts of rumours. Peter and Peggy have gone to the College.

At 1.30 Peggy and I went down, as the Depot should have opened. We went by Fitzwilliam Place and Baggot Street. Everywhere deserted and dead with a few people stealing about, or talking in knots, and children playing in the street. The police are confined to barracks, but this morning Peggy saw twelve of them taking shelter under an arch, while some small children played in the road with occasional bullets flying over them.

Mrs. Cole had driven the Professor in all the way from Carrickmines, in her car, and we all met at the College, and posted up a notice in the hall stating that the Depot would not open until the military regulations were relaxed.

It was such a heavenly sunny peaceful afternoon but every now and then the stillness was broken by the re-echo of shots. A boy went up on the College roof to look this morning, and was shot by a bullet, perhaps aimed at the Shelbourne.[17] The military are occupying the Shelbourne – they have cleared Stephen's Green; the Sinn Feiners have retreated into the College of Surgeons. We went back by the Plunkett House, where Mr Norman was trying to re-assure Susan for AE's absence. He was away with the Lysaghts but no word has been heard, and no one knows where he is.[18] H.N., Susan, and Peggy went home, and I went to the Winters. Dr Winter[19] said it all came as a great surprise, and broke out at midday on Monday. He was coming home by tram through Stephen's Green when he saw them digging busily in the Green, and heard what he thought were blank cartridges. He thought it rather odd. The next tram was stopped and seized for a barricade. We saw it lying derelict, and two overturned carts and a dead horse. The carter wouldn't stop and was shot dead. They took motor cars and anything that tried to cross the Green, and gave a receipt for everything, including 19 gallons of milk from a milkman, the receipt was dated '2nd Day of the Republic of Ireland'. Peter said on Tuesday he saw little children glued up against the railings of the Green looking in.

At 4.30 I started for the St. John staff meeting in Dawson Street, and remembering Dr Mather Thomson[20] [sic] was Staff Surgeon, went to his home. We walked down together, a fearful uproar of big guns and maxims going on continuously at Ringsend, they said at Boland's bread factory which the Sinn Feiners occupy. The firing was incessant. At the corner of Merrion Square and Clare Street a rifle cracked somewhere close to us. All shops are barricaded and closed. Some windows were broken in Nassau Street and the City is terrible, and Nobletts sweet-shop has been ransacked.

The office in Dawson Street was closed, so we came back. In Baggot Street we could see fighting at the Bag. St. [Baggot Street] Bridge end. Dr Thomson thought he saw a man fall, and went on ahead to see could he help. It was a sniper who had been caught red-handed. Two soldiers had crawled along the roof from one house to another and dropped on to the window from which he was firing. We came up Fitzwilliam Place, and on Leeson Street Bridge I met Dr. and Mr. Webb.[21] She had telephoned to the Vice-Regal Lodge for orders for the V.A.D.s, and got the reply we were to do nothing and above all not to wear uniform. Sir Matthew [Nathan] is at the V.R. [Vice-Regal] Lodge and we suppose Dorothy is with him. She was to go to Foxrock on Monday, but she cannot have got away.

I went to Mabel Dickinson[22] to tell her that much and she said troops had been arriving all day from England, and passing at the end of Marlborough Road. General Friend[23] has returned on a gun-boat, and Lord French[24] is said to be with him. The fighting has raged round Beggar's Bush Barracks, the Veteran Corps[25] is shut up in there, Charlie Dickinson, Prof. Wilson, and Mr R.A. Anderson among them. They have plenty of food, and are only short of tobacco and razors! The Veteran Corps had been for a long route march on Monday, simply because it was Bank Holiday, and were struggling home along Northumberland Road, when suddenly they were fired at from windows, and four killed instantly, and some wounded. They went into Beggar's Bush Barracks, which had been their headquarters, and are surrounded by Sinn Feiners, or at any rate totally imprisoned there.

A young man came in, belonging to the motor garage at the top of Dawson St. His chief is away, and the next in command dying from wounds in hospital and he is in charge. He cannot do very much except go and look at the place, and yesterday got a bullet through his hat cycling there. He was in Stephen's Green itself today, there were 3 dead men just inside the gates, he said the 'trenches' were pathetic, just little scooped out hollows and bits of bushes stuck in front, no cover at all. Countess Markievicz,[26] in men's uniform, with a cigarette in her mouth and a pistol in either hand was holding up the traffic. She shot a policeman dead.

Letter from Augustine Henry in London, to Elsie, 26 April 1916 –
'My dear Elsie, I wrote letters to you – one yesterday to Dublin, one today to Courtown. The news from Dublin came to me by [rumour] on yesterday 4 p.m. ... I sent on a letter then but it is doubtful if it reached you.

I soon found out it was impossible either to telegraph or to get to Dublin. I calculated that you would be intending to return yesterday from Gorey at 5 p.m.: but that you would not be allowed to enter Dublin ... At Euston the railway people say that they cannot book to Dublin. I went today and called at the Irish Secretary's office and a very civil official [confirmed] to all of us – namely no possibility of telegraph and no possibility of getting across to Dublin. Aunt ASG [Alice Stopford Green] much perturbed and alarmed yesterday: but I remained extremely cool indeed – mainly because there was nothing to do – except to accept the situation. This morning I recovered my things at Kew; and I am ready to leave here, as soon as I can. The civil official says he will telephone, as soon as the coast is clear and one can move.

I am sending this letter to Courtown, as possibly the mails may be carried there early from Kingstown and the official told me there was no chance of you being allowed into Dublin yesterday.

I presume the servants are peaceable and quiet and have not run away: and that Mr. Beattie[27] [sic] will look after things. Mr Wright may well have travelled to Courtown.

All that is happening may be different from this; but one can only go on surmises. I conclude that as you did not leave Courtown yesterday, that you are very well ... and I hope not duly alarmed.

Now for facts – I dined yesterday evening with Ms. Kennedy. Her sister, George and a young officer were there: asked much about you – and we discussed many things – I walked home by the Embankment at 11 p.m. and [while] sitting on a step I have seen guns fire at Zeppelins in the distance: and I saw the ordinary stars in the firmament shine out on a black night – and policemen [lingering?] at corners of streets every 100 yards or so ... This morning I went to Euston to make enquiries and then on to Kew. I got my belongings and I saw Prain:[28] return here to lunch: Simon was here and I heard him tell on the situation. Then on to the Secretary's office and got news ... The difficulty of telegraph is immense – no telegrams have come through for private persons, so far as I can learn.

At 1, de Walden Court yesterday, for tea – your Father is very well. Harriet is satisfied with his condition. He talked a good deal, and was very grateful for the eggs that I brought from our house. He was interested in the sphagnum, etc. ... London very warm and sunny ... I spent from 3 to 6 at the Natural History Museum ... I lay considerable stress on the possession by Mr. Wright of a motor bike: and presume you will have seen him and got news, etc.

I think the number of fools is too great for the world.

I must now conclude, and my last word is that I will cross as soon as I can. The Enquiry office telephoned at 9 p.m. to say they cannot[take?]

civil passengers to the other side. I love you very much and I hope to see you very soon.

Much love, Augustine'

THURSDAY 27 APRIL 1916

This morning there was a great rush for provisions. By 12 o'clock many shops in Ranelagh had been cleared out and were closed. Neither loaves nor butter to be had. The baker cannot reach us as he is the other side of town. It is extraordinary to see the shops emptying. Annie and I carried home oatmeal and some provisions: flour can hardly be had. This afternoon I went over to St Mary's; they are moving house.[29] The vans were there and the men quietly shifting furniture. The streets are quite empty except for people walking with provisions in their arms, and a few cyclists eagerly surrounded by pedestrians. General Friend has issued a proclamation ordering everyone to be in his house from 7.30 p.m. – 5.30 a.m., and not to approach the firing area, as the military won't be responsible.

From St. Mary's I went on to the Wrights. Mrs Fleming, one of our Depot workers, has been shot and is in a nursing home. There is still no word of AE.

Firing began at 4.30 this morning and has gone on intermittently all day. Peter saw a house in Harcourt Street on fire this morning, opposite the 'Winter Garden' pub. People strolled about but nobody did anything. Columns of smoke rose last night from the City, but impossible to locate it. After supper I went in to the Beattys. Joe Beatty was back on sick-leave from his regiment, but he has been called out again to act as guide. The British troops have been arriving on foot from Kingstown with <u>no</u> one to guide them geographically as to Dublin and they have been walking into death traps, particularly Carrisbrook house,[30] facing Ballsbridge. Joe saw Mr. Sheehy Skeffington and two men shot in Portobello barracks yard this morning.[31] He did not know the other two.[32]

There is a repeated report that a German boat has been caught off the Kerry coast with Sir Roger Casement and German officers on board.[33] But we are utterly cut off from all communications, and all sorts of wild rumours and stories are in circulation.

A mail boat got in about 11 o'clock today, and the passengers walked from Kingstown. Mr Beatty knew one man on it who got into Dublin this evening. He had a *Sketch* with him, and Mr Beatty says Birrell[34] is making jokes about the situation.

At 7 p.m. the gun-fire began in earnest. It has moved further citywards. We heard they were fighting in Brunswick Street[35] this afternoon, so they must have got Westland Row and be pushing towards the G.P.O. The city is very dark for there is no gas, and tonight there are no lamps lit at all in this quarter.

10.30 p.m. There has been a great flare of fire or smoke ever since 7.30, impossible to locate but in the Westland Row or Sackville Street[36] direction. The machine guns have never ceased since 7. The night is absolutely calm and still and the clocks strike the hours. The fire is awful, and the rattling guns.

The wretched men knew nothing of what was coming on Monday: only a minority of them knew. Most of them thought it was a Bank Holiday parade and many tried to get home after they realized, but could not. Connolly[37] (Larkin's man) is in command of the G.P.O. and Westland Row, it is said, and McDonogh[38] [sic] of the Northumberland Road end, and Countess Marckieviecks [sic] in Stephen's Green. But that is only hearsay.

11.45. The firing is getting worse.

FRIDAY 28 APRIL 1916

At 12.30 midnight the firing slackened, but began again about 2.a.m. fairly continuously. The firing continued all day. Dr Winter came 11 a.m. and reported Miss Reed[39] had returned from London and was in 'Ivanhoe', with the Sinn Feiners in her gate-lodge. He cannot get to Steevens [Hospital] as it is impossible to cross the city. Mrs Pollok[40] came at 11.30, Uncle Ned at 12. He tried to get to Plunkett House, but a sentry of whom he was trying to enquire the way, pointed a bayonet at him. AE has returned, last night, and had to walk from Clare, with an occasional car. It took him 3 days. Bea came at 2 and we walked together down Wellington Road to Landsdowne Road. Everything is quiet there, a lovely clear cloudless day. The fighting has been appalling – Evelyn and Con were shattered by it. Evelyn saw a woman throwing stones at a baker's boy this morning because he had no bread to give her. The shops are shut except for a few that have side doors, and there are queues of people waiting outside these.

The Wrights came at 4.30. [Peter brought flour]. Last night going home, they came on about 25 soldiers creeping along under the shadow of a wall at Oakley Road, close to MacDonagh's house, Sunnyside. They had their fingers on the triggers and motioned away the Wrights who hurried on. As they came to Rathmines church, a man ran out of a door, looked up and down the street and started to run, then thought better of it and dropped to a rapid walk till he got round a bend, then he just flew.

At 6 the Coles came. They had been in to Bray for provisions. The stock had given out and the grocers had met and decided to send a ship to Liverpool for more. Mabel [Dickinson] came in at 6. She has no further news about the Veterans at Beggar's Bush.

Another mail [boat] has come in from England, but no civilians are allowed on board.

Military have been pouring in from Kingstown in one unbroken line, horses and artillery. About 4.15 3 private motors packed with military tore past up to Clonskea, and two hours later heavy covered wagons containing men, came in from the Clonskea district; a motor ambulance followed.

8.30 p.m. The sky is still red with the same fire; it is said that the whole block between O'Connell Bridge and Abbey Street is destroyed. The firing goes on but nothing like so violent as last night.

Mabel found 4 or 5 soldiers sitting in a bunch in Marlborough Road, and seeing them very hot and tired, asked the officer mightn't she bring a bucket of water and give them drinks. He replied very curtly No. She said it was a pity, and he replied 'Those are the orders, and there is every necessity for them'.

Some of the soldiers thought they were in France, as they had been bundled off without any word, and had had a railway journey and a sea journey, and concluded they had reached France.

Every day feels like a whole week.

SATURDAY 29 APRIL 1916

Firing went on all night, with occasional big booms. At 11 a.m. I went down to see Dr. Ella Webb; she is working at the temporary hospital at 40 Merrion Square.[41] They would be glad of sphagnum dressings. I fetched Mrs Wright and Bea in a car, and we took a clothes basket. Connor put us down at the corner of Baggot Street and we walked to the College. As we went in, two repeated collapses of brick buildings rattled down somewhere near by. College looked barred and bolted. Empty. We left the basket and reported to Dr. Webb. She said the hospital was filling. So at Leeson Street Bridge we found an ancient growler [horse-drawn cab] and drove out to Anglesea Road. By infinite luck the Registrar [of the College of Science] was on his doorstep. We got the master key and returned by Ballsbridge and Baggot Street. The Horse-Show grounds are <u>full</u> of military and horses. At Boland's [*sic*] bread factory opposite a long queue of people were waiting to try and get bread. Military are on Baggot Street Bridge. We got down again to the College and collected the sphagnum pads and some lint and gauze for Nettie,[42] who has wounded in her home. We carried the things along Baggot Street and down Fitzwilliam Street into Merrion Square. The City of Dublin Red X people have a temporary hospital, at no. 40 further down. The fighting is all along Lower Mount Street. One man said 'Its a hot place you girls', but once into Merrion Square it was utterly deserted, just like 4 o'clock on a bright summer's morning. The birds all singing. There are sand-bags barricades all along the lower side of Merrion Square and the military firing from behind them. Soldiers were lying flat on the pavement, and taking cover behind lamp-posts. The firing was continuous and horrible. The column of smoke is still rising darkly from the Sackville Street direction.

Dr. Lumsden and other devoted men in white coats and red crosses were there and Miss Blandford doing secretarial work. A priest and a clergyman were standing in the hall. Miss MacDonnell has taken night duty as matron there. The packing room is turned into an extempore theatre with operating tables. There are about 20 cases upstairs. One boy is shot through the lungs and dying. A woman leading a child was coming out crying as I went in. It is awful. A rumour came through that the Sinn Feiners had surrendered, but was immediately contradicted by telephone.

We reported to Dr. Winter and Miss Winter gave us tea. We carried the dressings to Nettie and then tried to get home. Leeson Street Bridge was closed, so we went round Hatch Street to try Charlemont Bridge, meeting the Bests,[43] also homeward bound. Mrs. Best says it is true that Sir Roger Casement was taken from a collapsible boat landing in

Kerry on Wednesday and taken to the Tower and shot. We reached Charlemont Bridge, and the military were packed into the houses and on the roofs of the houses on opposite sides. The houses on the city side were crowded with people, and 'Halt' rang from all quarters. We 'halted' up against the advertisement hoardings, in the middle of nothingness. We should have got through, only that someone lost his head and became hysterical, and shouted and made such a fuss that he drew attention from all sides, and we quite expected he would draw fire. We retreated, they, the Bests, to the Lysters,[44] and we to Dr. Webbs, where we failed to get on to anyone by telephone. So, making one last effort to get home, we came up Leeson Street and marched on to the bridge. 'Halt!', and we threw up our hands at a sentry pointing a bayonet at us. 'We have finished work and are going home, may we pass!', 'Ow, Oi carn't let yer owver' [sic], said the distressed sentry, The sergeant came up with a re-assuring smile 'Pass!' and we 'passed' through a barricade of boxes, cases, old grates and all sorts. But for our uniform we shouldn't have got over.

Rumours keep rushing along that the city Sinn Feiners have given in, that the military are encircling the town, and are going to hem them in, and search the streets. There is nothing confirmed. Further rumours say a truce has been called to parley. No firing at all occurred from 5 till 7.30, then it began again intermittently. At 6.30 I got home to find kind Professor Cole had been in to say Augustine was in Kingstown, safe and well, and would get a military pass, and would arrive at 5.p.m. or, knowing we were all well, might cling to the baggage and stay the night in Kingstown. There are no Irish papers, but stray copies of the *Daily Mail* and *Sketch* brought over on the mail were selling for 1/- each. We have not had English or European news for five days, but the fictions have been stranger than Truth could ever have been.

Mrs. Rice, who works at the Depot lost her husband[45] in today's fighting. The great difficulty is to bury the dead. They buried some today at St. Bartholemew's church (Elgin Road), where no one has been buried before, but it is a terrible difficulty, and also identifying the dead Sinn Feiners, who have no identification discs, and nobody knows what they are doing with their dead, or how they are getting their wounded attended to.

Sunday 30 April 1916

The firing went on till 2 p.m., probably all night. Some seemed to be in Rathmines and big guns sounded from the direction of Ringsend. Another lovely cloudless day, and fruit blossoms in full bloom.

At 1.30 Augustine arrived and said he had left London on Friday evening.

[This section was written by Augustine] –

'was told at Holyhead that the passengers could not get beyond Kingstown, Dublin being in flames. Welshmen at Holyhead very excited. Arrived at Kingstown on Saturday morning, 29th, breakfasted with T.P. Gill at 4 Adelaide Street; could get no news at first as to whether Elsie was at Courtown or not. While waiting at the Town Hall (Asst. Provost Marshal's office) in the queue for a permit to go to Dublin, spied Prof. Cole with a bicycle, left the queue and heard the news that Elsie was in Sandford Terrace. Afterwards, about 3 p.m. returned to the queue, but did not get a permit [at] 6, when the office was closed. Saw various people and also Matilda and Mary Kerley,[46] who had lodgings at 3, Martello Terrace. Stayed at 3, Martello Terrace for the night.

Sunday 30 April got into the queue at 10, the office was opened, and secured permit at 12, hired a car and came on with luggage ... to Sandford Terrace, reached at 1.30'.

Papers from England.

Two small boys had looted toy guns and hats from Lawrence's toy shop opposite the Pillar [Nelson's Pillar in O'Connell Street], and were doing sentry-go with immense importance outside the shop on the pavement.

MONDAY 1 MAY 1916

Augustine went out early to Johnston Mooney and O'Brien[47] and secured two loaves. Firing is only spasmodic, the present rumour is that the Sinn Feiners have all given in, all except Connolly's 'Citizen Army'. The military cordon is exceedingly strict. Our orders were to give out sphagnum moss dressings from 11–12 at the College. Mr Dowling[48] said he would be there to open it. Going round by his house, we found him willing to confide the master-key to us two again, so Aug. and I went on to Ballsbridge for our pass. A queue 3 deep and stretching down the road, many Red X nurses waiting among them, quite hopeless. We went to the Masonic Girls' School, which is now the military head-quarters, and asked for an officer. By three relays of sentries we were led inside, and there transferred to Colonel Dent. He dispatched us to the Red X quarters, and finally I was dispatched off in a motor ambulance, seated by the stretchers and clinging desperately to a large paper bag of oranges! The ambulance was stopped both on Ballsbridge and on Baggot Street Bridge for its pass, although an official ambulance. At Merrion Square the firing is still progressing smartly. The patients in Merrion Square rejoiced over the oranges. It is very hard to get food in the city, but far worse on the north side. Two patients died last night.

Mrs MacVittie, Miss Shaw and another came with me to the College. Peggy and Bea were waiting, having crossed Leeson Street Bridge on the strength of their uniforms alone and sheltered Peter!! We went into the College, filled the baskets of dressings which Mrs MacVittie escorted back. She said they had all been sewing bandages, etc. on Tuesday morning at No. 40; they left at lunch time, and returned with bedding etc. at 2 p.m. and had casualties in at 4 p.m.! Completely organised by St. John volunteers. I went round by Dr. Winter's to Nettie O'Brien's home, 65 [67], Lower Leeson Street. Sniping is still going on near Leeson St. Bridge and somewhere in the direction of Portabello.

Nettie has had an exciting time. The Sinn Feiners demanded possession of her house, and fortunately she had her door on the chain when she opened it. She refused point blank. They hammered on the door a few blows and then went on to the next, leaving her alone. They have possession of a great many Leeson St. houses. On one side of Nettie is a man and his family. He promptly yielded up his house, carried away his family, and rushed off to tell the police to mind his house for him! On her other side is an old lady between 70 and 80, who replied 'I'm an old woman and I can't do anything against 4 armed men, but if you come in I'll make it so uncomfortable as ever I can for you'. They did come in, and occupied as usual the top floor. Nettie said she was greatly puzzled by an extraordinary noise that was repeated every hour till the next day. It was the old lady, who took her dinner gong up to the top floor every hour and battered it loudly outside the Sinn Feiners' door, remarking 'As long as you're in my house I'll take good care you don't get any sleep'. The Sinn Fein officer came round next morning and called them out, and one of them remarked to the maid-servant 'Thanks be to God we are getting out of this, and divil a foot will we set in here again!'.

Nettie went out into the street to carry in her Irish terrier, under cross-fire from either side of the street yesterday (Sunday) and also watered her plants in the garden to a cheery accompaniment of whizzing bullets. She had no cook, and today she is cooking and baking for 15 people in her house. She is a really wonderful woman. She is supplying 60 lbs. of homemade jam to the Castle Hospital.

Bea, Peggy and Peter went down to Sackville Street, a desolate wreckage. Everything on the right-hand side from O'Connell Bridge to past the Pillar is in ruins, and on the left-hand side everything except the first block. The G.P.O. had just been newly done up. The cleanest and best buildings are destroyed. The miles of slums are intact. Peter said a ghastly thing was the wide trail of blood from the road to a house in Grafton Street where a casualty had been taken in. The R.A.M.C. [Royal Army Medical Corps] boy who conducted me this morning said that there were many casualties not yet traced, probably taken into houses no one knows where. He added that on the 27th they had had 180 casualties in one regiment alone.

The Sinn Feiners had made an attack on the military headquarters in the Masonic School [Ballsbridge]. One Sinn Feiner firing from the roof of the end house had been sniping all night, they had expended '800 rounds of ammunition, and 15 shots from the big gun, and couldn't get him'. From all quarters we hear the Sinn Feiners are exceedingly good shots.

At 4 o'clock Dorothy Stopford turned up. She and Mrs Nathan and family[49] had been staying at the Under-Secretary's Lodge. On Sunday last Sir Matthew seemed very uneasy and on Monday said he must go to the Castle as usual, although it was Bank-Holiday [sic]. He started at 9, Dorothy thinks just too early for the snipers in the Park, but arriving at the Castle, was surrounded. The gates were just closed in time, but the policeman shutting them was shot. Sir Matthew has been imprisoned there ever since, but was able to telephone up to the Lodge. Mrs Nathan and the party at the Vice-Regal Lodge escaped in motor cars on Saturday afternoon by a very circuitous route around the Dublin mountains, and got into Kingstown in time to catch the boat. Dorothy went to the Charlie Dickinsons in Foxrock.

Charlie Dickinson had been ill on Monday and had not gone out with the Veterans, but as soon as he heard they were in Beggar's Bush Barracks he started to join them, in uniform. As he walked, a lady ran out of her house and told him he could not possibly escape the hail of sniping, if he went in uniform. She took him in and dressed him up in a long waterproof and a clergyman's hat, and he strolled into the barracks.

While Nettie was baking in her kitchen one morning, a man rushed down the area steps into the kitchen saying desperately 'Give me food, <u>any</u> food'. Nettie replied 'I haven't much to give you but anyhow I can't be seen with you leaving my house with your arms full of food. If you'll get some paper to wrap it in, I'll give you what I can.' The man rushed off again, and Nettie bolted the door.

On Sunday Nettie saw a milkman shot on Leeson Street Bridge. He was driving a milk cart and had a pass all right, but the sentry searched the cart. It was full of ammunition. The man tried to whip up and escape and he was shot.

TUESDAY 2 MAY 1916

The firing has stopped. A heavenly peaceful day. The military cordon is still very strict. Women, children and men over 65 may pass to and fro across the bridges, others must have passes.

The Bests got home safe on Saturday evening, (after trying several bridges), by Mrs Best producing an old bill for bacon or something!

They have arrested Mr. Macarthy, city architect. Last night they searched the houses in Castlewood Avenue for arms.

The sequel to our going into town yesterday was that the Registrar thought he would follow us to the College, so he hied him to Ballsbridge and applied at the Staff quarters for a pass, saying he wanted to go to the College of Science to give out dressings. 'No' they replied, 'We've heard that story before; a lady has been here already this morning, with the Key!'

The weather is perfect, and the gardens have never looked so lovely, with all the fruit trees in blossom, and the young green of the trees brilliant after the long winter.

An undertaker's cart went by, with five soldiers marching slowly beside it.

WEDNESDAY 3 MAY 1916

Sniping went on from 3 p.m. till midnight somewhere in the vicinity. A little sniping during the night, there was a good deal in Castlewood Avenue. Two policemen blossomed forth again like summer butterflies.

Dorothy arrived at 4. She got away from the Castle on Saturday. The Park had been full of snipers, and they had tried to blow up the power magazine, but only burnt one unimportant end of it. Dorothy, Mrs Nathan and two children were alone in the Under-Secretary's Lodge, with very little food, coal, or candles. The only time they got a bad fright was when a large shell burst in the garden <u>close</u> to the house. Mrs Nathan was in a panic, telephoned through to the Castle, to her brother. An A.D.C. replied soothingly not to mind in the least, as it was merely a little mistake in aim of our own artillery!

Dorothy brings the story that the cook at the Vice-Regal Lodge, on Friday when there was a shortage of food threatened, refused to cook for them, saying he wasn't going to serve them while his wife and family were starving in the city; threw the saucepan at the A.D.C.'s head and left.

Went over to Miss Reed. She had been entirely surrounded, the rebels were in Landsdowne station, her gate-lodge, the house next to it, and houses all up and down the road. Her windows have no shutters, and the bullets whizzed around the building the whole time. Her house was <u>quite</u> full. She and Miss Shuter [*sic*] went in and out foraging for food for the patients.

The Sinn Feiners have been most courageous, especially the unfortunate young boys who were led in all unknowing, and went on through with it, fighting desperately. They were so young, Miss Reed said, and so terrified, pale with fear and agitation, and scooping away the most pathetic little hollows, all the way up the railway line from Landsdowne Road to Westland Row. Miss Reed said they were spotlessly clean on Tuesday, but had blacked their faces intentionally the next day, so as not to be recognized. They used Miss Reed's hen-run as their means of communication, but they never touched an egg or a hen.

THURSDAY 4 MAY 1916

Down to the College. Leeson Street is open to everybody, but no other bridge. We sent out baskets of dressings to Patrick Dun's and City of Dublin Hospitals.

Mrs Jardin was at the College. Mr Jardin and the College men's V.A.D. have been used. Mr Jardin was sent to the City of Dublin Hospital for duty, to sew up 19 dead bodies for burial. But when he arrived the doctor said 'This is no work for you' and the medical men did it themselves.

Mr. and Mrs Walsh were prisoners in their own house for 4 days, and were allowed 150 yards for exercise. Friends brought them food.

A tram is seen, great excitement.

Returning from Miss Reed's I saw a Kingstown tram crossing Ballsbridge, carrying women and children only. Men must travel by themselves as they must all show passes.

We went up to see Professor and Mrs. Wilson. Professor Wilson was all through the Beggar's Bush defence. He looks simply splendid and years younger. They had a weary time, but they held the barracks although only a handful of men. Had the Sinn Feiners known, they could easily have rushed it. Mrs Robinson's husband, the Rev. Robinson, was one of their best shots. They were there from Monday night for a week. Occasional orders filtered through to them to direct their fire exactly as they [saw] the Lincolns[50] doing. So presently the fire was directed on a big building opposite, so the Veterans followed suit. They fired away the best part of the day, and gradually the windows of the opposite building began to whiten. The barricades broke down and the big sacks of flour behind oozed out. But no human body appeared. Prof. Wilson wondered wasn't it a waste of effort. Then, all of a sudden, in the evening the Lincolns ceased, so the G.R.s Veterans held their hand, then 'boom' went the big gun, clean over the building and into the distillery behind. The military had been persuading the Sinn Feiners that they thought the Sinn Feiners were in the flour building – they evacuated it and all day had been concentrating into the distillery. Charlie Dickinson and Mr. Robinson met yesterday and laughed at each other, Mr. Robinson saying 'When we last met you were the clergyman and I was the soldier'.

Judge Andrews occupies a corner house of Leeson Street, from which the Sinn Fein volleys were poured down Fitzwilliam Place. Judge Andrews is old and was ill in bed. The Sinn Feiners invaded the house and demanded to know where the food was. 'I shall not tell you' said the old gentleman from his bed 'You are not my guests'. They took possession of the house, and occupied the top floor from which they kept up the shooting. Mr. Hicks, the Unitarian minister, went every day to him, down in at the basement, with the S.F.s on the top floor, and brought the Judge bread and food, Mrs. Hicks carrying provisions also. Mr. Hicks has now brought the old Judge away to a relative in Rathgar. The house was taken by the military and closed and shuttered.

FRIDAY 5 MAY 1916

Very wet. Trams are now running on all lines as far as the bridges. Down to the College: we sent dressings to Mercer's [Hospital] and the

[Dublin] Castle Hospitals. Two posts were delivered today. The streets are busy. Barricades are still up across every bridge, old grates, boxes of jam jars, tin pails and broken boxes, such a conglomeration.

At 3.30 a post was delivered, bringing a letter a week old asking for tetanus serum for Augustine's brother[51] who has had a bad bicycle accident in Antrim. A. left immediately for Belfast.

SATURDAY 6 MAY 1916
Still raining heavily and very cold. No one at the College. Dorothy and I collected provisions. At 2.30 she went off to collect her luggage from the Under-Secretary's Lodge. Sir Matthew went to England yesterday.

SUNDAY 7 MAY 1916
Still pouring and very cold. Dorothy and I cheered each other. Augustine returned 6 p.m. by an odd train from Belfast. His brother is better. A young and enterprising doctor gave him 3 times the ordinary dose of serum and has saved his life.

MONDAY 8 MAY 1916
The Depot opened again. A fair number of workers working eagerly to make up for lost time.

Mr. Vernon's (Mrs Cole's brother) house has been fearfully damaged. One girl coming into her bedroom after her bath, heard a bullet whizz through the bathroom; she went into the second girl's bedroom to do her hair and a bullet buzzed through the looking glass. Poor Mr. Vernon is *plus royaliste que le roi*, but his china and furniture has been smashed and ripped. The house is in Wilton Place on the [Grand] Canal, opposite St. Margaret's school, where Miss Heusman resides. Miss Heusman and Miss Vernon were comparing notes at the depot this afternoon, when it transpired that Miss Heusman had opened her doors and welcomed in the military to demolish Mr. Vernon's house. She did not know it was Mr. Vernon's, but believed they were nice people and recommended them for mercy! But the interior was practically wrecked.

Letter boxes present a ludicrous appearance and are vomiting letters on to the streets. In Ranelagh an agitated lady who could only barely get one stuffed in, was mounting guard over it until a postman should arrive.

Lieutenant Valentine[52] has been killed in France.

Greville A.J. Cole, Kingstown and D.V.C. Headquarters, to Elsie, 8 May 1916 –
'I hope by this time you have had full news of your Father. I have been unable to get into Bray, being attached to the office in this very interesting armed camp; but I wrote to Bray Post Office for any letters that might be lying there to come on here. We shall all meet I hope shortly.'

Letter from Lauder Brunton in London to Elsie, 6 May 1916 –
'I sent on your letters to Aunt Alice. I have not seen her for a good while. I fancy she must be a good deal worried in regard to Roger Casement. I wrote about him to *the Times* to say I thought him insane, but the Editor declined my letter ... The question of Casement's mental condition will be thoroughly considered. I saw no evidence of mental disarrangement when I examined him but I thought he had some lesion in his brain as his tongue was protruded to the left. What an awful time you have been having! Nance has been in peace and quietness. I am thankful that things are quietening down.'

[TUESDAY] 9 MAY 1916
Staff meeting of St. John [Ambulance Brigade]. Mr. Stoddart,[53] one of the District Superintendants was killed during the fighting.

SATURDAY 13 MAY 1916

Martial law has been relaxed to a curfew at midnight till 5 a.m.

Miss Brereton (one of the V.A.D.) came in. She was doing 3 months work in Baggot Street Hospital, and stayed on to help during the troubles. She describes the battle at Baggot Street Bridge as frightful. It raged day and night; men and officers were killed, civilians and women. One man had rashly come out to get some tobacco, was shot and brought into the hospital. He asked would it be very long, as he lived alone and kept fowl, and the poor fowls would be starving. Before night he was dead.

The soldiers were in some cases exhausted, having been brought from England without a moment's notice, hustled on board, and started to march from Kingstown, with no food since leaving England. A great many thought they were going to France, and one, Irish born, told Augustine he was never so surprised as when he recognized they were steaming into Dublin Bay.

People gave the military food and drink as they came along, and as best they could. A cup of tea was handed to one Tommy from the doors of Baggot Street Hospital, but he scarcely reached the bridge, when he was brought back into hospital, dead. One lovely child of 15 was killed: she was said to be the loveliest in the neighbourhood, and she was just ready for mass when the bullet flew through the window of their house.

Miss Brereton usually poured out tea for the V.A.D.s at the head of a small table, she chose to move two cups over to one side, and a minute later a bullet whizzed through the window where she had been. The hospital suffered on both sides, but the most terrible thing was what to do with the dead. Dying and dead were all brought in.

Mr. Warwick, of the College, was going home on the 25th or 26th, having purchased a *Spark*, or *War Cry*,[54] from pure curiosity. He was stopped by the military and having no papers to identify him, was searched. The incriminating newspaper caused him to be shut up, where he was kept for 20 hours, until he could establish his identity. In the general scrimmage he missed his pocket book, containing notes. He returned home, minus the newspaper, sans pocket book, a sadder and poorer man.

It chanced that the sister of Mrs J. Clarke (formerly of the College and V.A.D.) came up from Kerry to pay her sister an Easter visit. Delayed on the far side of the city for three days, she at last struggled forth to reach her sister, steering herself across town by sentries. One of these was directing her on the best way, and they fell into general conversation. At parting he said 'By the way, you don't happen to know Mr. Warwick, do you?' 'No' she said 'but my sister does; her husband used to work with a Mr. F.W. Warwick'. 'Those are the initials' replied the sentry, 'Tell him that Private – of – regiment has found his pocket book with notes inside'.

Perhaps after all truth is stranger than fiction!

Letter from Sir Matthew Nathan from London, to Elsie, 13 May 1916 –
'Dear Mrs Henry,
Your letter was a very kind one and although I do not deserve the things you say of me in it I like very much that you should have said them. It was moss in the wound.

Yours very sincerely.'

SUNDAY 14 MAY 1916
To the Edward Stopfords in their new house. A friend of Miss Cunningham's met her in the street, 'Do you know the Stopfords?'. 'Yes' said Miss Cunningham. 'They are Sinn Feiners!'. 'Oh, no' said Miss C., 'I know them well'. 'Oh but they are, they have been taken and their house has been closed up'!

[16 MAY 1916]

The Marquis [MacSwiney] and Marchioness came today, poor things, a horrible experience.[55] The military searched their house, but went off again with all politeness and courtesy. However, presently an officer came back and took away the Marquis. He was put on an open motor lorry and taken round to Fitzwilliam Street where Count Plunkett[56] was arrested. The Sinn Fein snipers on the roof opened fierce fire, to prevent Count P. being taken, so the Marquis was under a volley. Finally they were both brought to the Castle, and imprisoned there for the night with a host of others in a tiny room, so that they had to stand all night. An officer assured the Marquis that he, the Marquis, was the head of all the trouble; and in the morning he would be tried by court-martial, and interned or shot.

Next morning early, he was released, without comment and returned home. The poor Marchioness hadn't a notion of what was happening all the time.

MONDAY 22 MAY 1916

Lunched with Susan and AE in the Homestead office. A great airship came sailing from Liffey-wards. It flew very low, crossed over the Museums, dipped nose first over the College of Science, and apparently didn't like the smell, for it rose hurriedly and made off over Merrion Square.

AE in despair over the new move with Lloyd George[57] in command. He read this poem wrathfully and then flung it into the waste-paper basket, whence I fished it [He gave me this] –

Conference

Come Ulster bigot and Munster goose

Leinster puzzler and Connaught rat

Come and call you muddlers all

Here's one will settle the fate of Pat!
One who can match you all with his wit
He is a canting hypocrite;
He is a muddler greater than you;
He is a rat with an eye on his fat
He can cackle enough for two...

Ulster bigot, Sir Edward Carson; Leinster [space], Redmond; Connaught rat, John Dillon.

AE believes from former conversations with Connolly during the strike times two years ago, that the Sinn Feiners believed Germany would ultimately win, and that Germany had notified the S.F.s that they must put up a fight on their own account in order to have an effect on the general 'morale'. Then when peace came, Germany would make special peace terms with Ireland, as a separate country. Connolly did not approve of the Hohenzollerns any more than the English throne, but his view was that the Labour party in Germany would not take more than 6 or 7 years after peace was declared, to overthrow the Hohenzollern monarchy, and then the German and Irish and other nationality Labour parties would all unite and obtain Labour government.

TUESDAY 30 MAY 1916

Dr and Mrs Mather Thomson to tea, later the Marquis and Marchioness. Dr. Thomson was waiting on a bridge at the end of the rising week, while a sentry examined his pass. Presently a motor crossed the bridge and went on. 'Hello' said Dr. Thomson to [the] sentry 'Do you know who you've let over in that motor?' 'No' said the sentry anxiously 'Who?', 'Birrell!', 'Who's that? Is he a Sinn Feiner?'. 'Don't you know 'im?' says a brother sentry scornfully 'Why B-A-R-R-E-L-L'.

The doctor finally got on his way to his Hospital (King George V) where they have Alderman Kelly, in bed, guarded by a sentry. He was better, and allowed to get up, but they wouldn't give him his own clothes, only the hospital blue overalls, so he refused to budge. 'Ah' said Dr. Thomson sympathetically 'You feel it a Government uniform, and you object to putting on any Government uniform?' 'Well no, doctor, it is not exactly that, but I've always been a bit aesthetic'.

The Marquis and Marchioness went away for a week to stay with Sir Thomas Esmond [*sic*][58] and recover their equilibrium. During their absence the nurse took Honoria and Bessie to paddle on the sands at Merrion Gates. A company of soldiers landed and the children started to cry. The nurse picked up one under either arm, and the two officers in charge of the soldiers bore down on her, and each gathered up a child while the sergeant followed behind with the shoes and socks. Honoria, aged 5, being comforted, the officer asked her 'But why did you cry?' To which Honoria [replied], 'Well you see, I thought you were Sinn Feiners, and what between Bessie and the Sinn Feiners my head has gone mad'. Bessie is aged four, and a champion chatterbox.

[*There is a gap in the diaries between the end of May 1916 and mid-December 1916.*]

SUNDAY 17 DECEMBER 1916

Got up at 6.50 and rushed through breakfast. Skated out of the front door in bright moonlight, to find Dublin one clear sheet of black glass. No horse and few men could stand. Impossible to reach train. Waited all day. Augustine tied brown paper over his boots, and I in galoshes, we pattered down by train with our luggage and got the night boat across. To Aunt Alice's. Shared a taxi, the only one, with a stray officer ordered direct from Dublin to Salonika. Top came, and we raced round together, Dawson's, and much business.

TUESDAY [19 DECEMBER] 1916

More flying round with Top – took Harriet [Jaffé] out to lunch. Arrived back at Grosvenor Road at [5.30] and flew off with Aunt Alice to madrigals in the Aeolian Hall. Left at 6.20 and stumbled round Bond Street and Regent Street, finally landing a taxi. London <u>very</u> black and also empty. Met at the Café d'Italie Arthur Hill, Top and Augustine and went on to 'Aïda'. Home by tram along the Embankment, crawling thither with an electric torch and in soon after midnight.

[WEDNESDAY 20 DECEMBER 1916]

With Top to interview Mr Murray R.A. about having Mother's miniature copied. He said 'It is a very fine subject' and then 'it is a great pity it wasn't taken from life by a first rate artist'. He lived next to the Dickenson's old house, in a vast museum of a studio, but had to be persuaded by Aunt Abigail to arise from bed to see us, at 11 a.m. He recommended Miss Worsefold, 29 Grosvenor Street. A great chase. Back to Grosvenor Road for lunch. George Wakeling there. He has undertaken to be Top's proxy during the war, as trustee and Executor. Spent the afternoon packing with Top at the Welbeck Palace Hotel. Back together to dinner with Aunt Alice.

THURSDAY [21 DECEMBER] 1916

Up at 6.30 after a night of alarms; booming; two fire engines in full flight, and search-lights, but 'nothing doing'. The taxi didn't come, we ran through pouring rain with our baggage to the Tube, caught the Mail [train], which was packed, and arrived home just before 9.pm. about 2½ hours late. Dublin is frozen hard.

Letter from Marryat Dobie, BEF, to Elsie, [no date] –
'My dear Elsie,

Thank you both very much indeed for your combined parcel of book and cigarettes ... I am always delighted to have a book; and the virtue of the present does not end in me, for it goes on and rejoices many. I generally pass on my old books to many people who are only too glad to get anything to read. I have not yet tried any of the cigarettes (I religiously refrain from eating, smoking, reading, wearing or playing with any Xmas presents before Xmas day) but if they are as good as the ones you usually send me they will be splendid; everyone appreciates them as they are a change from the usual old Abdullahs and De Retzes (I would never buy a De Retze on principle to punish them for their horrible advertisements) ... I have just heard that the man at Corps H.Q. (whose place I took just before I went on leave) is again going away so I expect a pretty busy Xmas week ... Tell your brother where I am – I think you know; I am always to be found at the station or the Town Major's office and we have a most jovial mess to which to welcome him.'

[MONDAY] 25 DECEMBER 1916
A perfect clear cloudless day and frost. James Stephens, Cynthia, Iris and Sonny to lunch and tea. To dinner with Uncle Ned and Aunt Lily.

[TUESDAY] 26 DECEMBER 1916
Another perfect day. Out to Dollymount with A. to see the sun on the sea. Miss Gleeson, Mrs MacCormack, Kitty, Gracie and May to lunch and tea.

[WEDNESDAY] 27 DECEMBER 1916
Hard frost and some fog. Uncle Ned and Aunt Lily and Mrs Horas Kennedy to lunch.

Letter from C. [Constance] Stopford to Elsie, [no date] –
'I had very interesting letters from Robert 2 days ago. They have started a mess for the [Training] Coy. And they are about 14 – and have also a canteen near ... the sandbags of his dug-out had fallen in on top of his desk and it was completely ruined but he said he was sleeping on a pile of hay on the floor and was very comfortable – he had been inoculated again as it is 2 years since it had been done last and he had no bad effects, except for a stiff arm for a couple of days. He had been sent on a job, very interesting work, to convoy up to the front line 2 battalions of the Revolutionary Greek army and he had to bring them through a [wood] part of our former trenches and through the Bulgars trenches we had taken the night before and so on to our very front line. He said the Greeks were a great set of men and as he was unofficially liaison officer, Supply officer and Transport Officer he had a busy time. Once at a stream they had to ford the Greeks [did] climb on his wagon (he had 24 wagons) and nearly upset them so he sat on his horse on the bank with a loaded revolver in his hand to keep them from climbing on the wagons. All the time there was a big 'Strafe' going on – so he is indeed in the middle of it.']

6

The 'flooding sorrow' of a World at War Continues:

The Diaries 1917[1]

INTRODUCTION

In 1917 the war became truly global when the last remaining powerful neutral country, the United States, entered the war on the side of the Allies in April 1917. However, revolution in Russia led to the new government there signing an armistice with Germany in December. Unrestricted submarine warfare contributed to continued shortages of commodities in Britain and Ireland and there were new domestic concerns regarding rationing.

In Dublin Elsie continued her war work in the Sphagnum Moss Sub-Depot but the political environment in Ireland was becoming more volatile. In July 1917 representatives of a wide spectrum of interests met in Dublin to attempt to find a constitutional settlement to the Irish question. However, there was a new brand of militant Irish nationalism. The executions of the leaders of the 1916 Rising and the indiscriminate arrests of thousands of suspected individuals, together with the imposition of martial law in Ireland had changed public opinion – something of which Elsie was made aware when she visited a sphagnum moss collection depot in Kilgarvan in April 1917.

The diaries contain newspaper articles and photos on the progress of the war, the launch in February of a National Service scheme to encourage volunteers to the armed forces – applied to England, Scotland and Wales (not Ireland)– the entry of the United States into the war, the Battle of Passchendaele, the war on the Italian Front, Allenby's entry into Jerusalem in December 1917, events in Russia and local Irish events.

✳

5 JANUARY 1917

Some unrest at the Depot. Mrs Cole [wife of Greville Cole, and the Depot Treasurer] flew into the office and began 'When I go to heaven, Peter will say, "and what have you done to deserve Heaven?" I shall say "I have worked with <u>that</u> woman (Mrs J. [Jardin²]) for the duration of the war!" And Peter will say – "Walk right in Mrs Cole and take the best seat you can find, close to the Band". She battered me for an hour and a half during the afternoon, then she relented and remarked, "Deceitful, unstable, and utterly worthless you may be, but articulate you are". This handsome apology was accepted and we return to status quo.

Letter from Top from Halifax, N.S., 17 January 1917 –
'My dear little sister ... I got to Montreal Friday night and reported to headquarters on Saturday. I was told to come down here on a course in artillery the same night so I was kept fairly busy. I rushed off and landed here Sunday night and reported at the school on Monday morning. The boy is well and weighs over 9 lbs now ... Betty looked rather tired when I arrived ... I expect her to come to Halifax this week-end for a short

visit. We have an excellent trained nurse and Mrs Porter will look after the baby.'

Letter from May, from Joyn de l'Argonne, Triancourt [Rouen], to Elsie, 22 January 1917 –
'... there is no space for looking after invalids ... the clearing base is very very damp ... I feel half dead when it is so cold.'

[1 February] 1917
First sign of Spring, a bitter hard frost, but a little sunshine at last. The black-grey sky has lifted after an unbroken spell almost since the new year, and a glint of blue appeared, becoming brilliant at midday.

5 February 1917
Frost harder than ever. People walking across the canal.

6 February 1917
17 degrees of frost last night, sponges all frozen on the nightstand this morning.

8 February 1917
Mrs Lewis[3] and Nance up. Annual meeting of headmistresses at Alexandra College. Prof. Houston gave a lecture with slides on the Meeanee plots for women at Terenure[4] now working about a year, and Nance spoke on gardening for women, and Ballingale. She had a great success. Everyone was delighted with her looks, her subject matter and the delivery.

*Copy of letter from Sir Alfred Keogh, War Office, London, to Elsie,
10 February 1917 –*

'Dear Mrs Henry,

I am very much obliged to you for sending me the two pamphlets
containing the records of the work done by the "Irish War Hospital
Supply" organization. The highest praise that I can give this work is that
I had no idea that its activities were so extensive.

I knew that it was going on, but you have accomplished it all so
quietly and without fuss that I had not gathered it was so widespread.
If your Committee will allow me, I should like to congratulate them on
what has been accomplished. It is no slight achievement.'

14 FEBRUARY 1917

Hard frost still every night, but a thaw during the day. Mrs Gower has
hacked down the weeping ash to make room for populous generosa,
and has torn up the grass patch between the two greenhouses to make a
potato patch. After 3 weeks search, we have achieved 2 loads of manure.
It broke the barrow to pieces, but Aug. rushed out for the Beatty's barrow
and saved the situation. Three fires are burning on the patch, to burn
up the skinned turf. All the paths are one welter of mud, and the sparse
gravel has been swallowed up.

16 FEBRUARY 1917

Great agitation has prevailed the last week because of the Invasion of
the Food Commission [into the College of Science building]. It wanted
the Sphagnum rooms, especially the top circular room, and said that
Providence had especially designed it for the Food Commission and
nothing was to stand in the way of the F.C. Then rose up the Professors
in a body, truly chivalrous. One and all they exchanged rooms, effaced
themselves into corners, did without, and so on, in order that the
Depot should not be disturbed. The Commission took it all, and still

cast covetous eyes on the ewe lamb. It must, and would, have that. Naboth's vineyard wasn't in it. The Dean (Professor Jeffcott[5]) hurled himself into the breach. He led them forcibly away. He showed them a beautiful laboratory (the life blood of somebody or another joyfully sacrificed). 'Yes' said the F.C. 'but look at the desks, they are too far from the floor'. 'Then' said Prof. Jeffcott, 'the floor must be raised to meet the desks'. And so it was! The Professors and Staff rose up and did battle, with a united front, for the I.W.H.S. Sub-Depot, so we continue to hum peacefully, as bees, D.V. [Deo Volente]

SUNDAY 18 FEBRUARY 1917
James Stephens has pneumonia. Cynthia sent for me. The children come tomorrow.

WEDNESDAY [21 FEBRUARY] 1917
Sonny discussed the matter of prayers while being put to bed. 'I said my prayers for Daddy and that the [hot water] jar might be just the right heat tonight, for I hadn't a chance with it last night'.

SUNDAY 25 FEBRUARY 1917
The first snowdrops and crocuses appeared, and there was sunshine yesterday. The children are blissfully happy rioting round the garden and wrestling with the new 'wheelbarrel'.

1 MARCH 1917
The first golden glow of crocuses of the year. They have been solitary buds. Today the sun shone and they opened and glittered ... The 'early' potatoes have steadily refused to sprout, so they were consigned to the grave this morning in the hopes of a more speedy resurrection. Sonny and Iris went to Miss Wilson's school this morning with great joy.

2 MARCH 1917

The Food Commission has reft the moss room from us. Mr Gill notified us this morning that the moss room must be cleared by tomorrow afternoon. Prof. Brown is giving us his own lecture room in the basement.

[4 MARCH] 1917

Another blizzard, snow and rain and high wind, the winter back in force.

Letter from Top in Halifax, N.S. to Elsie, 4 March 1917 –
'I do hope things are not too gloomy in Dublin but I suppose they are none too bright. We have just returned from a week of practical gunnery at McNab's island which is just off the mouth of Halifax harbour. We fired several rounds from guns and one series of which I had charge consisted of star shell at night. The people of Halifax imagined it was a wreck and sent a tug to rescue the ship in distress ... I am sending you a photo of little Ted which was sent down to me and I think he looks pretty lively on 3 months old.'

SUNDAY 11 MARCH 1917

A glorious morning ... Augustine and I went out to Dalkey and walked to Killiney; a smooth blue sea, and sweet air and pine woods, everything perfectly exquisite. The children spent the afternoon with their parents. Seamus Pere [James Stephens] looks very fragile.

14 MARCH 1917

The children went home. Seamus is recovering.

Letter from Alice Stopford Green in London to Elsie, 18 March 1917 –
'Darling Elsie,

Isn't the world upturning? Lord Haldane was here today, knows no more than we do, but sees we are only getting the news they care to let through (Lord [Milne?] knew nothing at all about it all!). Cabinets, he says, only get news an hour or two before journalists, but no better news. But the general feeling, which I share, is one of relief and hope. The world will change a good deal, and democracies will be as slow to learn their lessons as kings have been. Anyhow they can't be slower or bader [*sic*] than Carson of the Cabinet. And it is a move on, when more men are determined not to live in prisons for their belief. Lord H. brings accounts of a Germany <u>really</u> debilitated from want of food. He thinks there may be some desperate adventure – a sea raid – But he thinks the end will be in sight in three months.']

Letter from Elsie in Dublin to A.S. Green 19 March 1917–
'Darling Aunt Alice,

I'm feeling much better for the rest, and will soon be Richard [recovered] again! Do you remember Ted's scorn of the "good rest", which expression, originated by Aunt Connie, came to be regarded as the last word in opprobrium. A sense of degradation always attaches to the term. The flooding sorrow of the world is too great to realize, even though it keeps rushing in in personalities. Every member of the depot has a personal tragedy; one of our best workers is dying of cancer, Mrs Cole is threatened with a serious operation, her husband is dying slowly, the Wrights' baby took mysteriously ill and hovers between life and death, Miss Gleeson's maid's fiancé was drowned coming home on leave. There isn't any grasping it mentally, much less understanding it. I wonder if there is any hope of the war being over before Top is ready. The news is good now, only one doesn't know where the next German stand may be and what it may cost ... One of our poor ladies gave back her blue band of office because the Commandant[6] had "spoken" to her. I said sympathetically, "Yes, we'd all been through it, not once only from the Commandant, and we all lived it down", to which the poor lady replied "Yes, you may have been brought up to that sort of thing, but I haven't met it since I was a child and now I'm too old to learn". Wasn't it really pathetic, and so candid. The Commandant <u>is</u> always right when she "speaks" because she is the highest authority here on Hospital dressings, and the poor lady frankly recognized it to be so, but merely said she couldn't face it. Yours [Alice Stopford Green's letter of 18 March 1917] just come this minute. Isn't Lord Haldene "like a whale"? (this, I believe, is some dreadful slang expression for talking through a hat) ... Perhaps peace may really come before Top's battery is ready. <u>Of course</u> we never hear the truth at all, or anything approaching it, but don't you regret you are not a journalist these days? They are the real makers of History, and all through their hats whatever shape they fancy.'

20 MARCH 1917

Mr Fletcher came to tea at the Depot and says the Tillage scheme is going grandly, a success far beyond their wildest dreams.[7] The lady gardener, who paddles around the environs of Dublin says there has never been such activity and that it is grand to see the Citizens after office hours hurrying to their plots instead of to their pint at the pub. There is a grand new Something coming in the near Future – possibly a Prepared Pasture where the lion and the lamb may lay down together (without any inconvenience to either).

Letter from Alice Stopford Green in London to Elsie, 25 March 1917 – 'My dear,

<u>Just</u> as I sat down to write comes rumours of a German attempt to land

an army on the east coast. All last night soldiers sent on leave were called back from stations and everywhere, and hurried back on motor busses [*sic*] and every other vehicle. A battle supposed on land or sea. Till tomorrow we can get no news but so far this is authentic. A huge effort has been officially expected of late, possibly the whole German fleet to come out. Or it may have been a feint, to keep armies from reinforcing to the north of Arras, where some expect the next attack.

Oddly enough other rumours of the new Russia making a separate peace with Germany on the basis of Poland. And yet another, of a government encouragement here of a peace propaganda. I don't like to give names. But it is clear that the desperate situation is on the world very rapidly.'

Letter from Alice Stopford Green in London to Elsie, 28 March 1917 –
'That affair of the soldiers was brought home by a policeman who on his night's beat had watched the train of returning soldiers. It has turned out to be a War Office experiment to see how quickly they could be recalled. And the manoeuvre set everyone guessing. I suppose we'll many more guesses.

Rasputin's[8] body was thrown into the river with weights badly attached. His body rose with arms outspread. The tsarina saw an emblem in it and had the coffin made in form of a crucifix and it was carried through the city, to the universal emotion of the crowds, and buried in the Palace grounds. Now it has been taken up and burned. What a tale! Did I tell you that he refused to see man or woman except in Court dress – Generals with all their orders, ladies with all the jewels. If a name was brought to him – "Is she dressed properly?" "She is in furs". "Let her go home and dress!" And so they thronged his court to beg for favours. Then the Tsar had to fall for spiritual council in State affairs to table-turning with the Head of the Church. He got bad advice from the spirits. Now all wait for the end.'

Postcard from Bea [O'Brien] to Elsie, [28 March] 1917 –
'Dorothy had quite an exciting journey across, as 3 ships had been
torpedoed in the Irish Channel that morning. They came on a sailing
vessel and 2 boats tied together with 30 men from a torpedoed collier.
The mail [mail boat] stopped and was about to lower rope ladders to
take them on board when they were told then to go on that it was not
safe to stop and that they could reach port alright, so it went ahead with
great speed and arrived safely alright.'

31 MARCH 1917
Left Dublin in a snowstorm which lasted to Portarlington, then it
cleared, and further south were primroses and signs of spring. All along
the line from Dublin every property had its percentage for tilling newly
turned. Some had large portions, and in Co. Cork the soil was grand,
but in Kerry the land is an old bog, very poor, nevertheless the tillage
goes on and they are trenching deep drains. The men and women all
working in the fields give an extraordinary sense of life and vigour to
the country.

1–3 APRIL 1917
Great Southern Hotel; very comfortable. About 3–4 inches of snow lying
constantly, re-inforced by hourly snow-storms; very dark and cold.

4 APRIL 1917
Warmer, the snow has ceased to fall. Mr Maguire, the R.M. [Resident
Magistrate] from Tralee here; had an interesting case of a servant girl in
Tralee who got hold of her mistress's cheque book and wrote and cashed
4 cheques for £10 each over shop-counters during the afternoon, some
not dated and some not endorsed. She was cashing a fifth when she was
caught. She was going off to Queenstown to join a young man en route
to America.

Extract of letter from Elsie's cousin George Stopford, serving with the 11th Wing Royal Flying Corps 'somewhere in France' to Aunt Lily [wife of Edward Stopford], 2 April 1917 –

'One is really much more settled down out here (probably for 5 years I should think!). I am living in quite comfortable billets in a small village, not at all bad. We work all day and generally have time for a rubber of bridge after dinner, as you cannot go to bed early owing to the continuous telephone calls which so disturb the bridge. Aerial fighting has been brought to a high art these days, – most terrific fights occur between dozens of machines on each side at heights between 15,000 and 20,000 feet. If the war lasts another year I expect airmen will have to have oxygen helmets and diving suits to keep going. Every day with new machines the height increases as the highest man has the advantage, being able to dive head-first down at speeds of up to 200 miles an hour on to his opponents so that aerial fighting is becoming a sort of climbing match among other things. Each side also uses a sort of incendiary bullet which sends machines hurtling down in flames which is rather ghastly. However, everything is so ghastly one loses all proportion of things.'

Letter from Alice Stopford Green in London to Elsie, 4 April 1917 –
'My dearest friend and priceless confidante,
It is [seriously] hard now to get a letter in time for the 5.30 post. Scarcely any secretary help for a mass of business, current correspondence for the moment, and lack of coal, which chills all endeavours. We are at the last scraping of the cellar dust, and the study fire is a shabby picture. Today was our last scuttle – but from maddened appeals have wrung now a promise from my coal-merchant of 30 years to let us have some tomorrow. Our economy in warmth in the last two months has been a prodigy!

I forgot to tell you that on Thursday Nov. 27 I went to S. Paul's for the unveiling of the monument to Sir William and Lady Huggins.[9] The Chapter objected to the lady. The only monument to any woman except crowds of unnecessary angels weeping over heroes, has so far been for Miss Nightingale. So the accursed thing had made a chink. Through that Miss Montefiore[10] paraded in triumph. The Chapter was firm on one point. The lady's head must be smaller than the man's. So a usual bust was made of Sir William: below it a flat bar on the slab, and dependent from that a medallion of poor Madge. The ceremony was very moving. All the heads of all the scientific Societies came, Sir William Crookes tottering and Sir A. Geikie nearly as old. The Dean and a couple of canons said some prayers, inside a modern railing. Then were brought into the enclosure the Presidents of the Royal Society and the Astronomical Society, who made addresses. The Astronomical One, MacMahon, was worthy of his name and spoke from his heart – of esteem, honour and pride in the great names, and spoke of Madge's service to science. I went to thank him afterwards, and said how fine and noble it was; and he answered "At least it was true" The ringing out of truth and honour gave nobility to the scene, and the presence of all there who came out of pure regard and fellowship for great scientists (for there was no family to call them or anything but just respect). It was a unique scene, and a testimony to how deep in human hearts lies the fellowship of saints – the communion of those who have fought together to gain some foothold in the seen or the unseen.

And Miss Montefiore! Three executors were left £100 each. Not one but Miss M. would serve. She was a school-mate of Madge and a devoted friend. And poor Madge in a [sick [illegible] of mercy], after leaving her £100 a year, told her she could not afford it, and cut it down in the last weeks of illness, to £20 or less. And the good woman (who has small means to live on) fought the whole battle cut from the big sums left to rich endowments in London and Cambridge, and American colleges,[11] and arrangements for a Life, and a long conflict with the Chapter, and won success at every point. What a friend to have! I wish I had not to say she is a Jew.

Dear love, this is all I can do this evening.

A.S.Green'

4–12 April 1917

Snow almost every day; on the 11th a driving blizzard, and trees being blown down everywhere. Brilliant sunshine in between and the country looking very like the Bernese Oberland, with the piquant addition of a masted vessel and a steam tug in the valley. Lunched with Mr and Mrs Colomb at [Dromquina] and visited the moss depot on Tuesday, its working day. Everything admirably done throughout, a very large output of work and all of the highest standard. On Wed. to tea with Mr and Mrs Maxwell, Lord Landsdowne's agent. They have a lovely natural rock garden, from which they have scraped, bit by bit, the covering grass field. Augustine works all day and everyday at his lectures for the Chadwick Trust.

11 April 1917

Fierce snow blizzard, and after that spring seemed to come suddenly. On Thursday the sun came out warm, with fat, fleecy clouds, the snow melted, except on the range of the Reeks, and even the dog-violets [and] celandines glowed out into blossom.

Friday 13 April 1917

Went out to Ardtully, the Kilgarvan sub-depot. The Constables are all artists, and he is a grandson of the great Constable. They have a great cathedral like porticoed rambling house belonging to the Orpen family, and the entrance hall is used for the moss work, the workers in their white, looking like nuns, working on high backed carved wooden settles, some medieval [illegible]. The workers are all poor, mostly farmers' daughters, whose mothers do all their share of the home work in their absence; one post-office girl, two or three old Biddies; one of them Peggy (?) [sic] Shea, comes down 5 miles from the mountains on foot, at 10 a.m.; does all the carbolizing; gets into her uniform and works away at moss and returns 5 miles in the evening. After she carries a sack of moss down from the mountains on her back. The collecting has been difficult, as the Kilgarvan people have boycotted the workers, and also at first tried to prevent the collection of moss. They attacked the moss gatherers one day, men and women, and one woman scratched Miss Constable's face so badly that blood poisoning resulted. There is a strange and active bitterness which does not exist around Kenmare itself. The feeling is all anti-English, but the Kenmare depot itself has not encountered any active resistance.

There was a wonderful dignity in the workers at their work, exceedingly touching.

[There is a gap in the diaries between April and November 1917.]

[11 NOVEMBER 1917]

There is a story current of a padre who (on the advance to Gaza) discovered in an old monastery, buried under a tessalated pavement, the genuine remains of John of Antioch. Greatly thrilled he wired to the War Office 'Have found John of Antioch, can we remove the body?' Back came the reply, 'Has been missing some time, send identity discs'.

17 NOVEMBER 1917

Stephens, Evelyn [Gleeson] and Miss Collard to dinner. James Stephens had been talking to the men just returned from Italy who told him the first cause of the Italian débacle was a food riot in Turin. The Italian Gov. sent army aeroplanes over the town, flying low down and firing upon the civilians in the town, killing them. When the army at the front heard their own women and children had been killed, a whole army corps laid down their arms and allowed the Germans to walk through.

12 DECEMBER 1917

Adrian Thrupp came. He and Augustine made friends roving among the trees at Kew. He comes from Karnloops, B.C. and joined the Canadian Mounted Rifles when war broke out, aged 18. A delightful boy, keen on every single outdoor thing, but especially trees. He was sent out to France in Oct. 1916, the regiment having been turned into infantry, and was through the Vimy push, and just after they had got over the Ridge, was wounded in the head. He has been in hospital and is now marked for home service, and having 12 days leave came over to Dublin for part of it.

Nance arrived from Ballycarney after a desperately strenuous term, all the pupils and herself having been ill.

15 DECEMBER 1917

A fearful blizzard of snow, hail, water and wind. Two pails and a jug catching the drip upstairs and wads of bath towels in the other rooms. Our hospitality is now accompanied by the loan of cloaks to guests dining, on going into the dining room, and umbrellas to guests going up to bed.

7

Crisis in Ireland but Peace at Last:

The Diaries 1918–19[1]

INTRODUCTION

The war news for 1918 was mixed, with a German offensive on the Western Front early in 1918. Elsie's main concern was for her surviving brother, Top, by then serving in France but very unhappy in his first posting there. In October 1918 she was in London and left to travel back to Ireland two days after the sinking of R.M.S. *Leinster*.[2] The General Armistice in 1918 was celebrated with great joy by Elsie and her friends in Dublin and by Christmas the Henrys had had news of their Belgian friends, the Hegers, for the first time since 1915 – as Elsie wrote on 18 December 1918 – 'What a day of joys'.

Elsie herself, together with her cousin Beatrice O'Brien, was awarded the OBE [Officer] of the Order of the British Empire] for her services to the war effort in the Sphagnum Moss Depot at the RCScI.

The political environment in Ireland was very nationalist by 1918. Augustine commented to his sister in April that 'The political situation is extremely bad'. The proposal to introduce military conscription to Ireland in April 1918 brought together an alliance of Sinn Féin, the Irish Parliamentary Party, the Irish Labour Party and the Catholic church in opposition to the possibility. In May the government, abandoning the proposed implementation of conscription in Ireland, instead arrested seventy-three prominent members of Sinn Féin because of an alleged German plot. In the general election of December 1918 the old constitutional Irish Parliamentary Party was effectively destroyed when Sinn Féin, emphasizing their history of opposition to British rule, won seventy-three of Ireland's 105 parliamentary seats.

The diaries for 1918 and 1919 contain articles from newspapers reporting on the Italian campaign, the French counter-attack on the Marne in July, the British campaign in Russia, the second battle of the Somme, the campaign in Palestine, the German request for an Armistice in October 1918, the German surrender, the signing of the peace treaty, as well as events in Ireland, the conscription crisis in April 1918 and the trial of the 'man in the Tower'.[3] It contains articles from newspapers on the state funeral of Edith Cavell; also of later events in Ireland, the meeting of the Free State Dáil, and of Alice Stopford Green's funeral in 1929.

❀

10 JANUARY 1918
Great news. Bob[4] has returned from Ruhleben and arrived in Oxford.

TUESDAY 15 JANUARY 1918
Dobie arrived from Hazelbrook on leave, very short. Tuesday evening AE, Susan, James Stephens and Cynthia, and Dorothy came in. Dobie

wore mufti for the first time since Aug. 4th 1914. Also a pink carnation in his button-hole, which he might not sport in uniform, on account of the Army regulation, 'Soldiers must not wear flowers or other unsoldierly trinkets'.

WEDNESDAY 16 JANUARY 1918
Nance came up. Dobie, Aug. and Alice went to the Abbey Theatre.

THURSDAY 17 JANUARY 1918
It snowed, and Nance, and Dobie surveyed the Harcourt Street Gallery, and we all lunched at the Bonne Bouche, having gathered Bea and Norah from the Depot. We pranced off to the 'Homestead' into the arms of AE and Susan, and browsed around the main bookshops of the city. Home to tea and a fire almost swimming thither through the mud, Dobie departing by the evening Mail [train].

[SATURDAY 19 JANUARY 1918]
Nance left for Ballingale Saturday morning. The children and Alice in the afternoon for singing and dancing and tea.

Letter from Marryat Dobie in London to Elsie [no date January 1918] – 'I had a delightful journey, tell Dr. Henry that the drunkards whom we saw at the station did not travel in the train with me. It was calm on the sea that night and me sleeping well in my bunk, glory be to God. I felt rather sleepless in the train at first, so I opened your parcel and ate myself to sleep, and woke up wallowing in crumbs ... I'm not going to say any more in praise of the time I had in Dublin – it was by far the best leave I have ever had ... the most interesting experience I have had since Halloween 1914 when I first went into action.'

SUNDAY 20 JANUARY 1918

Gloomy and dull, prospect likewise. Me dressed in me owldest [*sic*], Glory be to God, and no curling pin in my head overnight, but looking out at the mud and thinking of the two left over sandwiches to make lunch with on Howth Head, so as to 'begin fresh on Monday'. And wasn't it the old growler that drew up at the door and Themselves [Elsie's brother Stopford and his wife Betty] stepped out! And it was the great lepp [*sic*] I took from the bottom step straight on to his neck, letting a yell that brought the neighbours to their doors. Mary Doody rather pained 'And you in your camisole, mam, and the cabman thinking it was your husband come home'. They walked in, their utterly adorable selves. They just said they had come over to take us out to lunch. So we sprang in to the train to Bray, sat up on a car and gondolahed out (the water had great liberty that day, between Heaven and Earth, so it had) to Enniskerry. The Collins did us proud and Betty and Aug. roamed in the misty demesne and Top and I dreamed before a blazing log fire. Jane had a bright fire and hot dinner for us, and the evening was joyous!

MONDAY [21 JANUARY 1918]

They fetched Bea and me from College and we rollicked off to the Bonne Bouche for lunch, and came back to the Depot where they were both hailed delightedly as the parents of the already renowned Edward Lauder. Miss Nolan, Mrs. Cole, Mrs. Fletcher, Mrs. Starkie[5] almost fell on their necks, all remembering Betty in the early working days when she ground moss with the best of them. Miss Connolly has just finished 40 pairs of socks for the Battery, and was charmed to meet 'the Captain'. 'He has a fine face and he looks straight at you and through you, and I'm proud to meet him'. We processed <u>royally</u>.

Then to Alice's[6] and Top and Betty stayed to tea and I came back before Mrs. Campbell and Miss Stack departed after tea. Aunt Alice came to dinner and Mary had found some hellebores and pansies in the garden and made a delicious table decoration. We had the fatted calf (French: lapin) and there were still cabbages, celery and apples off the estate, and another ecstatic evening. Alice came in and Augustine recited Walt Whitman, with intense feeling, particularly a poem about a suffering cow. Top plunged to the rescue with a ghost story *à haute voix.*

[TUESDAY 22 JANUARY 1918]

Tuesday morning we rattled about town, gathering oddments of usefulness and amassing quantities of matches for Betty's ménage and Aunt Connie's, it being illegal in London to sell more than 1 box of matches per day to one person, and apparently women may only have a box per week. Here there is no restriction, so there was a positive orgie [*sic*] of matches of all varieties in the hall by lunch time.

Nance arrived at 1.45, having made a sporting dash from Ballingale to meet them. Top and I went down town ... He dashed to Mitchells for chocs for Nance and we sped to the Clonskea bridge to meet Betty and Nance and go and see the Stephens. Seamus and Iris chanted the Little Nut Tree to them, and we hied ourselves into a Keb [*sic*] and so to Springvale.[7] The garden looked lovely, and the hills, and the first breath of spring was in the air and sky. Uncle Ned is in great form and much excited about the Convention.[8] At 6.30 Aunt Alice arrived and we had a send-off dinner – <u>not</u> a 'teetotal, Hallelujah feast', Aunt Alice contributing a *vrai* Xmas plum pudding, and at 8.15 they took the boat train.

Letter from Charles Holloway in London to Elsie, 20 January 1918 –
'Dear Mrs Henry,

My wife and I wish to thank you and Professor Henry very much for your kind letter of sympathy, more especially as you express our feeling so truly in your mention of Lieut. Brunton, as Walter was one of those quiet natures who always did the things undertaken well. Nature never meant for such brutal work as fighting so savage a foe.

I am pleased that you are all keeping well and sincerely hope you may have the strength and good fortune to live these bad times through and reap the benefit of the better times which I hope are in store for the future.'

[24] JANUARY 1918

On Thursday the Convention exploded. It was reported that the Ulster members after preserving a stony silence from the very beginning, suddenly became articulate and omitted [*sic*] a flow of venom unprecedented in history. The remaining members rose up and filed silently out of the room ... Uncle Ned thinks the sequence is unbroken, ending in Sir E. Carson's resignation on Monday.

SATURDAY 26 JANUARY 1918

The first crocus, and two snowdrops. Three days of glorious sunrises – weather very warm and stormy.

30 JANUARY 1918

Perfect Spring weather; hepaticas and iris reticulate in blossom; and the sweet peas germinating in the pots after one week only.

28 FEBRUARY 1918

A bed of hyacinths in full bloom.

TUESDAY 12 MARCH 1918

Betty sailed from Liverpool [home to Canada].

TUESDAY 19 MARCH 1918

Heard from Top in France [with his Canadian regiment].

23 MARCH 1918

A wonderful week, like mid-May. Brilliant sunshine and crystally clear. So warm that Alice and Mary [Wordsworth] came round for tea in the garden. The hyacinths are over, and the daffodils just fleets in full sail. The Beattys' patriarchal pear tree, and all the pear trees in the terrace are in blossom. From my bedroom window is a vista of lemon coloured forsythia, creamy pear-blossom, and scarlet japonica, and the grass a deep emerald beneath. Tortoiseshell butterflies are busy on the wall flowers, and the birds in gay chorus. The thrush sings alone in the evening as the dusk [gives] the pure Botticelli sunsets, so delicate and so intense in colour. The moon is nearly full. She rises over the great dark cork tree, behind the patriarch, and the thrush among the white blossom welcomes her with a shout.

25–29 MARCH 1918

To Kilcooley Abbey, near Thurles, Mr. and Mrs T.B. Ponsonby. A lovely day and a drive of 13 miles. Rather barren country rolling on to the Galtee mountains. The old Abbey stands in the fields, a beautiful ruin, with the first 'Gothic flamboyant' window in Ireland, in perfect preservation ... From about 1200 it became the centre of a school of learning much frequented by Germans. The family residence of the Ponsonbys' (a Cromwellian family) was attached to the Abbey, now in a ruined condition, but a billiard room with a wooden billiard table is still there. Most of it was burnt down about 80 years ago, and the present house built ... There is a goodly company of family ancestors (Romneys, Gainsborough, etc.) very charming and lively people, all <u>belonging</u>. Mr Ponsonby, having been through the South African war and afterwards lost one eye and almost the second, in a hunting accident, is unfit for active service and is doing tillage on a very large scale, using all his intensive and widely travelled knowledge, and modern appliances to make it scientific and economic. Mrs. Ponsonby was a Miss Poynter, sister of Brigadier Gen. Poynter, V.C. They have 3 charming children. The days were spent on this demesne, among the woods where Mrs. Ponsonby is doing considerable re-planting, at the saw-mill, in the new cowsheds in course of construction for the 88 cows. They are in charge of a Dane, and are milked by machinery, but the electric plant was out of order and the whole number, besides new calves arriving daily, were on the hands of three weary cowmen! ... This is the country of Mr. Carton, 'Woodcock Carton' a famous sporting character. He fell in love with a Miss [left blank] and laid careful plans for her abduction. She, her mother, and her married sister, rode to church in a coach on Sunday, and found, to their surprise, Carton attending the service. On the return journey their coach was suddenly set upon and all three ladies dragged out. The ladies fought vigorously, but they would have been overpowered, only that Carton's retainer, seeing how unwilling Miss [blank] actually was, deserted his master, and by that time the villagers were coming up. Carton, having bought beautiful horses and established relays of them as far as the coast, and there had a ship in readiness. His preparations cost him £5,000. He served a term of imprisonment, but after his release again attempted to kidnap his lady. He failed once again, and yet once more. She would not have him. Yet she married no one else.

FRIDAY 29 MARCH 1918

To Castle Martyr, Co. Cork. A more antique antiquità even than the last; a square tower built on the site of a monastery of the 6th century. The place belonged to the Fitzgeralds ... Castle Martyr passed into the Shannon family who evidently loved it and expended great thought and price on the laying out and planting of the demesne. The present house resembles a French chateau looking out on a sheet of water surrounded by woods. There is a beautiful ballroom 50 ft long by 25 high and 25 wide, with a lovely plaster ceiling ... the house was filled with fine pictures, statuary and china. But the family fortune was squandered and a great deal of this sold (about the middle of the 19th century), the estate mortgaged and finally bought by the Arnott family (Dublin drapers).

Mrs Dinan said they had furnished it like an expensive hydropathic. They were rich and smart and idle, and thoroughly demoralized all the tenantry. Lady Arnott let it to her children who started a family quarrel and refused to pay her rent. Finally it came on the market again and Mr. Dinan bought it in 1917 for the timber firm. They have hitherto dealt in foreign timber, and now there is none to be had and they must perforce fall back on the native grown. There are extensive woods – silver fir, spruce, Scots pine, some beech, on the estate. Mr. Dinan has a saw-mill up and a light railway is being fitted up on the edge of the demesne. They will cut down as they <u>must</u> now, for the war, but he will also re-plant. Hence the visit. He and Augustine ... spent every day going over the estate considering the question of re-planting, and the species. They have a family of 9 (3 sons have been killed in the war, there are now 4 sons and 2 daughters).

They are reviving the agriculture on the place, the cattle and the dairy ... Mr. Dinan is starting a hostel for wounded (abt. 30) soldiers in Castle Martyr village (Mogeeley) for them to learn gardening and tree-planting, they will do practical training on the estate.

The Dinans' own home is Knockaden, Queenstown. Miss Dinan told me she was in the garden the morning the *Lusitania* was torpedoed. Her father was expected home from England that day. The gardener came to her in great agitation to ask what route he was taking, and she told him the mail route via Dublin. It took a great deal to satisfy him, and she asked why. The gardener replied that there were 3 submarines lying just outside Queenstown waiting for the *Lusitania*. She said it was nonsense, but he was very agitated and said he had seen them. There were so many wild rumours just then they paid no attention to any. But that afternoon the *Lusitania* was sunk.

Letter from Top in France to Elsie, 12 April 1918 –
'Beloved little sister,
I am living on a farm, in other words I am on lookout duty away from the Battery (Dei Gratia) for a few days. Just before I departed, in fact while I was sitting in the side car ready to leave the mail arrived with as <u>always</u> your delightful letter and the pencil from Smyth. I hurtled the parcels in beside me and off we went. It is now 8.25 a.m. and I have just had breakfast. Bread and butter and strawberry jam with your <u>scrumptious</u> ginger and helped out by chocolates sent in an Easter egg by Mrs Stewart ... I am sorry you say you are uneasy about me for I have been really very comfortable and nowhere near any shells. It is a lovely day, the sun is shining and the air is warm and balmy. After all the rain we have had it is a great change and somewhat of a relief although I think it may help Fritz in his attacks. If you want to know nothing of the war come to France for we never have any news at all only red hot rumours which contradict each other immediately they appear. I can see the [dear] little Hun line here but no little Huns are visible as yet. However, we have hopes that we may be able to tickle their innards soon.

I am hoping to get out of the battery at the earliest opportunity for I really can't as Jeannie says 'thole' it any longer. I really have done my best but the position is hopeless. My Mr. Lewis is getting beyond a joke especially under these conditions. So far of course I have had no letter from Betty but I know she's safely back with the boy. So I am not bothering my head about her ... I am glad on all counts that I was able to get Betty back and I feel so relieved about her while I am here ... Owing to Mr. Lewis the censor stamps did not arrive for a long time so all the letters have been delayed about 10 days. Nobody was particularly pleased. I would be grateful also if you would send me some sort of a clothes brush ... Give Aug. my best regards and wish him well in his forestry, it is really important work. I am glad that the people liked to hear about Canada. They have done quite a lot and it was through you that Dr. P. [Porter] got going but it is really through your efforts that the IIS got into him for Sphagnum ... Thank you over again for the parcel of food. It sounds greedy I know but I did appreciate it so much and what is the good of appreciating it if I don't tell you.

How do you like the picture of E.F.L.B. [Top's son, Edward]. I think it is quite good. I should like to see the little person. Now that he is running about he must be very nice indeed. I suppose when I get back I shall have to be introduced to him and be on my best behaviour ... Best love

from Top'

[17] APRIL 1918

Extreme excitement prevails here. Miss Higginbotham just returned from Sligo, says the young men are all leaving the towns and making for the mountains with a view to guerrilla warfare. There were great crowds around the Mansion House during the meeting yesterday. Lord French arrived at Kingstown yesterday and is at the Shelbourne Hotel, sentries with fixed bayonets on guard. The rumours are the very wildest. The chief one is that the gurkas are arriving from India to garrison Ireland. This started today, from innumerable sources, just like the 'Russians through England' rumour.

[20 APRIL] 1918

Dorothy's car driver ended up an exhaustive exposition with 'I'll tell ye what, Miss, t'is the bigothry [*sic*] and inthollerance [*sic*] of the people of this country that have landed us in this co-ass (chaos)'.

Letter from Augustine to his sister Mary Crum, 21 April 1918 copied into her diary by Elsie –
'Two years after the rebellion.

The political situation is extremely bad.[9] All sections of nationalists are now combined. Bishops, Laity, Priests, Redmondites and Republicans and Bolsheviks, like Maud Gonne etc., not to accept conscription on any terms. They don't offer to do anything to fight the Germans. Sinn Feiners, when not drilling, are saying the rosary all day for the success of the Germans, I am informed. Rioting has begun in the ship-yards, Belfast. The Catholics took a solemn league and covenant today (à la Carson) never to accept conscription all over Ireland. Lord French is here. The military are taking precautions. Such a tragic situation! It promises to be "Russia" in Ireland.

If Lloyd George doesn't resign there is bound to be massacre, everyone believes. The bringing in of a Home Rule bill will not have any effect, as no one believes in that, now. Everyone believes in Hatred, and in some strange way, think that the moment has come when they ought to be "in the fight" – against the hereditary foe. In other words, National Feeling has triumphed – Carson is being imitated in every iota. The Covenant is avowedly based on his Covenant.

I think little of the wisdom of English Statesmen and of Irish Politicians. Everything is being done at the wrong moment by the Government. And all the time everyone is gay, because money is plentiful and food is in plenty. Food is dear, it is true, but wages are gone up, of labourers, mechanics, etc.

The Students of the Catholic colleges etc. are not returning after the Easter vacation to their classes. And a good many shop-boys are running from the cities home to the farms. The "Committee of National Safety" if it may be so termed, has decreed that all work will cease on Tuesday as a sign to the Government of their power to bring matters to a crisis when they like. In the French Revolution the clergy joined the National Assembly and made the Revolution possible. Acts of "passive resistance" etc. are acts of revolution – and the end of revolution, who knows? The peasants and labourers of Ireland are inflammable material, who are now led by skilful leaders, backed up by the late Insurrection, by song, ballads, and what passes for history and by a literature; and they are out or will be out soon – if conscription is imposed. That is my reading. These insane quarrels and misunderstandings, based on hatred, are bound to have a bad end'.

[MAY] 1918
The latest story of the moment Mary Doody heard being earnestly related by one member of the girls' club she attends, to another girl 'on the best authority' that Captain Redmond[10] is now in the Tower of London awaiting death, because he took off his uniform and beat Lloyd George <u>with</u> it.

4 MAY 1918
There is a great shortage of silver. Cork was destitute of silver on Thursday, and some of the southern towns. Now it has reached Dublin

and the banks and post offices refuse to give change. Several shops are also refusing to give goods unless the exact sum is paid – at any rate refusing to give change of any notes. All sorts of explanations are going, one is that the Jews started a story that the Germans will be in Ireland in a few weeks and only silver will be of any use, so there is a panic among the farmers, and the smart profiteers are buying up £1 notes all over the country, at 15/- in silver. The trams have put up their 1d. fares to 1½d., and have a dodgy way of never having enough halfpennies in which case they firmly annex a two pence from the victimised passenger.

14 MAY 1918

The situation [the Conscription crisis] is desperate and the nerves of every individual are taut. It is very obvious in every day existence, the sense of a sword of Damocles over each one.

And yet it is all such a perfect heaven of lilac and lilies of the valley, of perfect summer, fluffy clouds and glowing sunsets, and the unending choirs of blackbirds and thrushes. The old hawthorn in front is a perfect counterpane of pink. Mr. and Mrs Fletcher came to lunch. We sat all afternoon under the yew, talking ... It is perfect.

A letter from Top to Aunt Alice says all the officers notice the number of letters he receives, and comment on it, and he just told them he was very well loved and did not have to answer them; and he just swanked unashamedly, so that they got no satisfaction out of him.

Letter from Top, in France to Elsie, 7 May 1918 –
'Things have arrived at the finishing point in the battery and I feel quite convinced that the best thing for me to do is to get out quietly ... So far as I can see I have two courses open to me. One is remain where I am and keep my rank and lose all my self respect, the other is to get out and try to do some decent work elsewhere. The rank really doesn't matter as

army rank is a very changeable thing anyhow ... I am very glad Betty is back [in Canada] with Edward Lauder but I am concerned about you and Nance. I do hope they won't break out into civil war and do you in.'

22–23 MAY 1918

A heavy downpour lasting all day and night. A lovely morning: spring and summer were married, and the ground is strewed thick with wedding confetti. Pink hawthorn petals, yellow laburnum, and white chestnut blossoms.

24 MAY 1918

The honeymoon is hanging a little heavy on hand, a damp grey brooding atmosphere and the weight of summer foliage rather sudden and oppressive.

Letter from Top in France to Elsie, 1 June 1918 –

'Darling little sister,

I got your very nice letters and the butter, chocolate and sardines ... yesterday I had a day off after two days in the observation post. While up at the O.P. Fritz put over 21 shells fairly near us of which only one burst so that was a pretty good record, 20 duds out of 21 shells. The night or rather the evening before that was a beautifully clear one and we could see the Germans walking about behind the lines so we spent a very pleasant couple of hours chasing them up hill and down dale with shells especially some horse transport which had the temerity to come into open view.

Yesterday I had a side car and went off for a trip by myself. I went off to see Ted's grave and actually found it without much trouble. It is in very poor repair but has fortunately escaped the fate of some of the others in being destroyed by shell fire and it is still intact.'

24 JUNE 1918

Pictures are becoming more and more restricted in the daily papers, none are published now except those entirely uninspiring ones labelled 'official', so that the majority is made up of young women about to be married or doing justice to a new hat, with occasional portraits of Cabinet Ministers and escaped German prisoners (the latter really 'wanted').

Letter from Top in France to Elsie, 22 July 1918 –
'Dearest Elsie,

I have just had your first letter addressed to me as Lt. [Lieutenant]. I am delighted to get it and it has cheered me up immensely. After all what you say is quite true and when I look around at this game I realise that rank is not everything. I have just had a letter from Betty and one from Mrs P. [Porter] which I am sending on to you intact. I really am a most blessed person with Betty, Lauder and you and I certainly can look people in the face and tell them I have played the game fairly ... I shall be quite happy here as all the officers are very nice and quite ready to help me. As I think I told you the major is a public school man with (thank God) the manners, customs and traditions of his kind. I am very flourishing and very much interested in the new life and surroundings. I do hope you will be getting away soon for a holiday somewhere as the daily round of moss must be very tiring ... I am so sorry I can't describe our place of abode to you but we are mostly ensconced in the cellars of houses and I believe one building used to be the village school. [It was] a very amusing house or the remains of a house. There used to be a circular iron staircase in it apparently as a back stair and the house has been blown away so that the stair case sticks up in solitary grandeur. I am about half way between our old position and Ted's grave now and if I get an opportunity I am going to go over on the motor bike and try to tidy up the grave a little bit. I think Ted would like to feel a bit loved. Thank Aug. for his interest in my deeds and my welfare. I don't think I was cut out for much worldly success but I think I prefer affection and respect.

God bless you little sister and don't worry about me. I have grown very much older and wiser since the war and little episodes like this don't trouble me. What I really enjoy and live for are things like your love and Betty's and the great things of life like that.

Your devoted brother, Top'

1–8 AUGUST 1918
To Clohogue House, Luggalore, Wicklow, at the head of Lough Dan and in the beautiful valley lying between it and Lough Tay to stay with the Fletchers.

9 AUGUST 1918
To Rossnowlagh, near Ballyshannon.

11 AUGUST 1918
Gerty Kerley mentioned in dispatches for valuable services during the war (only 3 sisters and 1 other nurse besides her – St Thomas' Hospital).

Letter from Top in France to Elsie, 4 September 1918 –
'as things go I shall be getting leave about the end of this month and I hope we can meet ... Let us meet in London if possible ... Any suggestions you can make about plans will be greatly appreciated by your brother. With regard to your letter about transferring I am very much in agreement with you.'

FRIDAY 4 OCTOBER 1918

Nance and I crossed to London. Top met us at Euston. To the Redbourne Hotel, Great Portland Street.

SATURDAY 5 OCTOBER 1918

To the food office for emergency rations [card] and then to Scotland Yard and the D.G.V.O. [Director General of Voluntary Organizations]. A strong wind blowing, the Thames grey and lumpy and the Embankment smothered in fallen leaves. At 12.30 to 36, Grosvenor Road where Bob and Juliette and family are installed. Then over to Harriet's maisonette, 127, Maida Vale – perfectly charming – very snug and done up in white and pale tints, with all her Stratford Place treasures round her, the old drawing room chairs and the china and other things and pictures. All three sisters have beautiful furniture and a great love of it, and the home is really delicious. They gave us a gorgeous tea, other friends coming and going also; we taxied home and Top purchased a vast supply of oysters, and we had a [gorgeous] spree.

SUNDAY 6 OCTOBER 1918

A beautiful clear sunny autumn day. Top and I wandered round Stratford Place and Marylebone Lane and other Oxford Street haunts, and called on Col. Adami, while Nance was at church. We met at the hotel and went down to Kew which was looking perfectly exquisite. Sir David and Lady Prain at home and very kind, Miss Wilmot was there also, bemoaning the beautiful gardens with no one to run them, no labour, no coal to keep the orchids alive, etc.

From Kew we bussed back to Harriet's maisonette, where Dr. and Mrs. [Eichholz] were waiting to see us.

MONDAY 7 OCTOBER 1918

Ran about town; saw Dr. Law, got tickets at the Savoy while a wild storm raged. Then to Liberty and Hamley's with a view to Edward Lauder's birthday. Top went on the bend at Buzzard's and we capered back to the hotel with our spoils. A strenuous hour was passed translating a gunnery pamphlet collected by Top from a German trench, and then we separated, Top and Nance in one direction, and I to Squire's to 'sphag'. We re-united at Jim's house and on our way home looked into the exhibition of war models in Oxford Street. The submarine model was going up and down in water, a tank ramping along, ships on a rough sea, and models of many of the ships used for hospital and food transport, which have been sunk during the war.

Dinner at Jim's with Colonel and Miss Adami, and Miss Torrance, a very delightful, festive, pretty and pre-war entertainment, beginning with a cocktail and ending with real ice-cream.

TUESDAY 8 OCTOBER 1918

To Highgate: the anniversary of Ted's death.

Top went to see Captain Fairweather, and Nance and I to Winchester House, St. James Square, to interview Colonel Stobart about gardening work on the Graves Commission. The work now consists in keeping tidy the graveyards near the base, the women gardeners are not allowed nearer the front, and later on it is expected to develop into a very big work. There are two immediate vacancies but it is essential to join the Waacs.[11] In the afternoon we went to Grosvenor Street to pursue inquiries re Waacs. They were most anxious to swallow Nance whole on the spot. I saw Mr Caines, analytical chemist at Squire's, and he is going to look into the ingredients of 'sphagnol' for us, to give us a clue if possible to the properties of the moss. After there we bussed to Trafalgar Square where there is a huge thrill on. The whole square is staged as the ruins of Rheims to encourage the public to buy war bonds. All round was a tight throng of people, packed close. We walked along the Embankment to Scotland House. Sir John Duthie gave us half an hour's interview re Irish Sphagnum organization.

[In the evening] to the Coliseum to see the Russian ballet, *Carnaval*. Trafalgar Square was lighted up, and more amazing than by day, with a cinemadiagraph showing on the base of Nelson's pillar.

WEDNESDAY 9 OCTOBER 1918

About 10 a.m. we went round with Top to the Royal Society of Medicine where we translated gunnery instructions, till 11.30, when I flew down to Scotland House. But after 30 minutes weary wait, Sir J. Duthie still not materializing, I had to leave all information with Mr. A. Hutchings and hurry back to meet Aunt Elizabeth and Aunt Connie at lunch. Major Anderson from Toronto joined us at lunch. His wife is on the way back to Canada and he is very sad and anxious. It rained and blew; we skipped into a taxi with Aunt Elizabeth and span off to 1, Airlie Gardens to see the Simons. Lady Simon is <u>most</u> attractive.[12] John Simon is just back from the front and only just into mufti. He gave us a thrilling account of the Americans and Australians in the last big move. The Americans rushed forward and there were so delighted with their performance that they wouldn't stop at the point they had been ordered to. The Australians were to back up, but the Americans had torn ahead with so much vigour that they were completely isolated, and sandwiched solid between German masses. The Allies had to send aeroplanes with tons of food and drop it on the Americans like Elijah's ravens to keep them alive, and the Australians wasted all their strength hacking a way through.

Captain Fairweather from St. John, New Brunswick, came to dinner. He took over the battery from Top when Top transferred, but he had the same experience of the O.C. as Top had had. He was quite pleased to be wounded and out of it. He said the men were all devoted to Top, and that any statement Top made would be backed by the whole battery.

THURSDAY 10 OCTOBER 1918

To finish the gunnery pamphlet translation at the R. Society of Medicine, and took it to Miss Cheesewright to typewrite. Top and Nance went off together, while I tore down to D.G.V.O. to retrieve Hotson's[13] report. Mr Hutchings said Sir John was greatly impressed by the Canadian and American [sphagnum moss] movement. At 1 o'clock we met Col. and Miss Adami at the Gobelins restaurant and had a birthday dinner for Top – very festive and finishing with coffee and liqueurs and almost eternal friendships. We parted and Top, Nance and I taxied down to the Savoy to gather up Bob, Juliette, Nancy and Evelyn, who are growing up very pretty. *Nothing but the Truth* was exceeding funny and very well acted. We shrieked joyfully. We flew home to pack and Top and I escorted his trunks to Grosvenor Road, where both the little boy Venables hurled themselves on Top with embraces, and were greatly rejoiced by sweets. Top sent a box to Blanche to smooth my homecoming and we careered again by 7 o'clock when Jim and Betty came to dinner. At 8 we scrambled blindly into another taxi and deposited Top at St Pancras for the night train to Scotland.

FRIDAY 11 OCTOBER 1918

Left the hotel at 7 a.m. and, under mis-direction of the alien porter wasted precious time running about Tube platforms, then we rushed heatedly above ground, to walk to Euston, when an overnight growler crawled by. I asked him could he take us to Euston for the Irish Mail. He said 'Hope you'll have better luck than yesterday. They blew her [RMS *Leinster*] to bits yesterday'. At Euston no bookings were being made for Ireland, so I wired for a room at the Queen's Hotel Chester, and on reaching Chester, all civilians were turned off. We drowned our sorrows in sleep all the afternoon and went in the evening to *My Official Wife* on the Vitagraph.

SATURDAY 12 OCTOBER 1918

The station officials assured us boats were running again, so we chased off to Holyhead in a weary-Willie train at 10a.m. Arrived at 2 in Holyhead to be told that the boat had sailed early this morning. There is no one earlier till tomorrow morning and we must catch that, for although we were lucky enough to get a room in the Hotel and which is quite full, our funds are only just holding out over the extended pic-nic [*sic*].

The mail-boat is coaling up exactly under our window: there are four steamers in the harbour, all camouflaged in squares and stripes like Futurist pictures, all the camouflages are different, and there is one submarine, but he comes only partially into view: the storm of the past week is abating, it may be quite placid tomorrow.

Coming out from dinner we ran into AE!! who likewise seemed glad to collide with us. Everybody toddled to bed early, as we were to be called at 4 o'clock. No means of obtaining tea or anything, so we prowled about the platform in pitch dark, the three of us, and a Father Swiney from Yorkshire, going over there to a sick friend. It was very dark, very like Hell with the perpetual chance of missing the last train to Heaven. At last we got on board, everybody's passport was <u>minutely</u> examined. We started at 7 a.m. with two aeroplanes buzzing close over us, an airship and an American destroyer zig-zagging to and fro before across our route the whole way across. When the sun came up and shone on the silver airship it was most beautiful. The sky was clear and the sea a summer blue. The passengers were all put into life jackets – they were nearly all military, but among the civilians were some tragic souls – an officer who had lost his sister, a lady who had lost her sister, and others. The disaster happened only about 25 minutes out from Kingstown; just a bit beyond the Kish lighthouse – a small buoy was floating in the water with a black flag attached, over the spot, and a pathetic rusty old boat was mounting guard. It was infinitely sad, and all the more desperately sad for the smiling summery sea, and the shining airship and the powerful destroyer. They had <u>nothing</u> in that dreadful wintery gale on Thursday, and it was so long before any boat reached them. Sir Henry Thomson and Miss Doyle who was making maps for Augustine at the College in September are gone.

13 OCTOBER 1918

Captain Romanes told us there were three officers making for the mail train on the morning of the 10th. They started in a taxi and just missed the train from Westland Row. Their taxi had gone, but they picked up another one and started for Kingstown. At Ballsbridge they had a break-down and the chauffeur said he could get no further. By an extraordinary chance, – for it was then soon after 8.30 a.m. – they found a third taxi. They tore down to Kingstown, and caught the boat by the fraction of a minute. They were all three drowned.

28 OCTOBER 1918

[Added later to the entry for 13 October 1918]

Sir T.W. Russell[14] confirmed the above story. Lady Russell went down to Kingstown on Monday 14th to see her sister off. Professor Campbell was also on board. They were due to start at 2, but the crew gathered at the side of the ship, and refused to return to their posts until the American destroyer was sent for to escort them. She was at Holyhead, and was sent for. The crew remained perfectly quietly, lined up along the ship's rail. Lady Russell said that the moment the destroyer loomed in sight they went back each to his post and the mail boat started. It meant about 2½ hours delay.

18–19 OCTOBER 1918
Professor Henry[15] to stay. He told us stories of sacred trout in Ireland.

20–21 OCTOBER 1918
Gerty here. October 18th she went to Dundalk for two days. The Dundalk-Liverpool boat has been sunk, though there is no word of it in the papers. Out of 33 only 6 were saved. The manager, whose wife and children live in England, was over visiting them and returned on that boat. He has been lost. There is nothing left of the 'packet', ship and staff and management – all wiped out together, no one and nothing left of it to carry on.

Postcard from Marryat Dobie in France to Elsie, 23 October 1918 (it depicts the German Kaiser, William II, with the caption 'La Justice poursuivant la Crime') –

'My movements are a little uncertain now, so you had better address letters to me at Second Army Intelligence (b). I think this card must be very popular! I have seen it in shop windows for years.'

Letter from Mrs L. Studdert, Royal Herbert Hospital, Woolwich, Midnight 30 October 1918 –
'Dear Mrs. Henry,
The ward is quiet and I'm sitting down for the first time since I came on night duty a month ago!! Nearly all the surgical wards have been turned into medical to take all these flu and pneumonia cases that come pouring in from the camps. And as a number of the staff are ill with it too we are very short handed and are really having a dreadful time of it,

and so many cases end fatally and they so often go off their heads 3 or 4 days before they die. I've a ward of 44 pts [patients] and a Sister now every 4 wards. It is really terrible at night when you have 2 or 3 men delirious and trying to get out of bed and watch and attend them and do your ordinary nursing work at the same time. We are not getting quite as bad cases in the last few days. I think the authorities are sending the men to hospital sooner before they become really ill.

Before I went on night work I was in a surgical ward – since last Feb. ... it was a _very_ busy ward – being an emergency ward ... I think the work is very much the same as any other hospital and we are treated very well and have a great deal of liberty for a military hospital. At present the hospital is too busy to give the ordinary off duty half days or leave but we don't think it can last very long in this state. A good many of the VADs have been _very_ ill too ... I think the majority of us will be _very_ glad when the war is over, and we are also discharged, as well as the soldiers! I'm a 'Duration' VAD – so alas! may not get finished as soon as some! I suppose you have no idea what the 'duration' term means – I suppose as long as [I'm] wanted really. We are really very short of nursing VADs – a great many have resigned and taken up other jobs – and of course there are a number abroad.

Yours sincerely

L.F. Studdert

I hope Dr. Webb is well. I've not heard of or from her for a very long time – if you ever see her tell her I was asking for her – I've not been in Ireland for a long time now.'

11 NOVEMBER 1918

The news [of the Armistice] boomed round about the College about 11 o'clock. Bea and I were labouring over the moss collecting centres on the map for the annual report. We flew into our coats and dashed out. Flags were already waving out of many windows. It was a glorious clear bright sunny day and Grafton Street looked quite lovely, decked all the way down both sides. We picked up Mrs Ball and Norah O'Brien. Boys were yelling 'Stop-Press', and everyone buying, and then hurrying off to buy a flag. Woolworths was besieged. Grafton Street thronged with excited people. Trinity College students commandeered laundry carts and jumped on them 20 at a time, terrifying the drivers and even more so the horses. The military of every degree simply <u>beamed</u>. A growler proceeded down the street with a General (or something very nearly approaching to it), stuffing three or four Waacs inside, himself following them, and several Tommies sitting on the roof. We bought a tin trumpet, and took it in turns to blow. Life was utterly glorious; and everyone <u>so</u> happy. Mrs Ball and I flew into the Plunkett House blowing the tin trumpet and waving the Union Jack. It was rather like entering a cold-storage mausoleum. We climbed to AE's room and plunged in. There was a group of apparently soured and empoisoned Sinn Feiners, who sat stolidly glued to their chairs while we loudly mafficked with flag and trumpet. Susan was the only one who rose at all. We tooted down stairs again, having done our best in the Cause. The Depot rejoiced and rioted, each according to its own ... But <u>not</u> much work got done.

Silvery aeroplanes juggle in the air, doing their very giddiest; and all the forgotten barrel organs of the country resurrected by one accord and made the streets tuneful. Church bells are very cautious, after the fines inflicted in England on premature rejoicing, so we have been spared them so far, but everyone did their best.

The workroom closed at 4 and we hurried out to maffick further. The T.C.D. students had got an effigy of the Kaiser, escorting it round on a hearse, to make a bonfire later, but we couldn't trace this excitement. Grafton Street by this time was packed nearly solid in two streams, up and down, the trams, all crowded tight, and many more flags flying all over the town.

14 NOVEMBER 1918

Professor R.M. Henry to stay. He told us that a friend of his brother Paul Henry[16] was one of the men who went to meet Casement on his landing. The friend A. told him that the two motors started, with four men in each, the object being to capture Valencia Island, with the wireless telegraph station there, and get into communication with the German assistance.

Eight men, armed, were considered enough for the purpose. The directions given to the motor cars, were to start from a certain point and take the first turning to the left and then the first to the right, and that would bring them to the bridge connecting with the island. The two motors started, and A. was in the front one. It continued its journey till it almost reached the bridge, there it found that the second was not following. It turned round and retraced its way very slowly fearing to collide with the second car.

What actually happened was that the man giving directions had taken no account of a tiny boreen, which he had not reckoned a 'turning' but it lay between the starting point and the so-called 'first turning on the left'. The second car had taken it, plunged headlong down it, full-speed, straight into the water.

The first car returning, found the wheel marks and nothing more, saw what must have happened, put on full speed and raced for Dublin.

[14 NOVEMBER 1918 [IN 1916 DIARY]]

Professor Henry told us there was a priest in the Marlborough Street presbytery who was sent for to a wounded man in the G.P.O. after the rebels got into it. The priest went to him, and found Connolly, Plunkett and Pearce [*sic*]. They told him that a German force was at that moment landing in Dublin Bay and that they had only to hold on till relief arrived. The priest said that there was not a fraction of German assistance within 200 miles. Pearce said if they kept their flag flying for 24 hours, they were entitled by International Law to be treated as prisoners of war. The priest told him that International Law in Sackville Street was and would be exactly what the British Government chose to make it. He begged them to surrender. They shrugged their shoulders at him. So he talked to the men. This created some impression and the leaders called a council of war. They asked him to retire while it was being held. So he retired into an adjacent room, where the girls were doing the cooking. They were greatly excited and he stayed there trying to calm them. At that moment a shell burst against the wall of the room, opening up a gap. The gap was wide enough for a man to get through, so the priest collected all the girls who were willing to go, and escorted them through the gap into an adjoining restaurant, and so out by back ways, so that the party was not arrested when the G.P.O. was finally taken.

Letter from J.H. [Waddingham?], Section II, 46 DAC to Augustine Henry, 19 November 1918 –

'Dear Dr Henry,

Just a few lines to let you know how I have been getting on. What a great relief it is to be able to light a lamp and know we shall not be bombed. I think the absence of night bombing makes the armistice more realistic than anything else. Eight nights rest is what we have not had for a very long time. There was ... a great flap on 29 Sept.: three brigades of infantry swam the St. Quentin Canal, took the Hindenburg Line with 4,000 prisoners and 40 guns. Since then we had continued fighting till we reached the Oise Sambre Canal at Catillon. The 1st Division forced the Canal on the 4th: we went through the 1st Division the same afternoon and chased the Bosch till we reached the Belgian frontier east of [Auvergne] on the 11th. It was a most memorable time. It poured with rain, all bridges were blown up and pontoons had to be thrown across; roads were mined, and the craters so vast they had to be bridged, but in spite of all the difficulties we pressed the Bosch so close he never had time to occupy a defensive position. We generally reached a village less than an hour after the enemy had left.

The occupied country was devoid of [food and we] had to feed all civilians in the area. All horses, cattle and poultry had been taken away and many houses wantonly wrecked just before the German troops left. At [Landrecies] the Bosch tried to make a stand but lost all his guns and many [persons].

I suppose we shall be demobilised in due course and have to look out for something to do. At present we are resting and where we are going no one knows.

With kind regards to Mrs Henry.

Yours sincerely,

J.H. [Waddingham?]'

Letter from Top in Belgium to Elsie, 23 November 1918 –
'Dearest little sister,

You imagine me chasing Germans at a furious pace whereas I have been sitting still and doing nothing. I came from Lourdes to this place [Quiévrain] on the Belgian side of the Frontier and we have sat here ever since. We have been into Mons for one trip only but the place is quite interesting ... The Belgians have not suffered any like what the French have though they tell you the war is terrible.'

FRIDAY 13 DECEMBER 1918

Arrival of Brunton daughter. Cable received 11.30 p.m. Saturday 14th.

18 DECEMBER 1918

Last working day of 1918 at the Depot. The War Office is closing down cotton wool and bandage depots, but apparently requires moss ad lib, forever and ever. Mrs Cole said today with dangerous mildness 'The War Office is entitled to express any opinion it wishes, but after Xmas I am going to say "Nunc Dimmitis" and then I shall nunk'.

A telegram came for the James Wilsons that Logi is safe in Copenhagen, after being a prisoner 6 months in Straalsund. Professor Wilson and Mrs. Wilson and the 7 foot Carl were all rejoicing in the corridor together, and the stars of the morning that sang together simply wouldn't have had a chance.

Miss Nolan and I trotted home together, and Mrs. Nolan had gone voting;[17] so Louise asked her what she had done with the paper. Mrs Nolan probably doesn't know a vote from a torpedo, but she does know every animal that ever stood on a race-course, so she replied to Louise that 'the man' had told her it didn't matter how she folded the paper, so she had 'just closed it so he shouldn't see the horse'.

Great joy, after no news at all from all the Famille Heger since his letter after the sinking of the *Lusitania*, suddenly, by post a gay card with every single name complete, and winding up with Top's. What a day of joys.

Letter from Ethel Porter in Canada to Elsie [December] 1918 –
'We have just sent off 25 thousand sphagnum moss dressings with the Siberian expedition.'

Letter from G. Whiskard, Acting Secretary, Order of the British Empire, Home Office, Whitehall to Elsie, 18 December 1918 –
'Confidential, Order of the British Empire.
Madam, I have been directed by the Home Secretary to inform you that, in view of the service you have rendered on work connected with

the War, it is proposed to submit your name for appointment as an Officer of the British Empire.

The Home Secretary desires me to ask you to be so good as to fill up the enclosed form and return it to me in the accompanying addressed envelope <u>at your earliest convenience</u>.

I am, etc.']

[Elsie's cousin and colleague at the RCScI depot, Beatrice O'Brien, was also honoured.]

20 DECEMBER 1918

<u>London</u>, on our first real honeymoon trip since Aug. 1914.

25 DECEMBER 1918

Xmas Day beautiful, frosty, sunny and still. We did walk all morning in the Gardens, and the nurseries, and lunched with Sir David and Lady Prain, and afterwards went to 36, Grosvenor Square where Bob, Juliette and the children were celebrating their first Christmas together. When we left them we were 'upon the wide, wide, world' and we dashed round dark, silent, gloomy streets until we found a haven in the Charing X [Cross] Lyons, to celebrate really unconventional Xmas dinner. A letter also from the Hegers came by the Xmas morning post.

Letter from Paul Heger, Bruxelles to the Henrys, 5 December 1918 –
'Our little country has struggled beside yours for a beautiful ideal. What we have suffered physically or in morale would be difficult to say. During the German occupation one could not say anything for fear of prison or often of deportation. My Becker children have taken in three orphans, whose mother and father were shot in August 1914 together with 120 inhabitants of their village ... I have been very busy maintaining during

the war the school of Edith Cavell which was organised above all by Madame Depage.

8 JANUARY 1919

Top arrived quite suddenly and unexpectedly from France. Annette came up from Bognor for a night. <u>Grand </u>old razzle-dazzle, lunches, restaurants, shops, Academy, breathless ber-lissful [*sic*] joy.

[*Letters of congratulation to Elsie on her OBE from Arthur Stanley, Chairman of the Joint War Committee of the British Red Cross and Order of St. John (9 January 1919), Sir John Lumsden, Director in Chief of Joint War Committee of the British Red Cross and Order of St. John, Leinster, Munster and Connaught (9 January 1919), George Fletcher (10 January 1919).*]

Letter from [Bea O'Brien] in Dublin to Elsie, January 1919 –
'Dearest Elsie,

So the O.B.E. has come at last! I simply don't know what I shall do if you haven't. I heard all about it from Blanche and if you haven't got it at the same time as me I will be in a dreadful state ... I know I have done good work and grind but yours has been the inspiration, but of all loyal little souls you are the most so. I am keeping it dark till it is actually announced, in case anything happens! But I told Blanche who was at her engineering yesterday and Peggy and Miss Reed who I met in a shop ... Blanche thinks it has come at <u>the</u> right moment before we dissolve, and now we can sing "nunc"!'']

Letter from M.E. [Mary Elizabeth 'Aunt Lily'] Stopford in Dublin to Elsie [no date] –

'I am so glad, dear Elsie, that your work has been recognised and that you have the O.B.E. You were really the origin of the whole thing and in addition to your public work you have done a private work of great value, in starting Bea on her career. You discovered her, and enabled her to discover herself.

Ever your loving aunt, M.E. Stopford'

Letter from Marryat R. Dobie, now with the Second Army, BEF in Cologne, January 1919 (he was now part of the British Army of Occupation in Germany) –

'My job here is not at all exciting; the old game of issuing passes. I had, all through the years when I was preventing decent French people from travelling, looked forward to the day when I should do the same to Germans; and now that we have got here we have, according to instructions, to be infinitely more lenient to them than we have to the French.'

3–10 MAY 1919

To Courtown for a week with Iris and Seamus [James Stephens' children] – dream of loveliness, the sea, blackthorn in bud, carpets of bluebells through the woods, cascades of primroses down the banks, pools of brilliant kingcups, and hollows where the wild lilies of the valley were coming into bud. A multitude of lords and ladies, long stretches of purple ground ivy; birds and bees and insects; and over all the crystal exhilaration of the sea.

13 MAY 1919

To London, to meet Heger, bringing the body of Edith Cavell from Brussels. Stayed with Bob, Juliette and famille Venables at 36, Grosvenor Road. On Thursday morning Juliette and I went to the memorial service. London looking a radiant and glorious vision of old times. Clear, cloudless, sparkling weather, and the sun filtering through the fairy green of young lime and plane leaves on to the squares and pavements. The joyous stir and tear and bustle of demobilization, and a 'season' beginning. Only along Victoria Street, Parliament Square, and the route [of the funeral procession] to Liverpool Street [station] hushed and quiet, and silent crowds.

16–17 MAY 1919

Harriet and I spent mostly with Heger, he has not aged a day since July 1914.

His daughter Madame Becker has adopted 3 children, a girl and two boys, orphans of civilians, shot in the Ardennes, early in the war. The Germans entered the village of Rossignol, and ordered 125 inhabitants into a train. The bewildered peasants sought one of their number, called Huriot, who knew German, and said 'You come with us as interpreter'. Huriot got into the train, and Madame Huriot said 'if you go, I go too'. The train stopped a certain distance away. The Germans ordered everyone to descend, lined them all up against a bridge and shot them all. Madame Huriot was among the last. She was forced to stand on a heap of dead bodies, including that of her husband. She never flinched, at the last moment she tore open her blouse crying 'Fire: Mais Vivre la France'. The Germans thought there had been no witnesses, but the curé and one inhabitant of a neighbouring village had seen it, and reported it to Belgian headquarters. The Germans tried hard to make friends of the Belgians during the first year of the invasion, but when every means failed they took to terrorism. At a given moment the civilian inhabitants of many villages were conveyed away by train, lined up and shot, as in the case of Rossignol. Heger said the method was refined cruelty; a machine gun was turned on and they were mown down. After each mowing the officer cried 'Let everyone who is not shot, stand up'. The unfortunate souls who were only wounded gathered themselves up with hope – and the machine gun was again turned on all down the line.

While the efforts at friendliness were still in progress, the son of Von Bissing, Professor of Archaeology at Munich University, requested an interview with Heger, as President of the University of Brussels. 'I arranged that the interview should take place in his house' said Heger 'for if he came to me, I could not terminate the interview'. Von Bissing began by every possible attempt at friendly relations, he said that although they were at war, Science was above war, that scientists must co-operate in the cause of humanity, etc. etc., and then laid down the [terms] on which the Germans wished the University to come into line with them. Nothing doing. Von Bissing began to get angry, and shouted threateningly 'And what if we <u>command</u> you?' Heger replied with perfect gentleness and polish; – 'Cela serait comme si vous n'aviez parlé'.

He said the Germans were extraordinarily and invariably petty and bullying in mind, and gave as an example the way he took to get out of Brussels. In 1915, the Queen, then at La Paune, sent him a verbal message 'Venez'. He conveyed back that he would come ... So Heger reached La Paune, and while he was there he heard of the loss of the *Lusitania;* being already out of Brussels, he was able to come over to England to meet the body of his niece, Marie DePage, and take her back to Belgium. He said it was much more difficult to re-enter Brussels. But he managed that too, and during the whole time in Brussels with the suffering, and anxiety and sorrow he was never a day ill or doubtful until just before the end, when the Germans were sweeping towards Calais. He said for one moment then his faith flagged, and he got ill. He then got leave to go for a short holiday into the hills of the Ardennes. There he saw different animals but he also saw men – (but they were no longer men). They had no clothes, and they lived in holes, and had been in hiding for four years. The villagers around knew of them, and when they could, brought them crumbs of any food available.

He showed us a letter from Miss Cavell dated 22nd September, a very short time before she was shot. She and her friends believed the sentence would be imprisonment, and possibly removal to Germany. Heger had conveyed to her by a nurse that whatever money, etc. she might need, she was to let him know, and he would see that she had it all. Her letter in reply was quite unconcerned, saying that it was extremely inconvenient at the particular moment when she wanted to 'démenager', and her letter was so generally full of trivialities that she could not have been under any apprehension. Heger said that nobody was, for it wasn't legal in Germany to punish the offence with death, and he said, 'It might have happened to any one of us, we every one of us were constantly doing it [hiding prisoners of war], all the time'.

He showed us a photograph of the notice posted up in 3 languages in Brussels by the Germans. Now in Edith Cavell's notes she wrote 'Condemned to death 8th Oct.' but the German notice says Condemned to death Oct. 9th. Heger says they actually did condemn her on Oct. 8th and within the next 24 hours they passed a law in Germany making it legal.

They had no particular wish to condemn the other people mentioned in the same list, but they couldn't shoot one single woman alone, so they condemned a handful for the sake of appearances. The only other woman was let off.

Postcard from Nance, from Aubreville (Meuse) where she was serving with the Service de Santé Militaire, Societé des Amis to Elsie, 1 September 1919 –

'The ink spot is about where our équipe is; just above the village. The trees make it look not quite so desolate and all the little wooden houses have been put up by the Mission. The little house end on in the foreground is the bakers where we get our bread; he has just got his oven built; before he used to walk to and fro from his oven at Augeville 4 miles away every day. It must have been a lovely place before it was destroyed. It is all surrounded by orchards. I live in a little house just like these.'

8

Postscript

Augustine and Elsie Henry continued to live in Dublin after 1919, witnesses to the War of Independence, the Civil War and the birth of the new independent Irish State. Elsie does not appear to have continued her diary but she did describe one of her experiences during the Civil War to her sister Nance:

> We left Dublin on Thursday night, but couldn't get to Westland Row, because of the ambushes, but got a taxi to drive us to Kingstown, and were held up twice by Free State troops ... Today's papers say the Four Courts[1] have been entirely blown up in one final terrific explosion and Rory O'Connor[2] and his crowd surrendered. The buildings are destroyed, and all the documents, historic and otherwise, in them ... Bullets were whizzing round College Green and Dame Street on Thursday morning when I was down there ... A. [Augustine] crossed Leeson Street Bridge on Wednesday ten minutes after a bomb was thrown on the bridge, which killed four Free State soldiers.[3]

Elsie's aunt Alice had moved to Dublin in 1919, establishing herself in a house in St Stephen's Green where nationalists and journalists could meet – a house which was raided by police and the British military forces during the War of Independence. When the War of Independence came to an end in 1921, the possibility of peace in Ireland vanished with the disputes about the Anglo-Irish Treaty and the subsequent Civil War (1922–23). Alice Stopford Green and two of her Stopford nieces, Alice and Edie, supported the Anglo-Irish Treaty and the new Irish Free State. This put them at odds with Dorothy Stopford, who by 1922 had qualified as a doctor, was working in Kilbrittan, Co. Cork and had become a republican and supporter of the anti-Treaty forces. Her sister Edie recalled:

> I joined my sister Alice Wordsworth in Dublin. My sister, my Aunt Alice and I were all Free Staters or Cumann na nGael (I being specially concerned to support Irish labour); but Dorothy remained a Republican, along with Erskine Childers, Bob Barton and others: so that our relations with her (as in the case of so many other families) were for a time rather strained.[4]

Despite their political differences, in January 1925 when Dorothy married Liam Price,[5] Edie, Alice, Alice's daughter Mary and their brother Robert were at the wedding, although their aunt was not well enough to attend. By then Dorothy had left Cork and was establishing her medical practice in Dublin. Alice Stopford Green died in 1929, having been one of the four women who were elected to the Senate of the Irish Free State. Alice Wordsworth and her daughter remained in Ireland but Edie returned to England, where she held various posts and took care of her mother.

Of Elsie's immediate family, her surviving brother Top returned to his family in Canada after the war. Her sister Nance worked with the Society of Friends relief corps in France in 1919 and in Austria in 1921, her aunt writing to a friend that 'one of my nieces is away in Vienna saving the starving children there and growing into skin and bone herself'.[6] She subsequently worked in Salonika, Poland, Bulgaria and Russia. In 1928 she married a Ukranian named Adolf Kruming and they emigrated to Canada.

Unlike some of his colleagues in the RCScI who left Dublin after the transfer of power from the British government to the new Irish Free State, Augustine continued teaching at the college. He remained as Professor of Forestry after the RCScI became part of University College Dublin (UCD) in 1926, retiring the following year. The Henrys travelled in Europe during the post-war years, visiting France and Poland, and Augustine continued his research.[7] He died in 1930 and after his death Elsie presented Augustine's collection of specimens under a 'Deed of gift' to the National Botanic Gardens in Glasnevin to be known as the Augustine Henry Forestry Herbarium.[8] Much of her time after 1930 was devoted to cataloguing this collection of over 9,000 specimens that he had collected – a task that had not been completed by the time she died in March 1956. In 1957 the task was completed, a catalogue of the collection was published and to mark Elsie's contribution and a plaque in her honour was placed in the herbarium in the Botanic Gardens:[9]

> This plaque is erected in memory of Mrs. Alice Henry, wife of Dr. Augustine Henry. She was a constant source of strength and assistance to her husband in his botanical explorations in Europe, Africa and America. After his death she assembled and arranged his specimens to form the Augustine Henry Forestry Herbarium, a task which took her eight years to complete. She then generously presented it to the National Botanic Gardens, Glasnevin. She also

presented many valuable plants, books and pamphlets and
was in every way a good friend to the garden until her death
in March 1956.[10]

Apart from her work on Augustine's collection, Elsie became involved in
the Irish Roadside Tree Association,[11] that encouraged all Irish forestry,
fostered public interest in trees and planted the streets of Dublin
with ornamental trees. She was also an active member of the Dublin
Naturalists' Field Club from 1931[12] and a member of the Irish Society
for the Protection of Birds.[13] She also continued with her own research.
In August 1939 she was in Sussex, where she visited and compiled a
report on the area and forestry around Kingley Vale.[14] In 1940 Elsie left
the house in Ranelagh that she had shared with Augustine and moved
to 21 Clyde Road, Ballsbridge. She died in 1956 and was buried with
Augustine in the cemetery at Deansgrange, in Dublin.

Elsie kept in contact with her family throughout her life, remaining
close to Alice Wordsworth and her family, with Robert Stopford and
with her sister Nance in Canada. She also kept in touch with Augustine
Henry's nephew Peter Kerley.[15] Childless herself, she had 'god-
mothered' James Stephens' two children, Iris and Seamus, and in later
years Alice's granddaughter recalled visits to the house in Ranelagh
whilst a daughter of Peter Kerley has happy memories of herself and
her sister being treated to lunch (including an ice-cream concoction,
Knickerbocker Glories) in Switzer's restaurant in Dublin.[16]

Elsie is remembered by one of them as a 'tiny figure but with a very
strong personality, but she was always very kind'. These qualities of
kindness and strength of character (together with a sense of humour)
are the qualities which are so evident in the diaries of Elsie Henry.

Notes

1. Introduction: Elsie Henry and her Diaries

1. Sir Thomas Lauder Brunton, 1st Baronet (1844–1916) was a highly successful doctor who was also a lecturer in Materia Medica and Pharmacology at St Bartholomew's hospital. He made numerous original contributions to medicine and pharmacology, including studies on the effect of digitalis for heart conditions. He was one of the founders of the National League for Physical Education, and was a steadfast and active advocate of schemes in favour of national health, school hygiene and military training. Knighted in 1900, he was given a baronetcy in 1908.

2. The entry for Thomas Lauder Brunton in the *Oxford Dictionary of National Biography* states that the Bruntons had six children. However, there is no record of there being any more than four; J.A. Gunn, rev. M. Earles, 'Brunton, Sir Thomas Lauder, first baronet (1844–1916)', http://www.oxforddnb.com/view/article/32139.Two children may have died in infancy in an era of high infant mortality.

3. James Stopford ('Top') Brunton (1884–1943) emigrated to Canada and worked with the Canadian Geological Survey from 1912–13. During the First World War he served with Canadian troops in Canada and France, returned to Canada at the end of the war and worked as a mining geologist.

4. Edward Henry Pollock Brunton (1890–1915) graduated from Cambridge with a Bachelor of Arts (BA), was registered as a Licentiate, Royal College of Physicians, London (LRCP) and as a Member, Royal College of Surgeons (MRCS). He fought in the First World War and gained the rank of Temporary Lieutenant in the service of the Royal Army Medical Corps, attached to the 4th Battalion, Grenadier Guards. He

died on 8 October 1915 at age 25, killed in action at Loos.

5.   Anne Brunton ('Nance') (1888-1956) did a course in Rural Science for Teachers at the Royal College of Science for Ireland (where Augustine was professor of forestry) in 1913. She came back to Ireland in 1914, spent some of the war working in the Spring Rice estate in Foynes, Co. Limerick and spent 1916–18 teaching at a College of Gardening for Women in Wexford. After the war she worked with the Society of Friends relief corps in France and Austria and later in Salonika, Poland and Russia. In 1928 she married a Ukranian named Adolf Kruming and they subsequently emigrated to Canada. Her diary (from January 1913 to May1915) is now in the National Library of Ireland (NLI) (Diary of Annie Brunton, afterwards Mrs Anne Kruming, January 1913–April 1915 (NLI MS 13,620 [1-2]).

6.   For more on the Stopford family see Leon O Broin, *Protestant Nationalists in Revolutionary Ireland: The Stopford Connection* (Dublin, 1985).

7.   Elsie's aunt, Alice Sophia Amelia Stopford Green (1847–1929) was a historian and anti-imperialist. In 1901 she was a founder member of the Africa Society and its vice-president. She met Roger Casement when both were active in the formation of the Congo Reform Association (1904). In 1914 she was chairman and primary funder of the committee set up to organize the importation of arms into Ireland for the Irish Volunteers. She was horrified by the Easter Rising and in the Treaty debates she supported the Treaty, subsequently becoming a Senator in the Irish Free State.

8.   Elsie's cousin, Dorothy Stopford Price (1890–1954) was the daughter of Jemmett and Constance Stopford. She began her medical studies in Trinity College Dublin (TCD) in 1916. In 1925 she married Liam Price, a barrister and district justice in Co. Wicklow. Her medical career was based mainly in St Ultan's Hospital for Infants and the Royal City of Dublin Hospital, Baggot Street, and through her research she made major contributions to the eradication of tuberculosis in Ireland.

9.   Robert Jemmett Stopford (1895–1978) served in the First World War, first as a member of an ambulance brigade in Belgium, and later with the army in Salonika. After the war he served on a number of government commissions in India and in Czechoslovakia. From 1956 to 1968 he was vice-chairman of the Imperial War Museum in London.

10. Alice married a Christopher Wordsworth and they went to Bombay where Christopher was working. After his death she returned to England with her daughter, Mary, and eventually they settled

in Dublin. In the 1920s Alice acted as housekeeper for her aunt Alice Stopford Green.

11. Elsie's cousin, Edith Stopford (1890–1960) won a scholarship to Cambridge, had a brilliant academic career, with a Double First (English) from Newnham College, Cambridge, as well as a triple Blue (hockey, tennis and cricket). She worked with a section of the Board of Trade (later the Ministry of Labour) during the First World War and with the Peace for Ireland Council in 1921. She lived in England for most of her life, taking care of her mother until her death in 1939.She died in London in 1960.

12. Augustine Henry (1857–1930) studied science at Queen's College Galway and then studied medicine in Queen's College Belfast. In 1881 he joined the Chinese Imperial Maritime Customs Service, where he became interested in botany. By the time he left China in 1900 his interests had turned to forestry. He studied forestry in France and then in 1907 he was appointed the first Reader in Forestry at Cambridge. That year he gave expert evidence to an Irish departmental committee, advocating conifer cultivation in Ireland as part of a new Irish forestry policy and in 1913 was appointed as the first Professor of Forestry at the RCScI. He continued his research during the First World War. After the RCScI

became part of University College Dublin (UCD) in 1926 he remained on as Professor of Forestry.

13. George Russell ('AE') (1867–1935), poet and theosophist, became editor of *The Irish Homestead*, journal of the co-operative society, the Irish Agricultural Organisation Society (IAOS) in 1905. The headquarters of *The Irish Homestead* was at 84 Merrion Square, also named Plunkett House.

14. Evelyn Gleeson (1855–1925) a lifelong friend of Augustine Henry. She was the founder of the Dun Emer Guild, a workshop of the Arts and Crafts Movement in Ireland and Augustine had funded some of her activities. There is a large collection of the correspondence between Augustine and Evelyn in the National Library of Ireland (Letters of Dr Augustine Henry to Miss Evelyn Gleeson, 1901–1930, NLI MS 13,698).

15. Elsie's uncle, Edward Adderly Stopford ('Uncle Ned') and his wife Mary Elizabeth ('Aunt Lily') lived in Dublin. A retired tea merchant, he worked with Sir Horace Plunkett in the IAOS. A niece Beatrice O'Brien, who lived with them, became one of Elsie's closest friends.

16. Now 47 Sandford Road, Ranelagh.

17. Henry John Elwes (1846–1922), natural historian and traveller. Augustine Henry's collaborator on the seven volume publication, *The*

Trees of Great Britain and Ireland (1906–13).

18. Sir Horace Curzon Plunkett (1854–1932), pioneer of the co-operative movement in Ireland. He founded the Irish Agricultural Organisation Society in 1894 and was the author of *Ireland in the New Century* (1904).

19. James Stephens (1880/82–1950), author and co-founder of the *Irish Review* (1911–14).

20. Sarah Henrietta Purser (1848–1943), painter and stained-glass artist.

21. Diary of Annie Brunton, afterwards Mrs Anne Kruming, January 1913–April 1915 (NLI MS 13,620 (1-2)).

22. Herbert Henry Asquith, first Earl of Oxford and Asquith (1852–1928), a Liberal politician and Prime Minister from 1908 to 1916.

23. Elsie's cousin, Bob Venables and his family were in Mulhausen, Germany when the war began. Bob was interned but his wife, Juliette, and their children travelled to England, settling in Oxford for the duration of the war. His parents were Gilbert Venables, a London journalist and Elizabeth Venables (née Stopford) who was an older sister of Alice Stopford Green.

24. Irish War Hospital Supply Organisation. Royal College of Science Sub-Depot Sphagnum Department, *Annual Reports* (Dublin [1915–19]).

25. Alice Helen Brunton Henry diaries

1913–1919 (NLI MS 7981–7988). Two diaries are missing, covering the periods from the end of May to 19 December 1916 and from April to November 1917.

26. Alice Helen Brunton Henry diary 1913–1914 (NLI MS 7981).

27. These letters to Elsie are included in the text on the date they were written, rather than the date they are inserted into the diaries.

2. The Last Days of World Peace but Conflict in Ireland: The Diaries 1913–14

1. Alice Brunton Henry diary 1913–1914 (NLI MS 7981).

2. In August 1913 a group of Dublin businessmen, alarmed by the numbers of workers joining the Irish Transport and General Workers Union (ITGWU) attempted to force their employees to leave the ITGWU or face dismissal. By the end of September over 20,000 workers, mainly unskilled, were either on strike or locked out. The result was a long and bitter dispute that lasted until January 1914 and caused untold hardship to the striking workers and their families.

3. Built in the Belfast shipyard of Harland and Wolff, the passenger ship, the *Titanic* was the largest ship afloat at the time of her maiden voyage in April 1912. She sank on

15 April 1912 after colliding with an iceberg, resulting in the deaths of 1,514 people.

4. Ardglass is a small coastal village in Co. Down. In 1911 F.J. Bigger bought Jordan's Castle in Ardglass and restored it, renaming it Castle Shane.

5. Francis Joseph Bigger (1863–1926), antiquarian, nationalist and supporter of the Celtic Revival.

6. William Gibson (Liam Mac Giolla Bhríde) (1868–1942), 2nd Baron Ashbourne, an Irish language enthusiast and president of the London branch of the Gaelic League from 1908 to 1914.

7. Sir Roger Casement (1864–1916). He joined the British consular service and went back to the Congo as British consul. In 1904 he published a report condemning the colonial policies of the Belgians in the Congo. He became a committed Irish nationalist. In 1913 he retired from the Foreign Office, joined the Irish Volunteers in 1913, travelled to the United States (July 1914) seeking aid from Clan-na-Gael for them and then to Berlin seeking German aid for an insurrection in Ireland. Arrested in 1916, he was tried for treason and executed in August 1916.

8. Dublin Bread Co. dining and tea rooms, 33 Dame Street.

9. John Campbell Gordon (1847–1934), 7th Earl of Aberdeen and 1st Marquess of Aberdeen and Temair. He was Lord Lieutenant of Ireland in 1886 and from 1905 until Feb. 1915. His wife was Lady Ishbel Gordon (née Marjoribanks) (1857–1939). In her time in Ireland Lady Aberdeen encouraged charitable work and Irish craft industries, healthcare, the promotion of women's role in society and she was associated with an anti-tuberculosis campaign in Ireland spearheaded by the Women's National Health Association.

10. Inset by Elsie Henry at end of page identified him as 'Moore, Bog rope maker, Queen Street, Coleraine'.

11. Charles Dawson.

12. In their opposition to the imminent passing of the Home Rule Bill which would give Ireland its own parliament, in 1911 the Unionist movement, mainly concentrated in the industrialized north-east of Ireland, initiated a massive protest movement. In September 1912 half a million people signed A Solemn League and Covenant to defend the union of Britain and Ireland and by the end of the year a citizen militia, the Ulster Volunteer Force, had been formed. A 'provisional government' was also formed in preparation for the day that the Home Rule Bill was passed.

13. The restaurant Jammet's was established by two French brothers,

Michel and Francoise Jammet, in Dublin in 1901. Located at 46 Nassau Street it was well known for its French cuisine. It closed in 1967.

14. Angel Bickerdike (née Stopford), aunt of Elsie.

15. Elsie's brother Stopford Brunton and his fiancée, Elizabeth Porter.

16. Susan Mitchell (1866–1926), essayist and poet, was a lifelong friend of George Russell and a supporter of Sinn Féin.

17. The headquarters of The *Irish Homestead* was at 84 Merrion Square, also named Plunkett House.

18. Sir William Rothenstein (1872–1945), an artist and art administrator who, in 1910, established an India Society to educate the British public about Indian arts. He was later knighted for his services to art.

19. Alexandra College, Dublin was founded in 1866 by Anne Jellicoe to provide a wider and more complete education for girls, and it played a significant role in the campaign for the access of women to higher education in Ireland. From 1866 Alexandra College was based in Earlsfort Terrace in Dublin, before it moved to its present location at Milltown in the 1970s. The Hermione Lectures in art were endowed by Hermione, Duchess of Leinster in 1896.

20. Helen Laird (1874–1957) was an actress, a science teacher and a member of the Gaelic League and Inginidhe na hÉireann. She was active in the Irish Women's Franchise League (IWFL) and she helped form the Ladies' School Dinners Committee, which fed children from Dublin's poorest schools.

21. Liberty Hall in Dublin was the headquarters of the Irish Transport and General Workers Union. It was badly damaged in 1916 during the Easter Rising.

22. James Robert ('Jack') White (1879–1946) was a former soldier who had served in South Africa and had been awarded a DSO for bravery. In 1913, he offered his services to the ITGWU strike committee and he became a central figure in the subsequent formation of the Irish Citizen Army (ICA) in November 1913.

23. The Irish Citizen Army (ICA) was set up in 1913 to protect demonstrating workers and pickets during the Dublin strike and lock-out.

24. James Larkin (1876–1947) was a labour leader and founder of the ITGWU in 1909.

25. Eoin (John) MacNeill (1867–1945), a Gaelic scholar and nationalist politician. As a result of his article, MacNeill was approached by a group of separatists associated with the IRB, who asked him to take the lead in organizing the Irish Volunteers

(launched 11 November 1913). He became chief-of-staff of the Volunteers.

26. The Irish Volunteers, established in reaction to the establishment of the Ulster Volunteers the previous year. By June 1914 it had about 160,000 members. The movement split after the outbreak of the First World War when the majority supported John Redmond's call to support the war effort and a minority, led by Eoin MacNeill, opposed it.

27. Harriet Jaffé, Lauder Brunton's secretary. Sir Lauder Brunton bequeathed her £2,000 on his death in 1916, for her twenty-one years' service.

28. The artist Hubert von Herkomer (d. 1914).

29. Sir William Whitla (1851–1933) was senior physician to the Royal Victoria Hospital in Belfast, as well as consultant at the Ulster Hospital for Women and Children and the Belfast Ophthalmic Hospital.

30. Elsie's cousin Beatrice O'Brien, who lived with Elsie's uncle Edward Stopford and his wife Lily.

31. Irish Agricultural Organization Society (IAOS) established in Dublin in 1894 by Sir Horace Plunkett to promote co-operative organization among Irish farmers.

32. Willoughby J. de Montmorency (1868–1917) 4th Viscount. An army officer, he later became an officer in the National Volunteers.

33. Douglas Hyde (Dubhghlas de hIde) (1860–1949), Gaelic scholar, founder of the Gaelic League, and first president of Ireland.

34. Thomas Finlay, SJ (1848–1940) was appointed joint Professor of Philosophy at UCD in 1883 (together with his brother Peter). He was deeply involved in the Irish co-operative movement and was the founder of the *Irish Homestead*.

35. The Stopfords had grown up in Co. Meath.

36. Horas Tristram Kennedy (1899–1917) a relative of the Stopfords, was a geologist with the Geological Survey of Ireland. He was killed in action near Ypres in June 1917.

37. J.J. Walsh, chairman of the Cork county board of the Gaelic Athletic Association.

38. Thomas Patrick Gill (1858–1931), journalist, politician, and secretary of the Department of Agriculture and Technical Instruction (DATI) from its establishment in 1900 to 1923. He was also a commissioner of intermediate education (1909–23) and a senator of the NUI.

39. Sir William Barrett (1844–1925) was Professor of Physics at the Royal College of Science for Ireland. His sister Rosa (1854–1936) was a philanthropist who established Ireland's first crèche.

40. Grubb's was an engineering works

which specialized in manufacturing optical telescopes and instruments. The manufacturing works were at Charlemont Bridge in Dublin until 1916, when, for security reasons, it moved to England.

41. Sir Howard Grubb (1844–1931) an engineer and manufacturer of optical and astronomical instruments in Dublin.

42. Mary Emily Connolly Norman (née Kenny), wife of the psychiatrist, Conolly Norman (1853–1908), who had been medical superintendent to the Richmond district asylum, Dublin.

43. The Research Defence Society was founded in 1908 by Stephen Paget (1855–1926), a writer and doctor, to support vivisection in medical research.

44. Dr Charles Edward Fitzgerald, president of the Royal College of Physicians of Ireland, 1912–13.

45. Olivia Charlotte Guinness, wife of Arthur Edward Guinness (1840–1915), Baron Audilaun. She was the daughter of the 3rd Earl of Bantry.

46. Andrew Reginald Nicholas Gerald Bonaparte Wyse (1870–1940), was a civil servant who became an inspector of national schools for the commissioners of national education in Ireland in 1894, and in 1914 was private secretary to W.M. Starkie, the resident commissioner for national education. His wife was Marie, daughter of Count Dmitry de Chirpunov of Orel, Russia.

47. James Owen Hannay [*pseud.* George A. Birmingham] (1865–1950), Church of Ireland priest, novelist and playwright. His interest in Irish affairs led him to assist Douglas Hyde in the early years of the Gaelic League.

48. Now Cobh, Co. Cork.

49. Elizabeth Venables (née Stopford). She was an older sister of Alice Stopford Green, married to a London journalist, Gilbert Venables.

50. Robert Lloyd Praeger (1865–1953), was a naturalist, botanist and author. He originally qualified as an engineer, but abandoned his engineering career in favour of natural history and became a librarian at the National Library of Ireland. His wife was Hedwig ('Hedi') Magnusson (d. 1952).

51. Robert Francis Scharff (1858–1934), was a zoologist and keeper of the natural history collections at the Dublin Museum of Science and Art from 1890 to 1921.

52. James Wilson, Professor of Agriculture at the RCScI from 1901.

53. Richard Burdon Haldane, Viscount Haldane (1856–1928), was a barrister and a Liberal politician; he was Lord Chancellor from 1912 until 1915.

54. Probably the archaeologist Robert Alexander Stewart Macalister

(1870–1950), Professor of Celtic Archaeology at UCD (1909–43).

55. Jack Butler Yeats (1871–1957), artist and brother of William Butler, Elizabeth ('Lollie') and Susan ('Lily') Yeats.

56. Alfred Emmott, Baron Emmott (1858–1926), cotton manufacturer and Liberal politician.

57. Herbert Louis Samuel, first Viscount Samuel (1870–1963). Elected to the Westminster parliament in 1902, he endorsed the condemnation of the former British consul there, Roger Casement, against the colonial policies of the Belgian government in the Congo.

58. This may be 'Miss Whitty, Old Bawn, Old Connaught, Bray'; *Thom's Official Directory of the United Kingdom and Ireland for the year 1915* (Dublin, 1915), p.2195.

59. Sir Frederick William Moore (1857–1949), curator and later keeper of the Botanic Gardens, Glasnevin, Dublin from 1879 to 1922. He father was David Moore (1808–79), who had been curator of the Gardens at Glasnevin from 1838 to 1879.

60. Arthur C. Forbes (b. 1869), Inspector of Forestry at Avondale, Co. Wicklow from 1906 to 1935.

61. Francis Crosbie, Riverdale, Dundrum Road, Dundrum; *Thom's Official Directory of the United Kingdom and Ireland for the year 1915*, p.1957.

62. Elsie's uncle, Col. James G.B. Stopford ([1838] – 1916), a brother of Alice Stopford Green. He had served in the 8th Hussars and later was in command of the 1st Batt. Duke of Cornwall's Light Infantry. His only child was George B. Stopford, who served in the Royal Flying Corps (RFC) during the First World War; *Irish Independent*, 17 March 1916.

63. Constance Stopford (née Kennedy), the widow of Jemmett Stopford, an engineer, and the mother of Alice Edith ('Edie'), Dorothy and Robert Stopford.

64. Elsie's cousin, Edith Stopford (1890–1960), daughter of Jemmett and Constance Stopford.

65. Elsie's cousin, Dorothy Stopford Price.

66. In March 1914 Brigadier-General Hubert Gough and a number of officers based in the Curragh army camp in Co. Kildare resigned their commissions rather than participate in what they believed was a government plan to deploy troops against the unionists in Ulster in their opposition to Home Rule in Ireland. Often referred to as 'the Curragh mutiny' the political fall-out from this incident caused the resignation of the Secretary for War and the chief of the Imperial Staff. See *Sunday Independent*, 29 March 1914.

67. HMS *Pathfinder* under Capt. Francis Martin Leake was lost in September 1914; *Sunday Independent*, 6 September 1914.

68. John Edward Bernard Seely, first Baron Mottistone (1868–1947), a soldier and later first a Conservative and then Liberal politician, Secretary of State at the War Office in 1914, was forced to resign his post after the Curragh incident. He subsequently served with distinction in France during the First World War.

69. Herbert Henry Asquith, first Earl of Oxford and Asquith British Prime Minister in 1914.

70. Agnes Winifred O'Farrelly (Úna; 'Uan Uladh' Ní Fhaircheallaigh) (1874–1951). A graduate of the Royal University of Ireland (BA 1899, MA 1900), she was appointed a lecturer in Irish at Alexandra and Loreto colleges. Appointed lecturer in modern Irish at UCD in 1909, from 1932 to 1947 she was Professor of Modern Irish in University College Dublin (UCD). A campaigner for equal access of women to university education, she was a founder member of the Irish Association of Women Graduates and was president of the Irish Federation of University Women (1937–39) and of the National University Women Graduates' Association (NUWGA) (1943–47).

71. Susan Mitchell, 'Belfast Street ballad, 1916', *New Statesman*, 6 May 1914.

72. Alice Wordsworth first cousin of Elsie.

73. Sir Roger Casement travelled to the United States (July 1914) seeking aid from Clan-na-Gael for the Irish Volunteers.

74. John Dillon (1851–1927), Anti-Parnellite Irish Parliamentary Party MP and party leader from 1918.

75. The Irish Parliamentary Party (otherwise the Nationalist Party or Home Rule Party) formed 1874.

76. Timothy Healy (1855–1931) a former Irish Party MP expelled in 1902 following disagreements.

77. William O'Brien (1852–1928), editor, author and Irish Party MP.

78. John Redmond (1856–1918) MP, Leader of the Irish Party (1900–18).

79. Joseph Devlin (1871–1934), Irish Parliamentary Party MP and General Secretary of the United Irish League (1903).

80. Clongowes Wood College, a Jesuit school in Clane, Co. Kildare, attended by Redmond. He spoke at its centenary celebrations in May–June 1914.

81. Ancient Order of Foresters Friendly Society and the Ancient Order of Hibernians, nationalist cultural societies.

82. William Butler Yeats (1865–1939), poet, dramatist and founder of the National (Abbey) Theatre 1904.

83. Francis Thompson (1859–1907), religious poet and writer.

84. A private club at 94 Piccadilly, London which was founded in 1862 for junior officers.

85. Gertrude and Constance Pim, sisters resident at 12 Landsdowne Road, Dublin. Possibly connected to the Pims of Cabinteely House, which was used as a sphagnum moss sub- depot during World War I. The Pim sisters had been students at the RCScI.

86. James Standish O'Grady (1846–1928), historian and early novelist in the Irish literary revival.

87. Charles Fourrier (1772–1837), Utopian Socialist.

88. Horatio Herbert Kitchener, Earl Kitchener of Khartoum (1850–1916). An army officer, Kitchener served in Egypt, the Sudan, South Africa and India; he was Secretary of State for War from 1914 to1916. In this role Kitchener chose to create a new mass volunteer army, known as the 'New' army, to supplement the existing regular army. He died in June 1916 when the cruiser HMS *Hampshire*, on which he was travelling to Russia, sank off Scotland.

89. Professor Paul Heger (1846–1925), Professor of Medicine at Brussels University and director of the Solvay Institute in Brussels.

90. Sir Edward Henry Carson (1854–1935), a Dublin-born lawyer and politician. He was a committed Unionist and from February 1910 he was chairman of the Irish Unionist Parliamentary Party.

91. Silas Weir Mitchell (1829–1914), president of the College of Physicians in Boston.

92. Owen Wister (1860–1938), novelist. He favoured American entry on the Allied side in the First World War.

93. William Paton Ker (1855–1923) was a literary scholar, and the first holder of the Quain Chair of English Language and Literature in University College, London from 1899 to 1922.

94. Rural district twelve miles south of Brussels. The trees Elsie described were all gone by the end of 1914 for military uses.

95. Belgian Independence Day, 21 July.

96. Eugene, 3rd Count Goblet d'Alviella (1846–1925). His wife was an American, Margaret A. Packard.

97. John Millington Synge (1871–1909), musician, author and playwright. His play, *The Playboy of the Western World*, provoked public protests on its opening week at the Abbey in 1907.

98. Walter G. Phillimore (1845–1929), Lord Justice of Appeal and Privy Councillor (1913).

99. The Buckingham Palace conference was called in July 1914 by King

George V. Irish nationalist and unionist leaders were invited to attend and the conference was an attempt to avert a possible civil war over the introduction of Home Rule to Ireland.

100. The Irish Volunteers landed arms at Howth, Co. Dublin on 26 July 1914, and also at Kilcoole, Co. Wicklow. The guns landed at Howth had been brought to Ireland by Erskine Childers in his yacht, the 'Asgard', and the crew included Childers, his wife Molly, and Mary Spring Rice. The purchase of the arms had been funded in part by Alice Stopford Green. Later that day some soldiers, challenged by Dubliners, opened fire on a crowd at Batchelor's Walk in Dublin, killing three civilians and wounding thirty-eight.

101. Mary Spring Rice (1880–1924), a daughter of Baron Monteagle of Brandon. She was a nationalist and a member of the Gaelic League.

102. Andrew Bonar Law (1858–1923), Unionist Conservative politician and Prime Minister (1922–23).

103. Stewart and Mary Crum. Mary was Augustine's sister.

104. H. Charlton Bastian (1837–1915), a prominent though controversial physician and neurologist.

3. A World at War: The Diaries August – December 1914

1. Alice Brunton Henry diaries, 22 August 1913 (NLI MS 7981), 23 August 1914–2 March 1915 (NLI MS 7982).

2. Founded in 1905, one of many privately run organizations established to promote health, sanitation and reduce infant mortality. Sir Lauder's motivation was his anticipation of a war with Germany.

3. This reference is probably to John Redmond's declaration in Parliament of the Irish National Volunteers willingness to join the Ulster Volunteer Force in defending Ireland; *Evening Herald*, 5 August 1914.

4. Sir John Foster George Ross of Bladensburg (1848–1926), Chief Commissioner of the Dublin Metropolitan Police (DMP) (1901–14). He resigned in protest at the government's decision to suspend his assistant over the Bachelors' Walk shootings.

5. Robert Erskine Childers (1870–1922), author and Irish Nationalist. English born, he served in the British army during the Boer War, later became a civil servant, but he moved politically from pro-Imperialist to an Irish nationalist stance. His yacht, the 'Asgard', was used to bring arms into Ireland for the Irish Volunteers

in 1914. A lieutenant in Royal Naval Volunteer Reserve in 1914, he served in the armed forces throughout the First World War as an intelligence officer, being awarded a DSC in 1917. In 1919 Childers became involved in the War of Independence, and used his literary skills to aid Sinn Féin propaganda. An opponent of the Treaty, he was executed as an Anti-Treaty activist during the Irish Civil War.

6. Conor O'Brien (1880–1952), architect, writer and yachtsman and an early member of Sinn Féin.

7. Bulmer Hobson (1883–1969), an author and a nationalist. He was a member of Sinn Féin and of the Irish Republican Brotherhood (IRB). Founded Fianna Éireann (1908) and was a founder member of Irish Volunteers (1913).

8. Maurice George Moore (1854–1939), a soldier who served in South Africa, was a supporter of the Gaelic League and of the co-operative movement. In 1913 he was on the provisional committee of the Irish Volunteers, was inspector general of the Volunteers and spent much of 1914 organizing Volunteer corps throughout Ireland.

9. Col. Richard Cotter (1891–1929) joined the National Volunteers (1913). He fought with the Irish Volunteers at Jacob's factory during the 1916 Rising. He helped reorganize Sinn Féin for the anti-conscription campaign of 1918.

10. A spy story by Erskine Childers, *The Riddle of the Sands* was published in 1903.

11. Sir James Cantlie (1851–1926), physician, was an advocate of improved army medicine, and with his wife promoted first aid training for civilians through the British Red Cross Society during the war.

12. Gertrude Kerley was a niece of Augustine Henry who spent the First World War as a nurse in London. She was a daughter of Augustine's sister Matilda and Michael Kerley, a grocer and egg exporter in Dundalk.

13. Elizabeth Bloxham, a Protestant, born in Westport in 1878. Her father was a member of the Royal Irish constabulary (RIC). A domestic science teacher, she became involved in the Irish nationalist and the Irish suffrage movements, contributed to Arthur Griffith's *United Irishman* and later to Sinn Féin and was the national organizer of Cumann na mBan.

14. Antony Patrick MacDonnell (1844–1925), Baron MacDonnell of Swinford, civil servant. In 1865 MacDonnell joined the Indian civil service, initially serving in Bengal and later as chief commissioner of Burma (1889–90), chief commissioner of the Central Provinces (1891–93), acting

lieutenant governor of Bengal (1893), and member of the viceroy's council (1893–95). He was Under-Secretary for Ireland from 1902 to 1908, supported the 3rd Home Rule Bill and was a member of the Irish convention (1917–18).

15. In a speech in parliament on 3 August Redmond had suggested that all British troops should be withdrawn from Ireland and that the hitherto rival Volunteer forces (the UVF and the Irish Volunteers) would defend the island.

16. Osborn Joseph Bergin (1873–1950), Professor of Early and Medieval Irish at University College Dublin (1909–40).

17. Edward Grey, Viscount Grey of Falloden (1862–1933) was Foreign Secretary from 1906 to 1916.

18. Patrick A.E. Dowling was the Registrar of the RCScI.

19. Sophia Rosamond Praeger (1867–1954), sculptor, illustrator, author, and poet. In 1931 she was one of the founder members of the Ulster Academy of Arts, where she exhibited until 1949 and she was a member of the Guild of Irish Art Workers.

20. The Soviet government subsequently changed the name to Leningrad; it reverted to St Petersburg after the collapse of the USSR.

21. The 1st Cheshire Regiment, as part of the 1st Infantry Brigade of the British Expeditionary Force, suffered severe losses as part of the rearguard during the retreat to the Marne in August 1914.

22. Sir William Somerville (1860–1932), Professor of Agriculture at Cambridge.

23. Élisabeth Louise Vigée-Le Brun (1755–1842), French painter of romantic portraits.

24. Extract from the *London Gazette Supplement*, 3 September 1914, announcing that Lieut. G.B. Stopford, RA is 'promoted as a Flight Commander in the RFC Military Wing and is to be granted the temporary rank of Capt.'.

25. Sir William Leishmann (1865–1926), bacteriologist and pathologist who developed an anti-typhoid vaccine.

26. Robert S. Baden Powell (1857–1941), army officer and founder of the Boy Scouts and Girl Guides.

27. Rostrevor House, Co. Down.

28. Parliament passed the Government of Ireland Bill into law at the same time as the Government of Ireland and Welsh Church Suspensory Bill was passed on 17 September 1914. The Suspensory Act held the Government of Ireland Act in abeyance until after the end of the war.

29. Mather Thomson was a doctor at the

Mater Hospital and the George V Military Hospital in Dublin.

30. Frederick Sleigh Roberts, first Earl Roberts (1832–1914), an army officer who had served in India and South Africa. He was commander-in-chief of the British army from 1900 to 1904 and returned as colonel-in-chief of the empire ('overseas') troops in France in 1914.

31. William Bourke Wright (1876–1939) was a senior geologist at Geological Survey of Ireland. Mabel Crawford Wright (née MacDowell) was a geologist and had been a student of G.A.J. Cole at the RCScI.

32. Charles-Marie Le Bon (1841–1931), the French sociologist and educationalist who wrote *Psychlogie des Foules* (Crowd Psychology) in 1895. Promoted popular understanding of science and psychoanalysis.

33. Marryat R. Dobie (1888–1973), a family friend of the Bruntons. He had been an assistant at the British Museum. He enlisted as a private in 1914, was commissioned in 1915 and was an officer in the Intelligence Corps from 1915 to 1919.

34. The 14th (County of London) Battalion, The London Regiment (London Scottish). The first Territorial infantry battalion in action against the Germans, at Messines on 31 October 1914.

35. John Allsebrook Simon (1873–1954)

1st Viscount Simon Politician, lawyer, Attorney General (1913–15), later Home Secretary (1913–16). Subsequently held other Cabinet posts. He was connected to Alice Stopford Green through his first wife, Ethel Venables, a niece of John Richard Green.

36. Possibly daughter of Henry Harrison, Home Rule Party MP involved in the IAOS.

37. John Denton Pinkstone French, first earl of Ypres (1852–1925). An army officer, he served in South Africa, he became chief of the Imperial General Staff (CIGS) in 1912, and was promoted field marshal in 1913. In 1914 he was appointed as commander of the British Expeditionary Force (BEF) resigning in December 1915 after the Battle of Loos to become commander-in-chief of home forces. He was Lord Lieutenant of Ireland from 1918 to 1921.

38. Iris and Seamus were the two Stephens' children.

39. Logi Wilson was the son of James Wilson, the Professor of Agriculture at the RCScI .

40. Neither Horas Kennedy nor Robert Valentine survived the war. Robert Valentine died at Loos in 1916 and Horas Kennedy was killed in action near Ypres in June 1917.

41. George Fletcher was assistant

secretary in regard to technical instruction at the Department of Agriculture and Technical Instruction (DATI). His daughter was Constance Heppell-Marr.

42. Probably J. R. Campbell, BSc., assistant secretary in respect of agriculture at DATI.

43. Mount Trenchard, Foynes, Co. Limerick was the home of Thomas Spring Rice (1849–1926), 2nd Baron Monteagle, a co-founder of the agricultural cooperative movement. His daughter was Mary Ellen Spring Rice (1880–1924), the Irish nationalist.

44. Grenville Arthur James Cole (1859–1924), Professor of Geology at RCScI from 1890 to 1924 and Director, Geological Survey of Ireland from 1905 to 1924. His wife was Blanche Cole (née Vernon) who had been a student at the RCScI. The Coles had two houses, one at 10 Winton Road, Leeson Park (1902–20), and Orohova (later Glenheather), Carrickmines (1902–24).

45. Mary Doody, servant in the Henry household.

46. Mary Crum (née Henry), Augustine Henry's sister. During the First World War she was superintendent of a Red Cross hospital in East Grinstead. Her husband, Stewart, who had served with the army in South Africa and India, was called up in 1914 and promoted.

47. Sir Arthur Gerald Chance (1859–1928), surgeon at the Mater Misericordiae Hospital, Dublin.

48. Three Barton brothers served in the British armed forces during the First World War. Robert Childers Barton (1881–1975), had been a member of the Irish Volunteers and became resistant to Col. Maurice Moore. In the First World War he served in the Royal Dublin Fusiliers. He resigned his commission after 1916, joined the Volunteers, and in 1918 was elected Sinn Féin MP for Wicklow West. He voted for the Treaty in the vote in the Dáil but subsequently joined the anti-Treaty side in the Civil War. He was a cousin of Erskine Childers (1870–1922). Both Robert Barton's brothers' served in the Royal Irish Rifles during the First World War – Thomas Eyre Barton was killed in the Somme offensive in 1916 and in 1918 Charles Erskine Barton died in France.

49. The *Audacious* was a dreadnought of 28,000 tons and carried ten 13.5 inch guns and sixteen 4 inch guns. She was completed in 1913 and sank after striking a mine off the north Irish coast on 27 October 1914. In the *Daily Mail* of 15 November 1918 the Admiralty confirmed the sinking –'This was kept secret at the urgent request of the Commander-

in-Chief, Grand Fleet, and the Press loyally refrained from giving it any publicity'.

50. The *Freeman's Journal*, founded in 1763 and ceased in 1924, after its presses had been destroyed by the anti-Treaty IRA, and it merged with the *Irish Independent*.

51. Sir Matthew Nathan (1862–1939), soldier and administrator. He was commissioned in the Royal Engineers (1880) and later served as governor in Sierra Leone and the Gold Coast (1899–1903), Hong Kong (1904–07), and Natal (1907–09). In 1914 he was appointed to be under-secretary for Ireland but resigned in 1916 after the Easter Rising.

52. A Papal knight, Patrick Valentine Emmanuel MacSwiney (d. 1945), an Inspecting Officer with the National Volunteers, was arrested after the Easter Rising and in 1923 was an Irish Free State delegate to the Vatican.

53. John George Adami (1862–1926). A pathologist, he was appointed as Professor of Pathology and Bacteriology at McGill University, Montreal in 1892 and he campaigned in Canada for public health and in particular child welfare and measures against tuberculosis. In 1914 he became assistant director of medical services (in charge of records) to the Canadian expeditionary force.

54. Henry Nevinson (1856–1941), a journalist with very liberal views, reported on the First World War from Gallipoli and the Western Front. He was a friend of Alice Stopford Green.

55. John Edward Bernard Seely, served on General Staff in France from 1914 to 1918.

56. (James) Ramsay MacDonald (1866–1937), member of the Labour party and prime minister 1924, 1929–35.

57. George Wakeling was a relation and family friend of the Stopfords.

4. A Year of War Work and Personal Loss: The Diaries 1915

1. Alice Brunton Henry Diaries, 23 August 1914 – 2 March 1915 (NLI MS 7982), March 1915 – October 1915 (NLI MS 7983); October 1915 – 6 June 1916 (NLI MS 7984).

2. Angel Bickerdike (née Stopford), Elsie's aunt and elder sister of Alice Stopford Green.

3. The United States had invited the various American nations to a conference in the spring to discuss the financial and commercial problems arising out of the war, and suggested that New York would become a competitor with London as the world's financial centre. The *Dacia* was a German ship, interned in the United States and sold in January 1915.

4. In 1914 Roger Casement travelled to Berlin as the envoy of Irish-American leaders. He persuaded the German government to declare that if its forces landed in Ireland they would do so as liberators. He also tried to induce captured Irish prisoners of war to change sides and to join an 'Irish brigade' which would support the central powers by liberating Ireland.

5. This may be the poet Sidney Royse Lysaght (1856–1941). The Lysaghts had an estate at Hazelwood, near Mallow, Co. Cork and also had an extensive property at Raheen Manor, Tuamgraney, Co. Clare.

6. D. Houston, FLS, lecturer in agricultural biology and agricultural chemistry at the RCScI.

7. Seamas O'Sullivan (1879–1958), writer, poet and contributor to the *Irish Homestead*. In later years he founded and edited the *Dublin Magazine* (1923–58).

8. Edmund Joseph McWeeney (1864–1925), Professor of Pathology at Catholic University of Ireland medical school from 1890 and from 1908 in University College Dublin (UCD).

9. Captain T.H. Gibbon, RAMC, who gave a lecture on 'Treatment of the sick and wounded from the firing line to the hospitals at home' at the RCScI; *Irish Times*, 13 March 1915.

10. Subsequently Griffith Barracks, South Circular Road, Dublin.

11. Belfast shipbuilders.

12. The *Lusitania* was sunk by the German submarine, U-20, off Queenstown [Cobh] with the loss of over 1,000 passengers and crew, including the art collector Sir Hugh Lane (1875–1915). This caused an international incident as the previous February the United States had issued a warning that Germany would be held responsible if any American ships or shipping were lost as a result of the German submarine blockade of Britain.

13. Madame DePage, head of the Belgium Red Cross Society, a niece of the Henry's friend, Paul Heger.

14. Probably Dame Edith Sophy Lyttelton [née Balfour] (1865–1948), a writer and widow of the politician Alfred Lyttelton (1857–1913).

15. Kuno Meyer (1858–1919), Celtic scholar, philologist and translator.

16. Jocelyn Gore-Booth (1869–1944), 6th baronet, who was active in the Irish co-operative movement. His sisters were the nationalist and republican Constance, Countess Markievicz (1868–1927) and the poet and suffragist Eva Gore-Booth (1870–1926).

17. Thomas Spring Rice (1849–1926), 2nd Baron Monteagle and co-founder of the agricultural cooperative movement in Ireland. His daughter

was the nationalist Mary Spring Rice (1880–1924).

18. (Phoebe) Sarah [Hertha] Ayrton (née Marks) (1854–1923), a suffragist whose husband William Edward Ayrton (1847–1908) was also an electrical engineer. During the First World War she developed the Ayrton fan, or flapper, used in the trenches to dispel poison gas.

19. Sir Alfred Keogh (1857–1936), an army medical officer and director-general of the Army Medical Service from 1905 to 1910. In 1914, Keogh took charge of the Red Cross committee which coordinated voluntary medical aid in France and Flanders in 1914, and resumed his post as director-general of the Army Medical Service in Britain.

20. Douglas Haig, first Earl Haig (1861–1928), an army officer who served in the Sudan, South Africa and India. In 1915 he was commander of the First Army in France with the rank of general and by the end of the year he had replaced Sir John French as commander-in-chief.

21. John Lumsden (later Sir John) was the Commandant and medical officer of the Royal College of Science, Woman's VAD. He was physician to Mercer's Hospital in Dublin and chief medical officer to the Guinness brewery.

22. Alice Stopford Green's house in London.

23. Sir Lauder Brunton's apartment in London.

24. Sir Donald Macalister, principal of Glasgow university and president of the General Medical Council.

25. Edward George Villiers Stanley, seventeenth Earl of Derby (1865–1948), a friend of Lord Kitchener, he became director-general of recruiting on 5 October 1915 as a final attempt to sustain the voluntary principle for military recruitment.

26. Edith Louisa Cavell (1865–1915), a nurse and from 1907 director of a nurses training school and clinic in Brussels established by Antoine DePage. She was arrested by the Germans in August 1915, accused of assisting the enemy, was convicted and shot.

27. 'Supernumeraries' were described in the annual reports as 'having joined this V.A.D. in order to enter Military Hospitals as Cooks, Clerks and Dispensers'; *Royal College of Science, Women's V.A.D., St John Ambulance Association Dublin, No. 748: annual report*, December 1915, p.[2].

5. Conflict in Ireland: The Diaries 1916

1. Alice Brunton Henry Diaries, 23 October 1915 – 30 May 1916 (NLI MS 7984), 14 December 1916 – 19 April 1917 (NLI MS 7985).

2. The term 'Sinn Feiners' was used by the British authorities to describe the militant nationalists, very few of whom were members of the Sinn Féin party.

3. Island in the Aegean Sea.

4. 'Flags' and 'Arf-a-mos' were popular brands of cigarettes during the First World War.

5. Cape Helles was one of the landing places during the ill-fated Gallipoli campaign in 1915.

6. This refers to a very popular poem, 'Casabianca', written in 1826 by Felicia Dorothea Hemans, and which begins, 'The boy stood on the burning deck, when all but he had fled'.

7. Elsie's sister, Anne ['Nance'] Brunton, was working in the gardens at Mount Trenchard in Limerick in 1916.

8. Charles Cathcart (1853-1932), resident surgeon at the Edinburgh Royal Infirmary from 1878.

9. After this visit, when Betty returned to Canada, she introduced the possibility of the use of sphagnum moss as a surgical dressing to the Canadian medical authorities.

10. *The Torch: Journal of the Royal College of Science for Ireland.* Elsie wrote an article on sphagnum moss for *The Torch* in 1916; Alice Henry, 'Sphagnum Moss' in *The Torch: Journal of the Royal College of Science for Ireland,* 1 (1916), pp.6–7.

11. Alfred Fannin, managing director of a surgical and medical supply company in Grafton Street, Dublin.

12. Military hospital at Woolwich.

13. An incident when a hostile crowd marched to the offices of the Irish Volunteers and Cumann na mBan in Tullamore and attacked it.

14. This may be a reference to the fact that Sir Matthew Nathan's parents were Jews.

15. Westland Row was a main railway station of strategic importance and was occupied by Irish Volunteers until 3 May 1916.

16. Harcourt Street railway station, briefly taken on Easter Monday.

17. The Shelbourne Hotel, founded in 1824, is located on the north side of St Stephen's Green.

18. AE travelled to the home of the MacLysaghts in Co. Clare on Good Friday and did not arrive back in Dublin until the following Wednesday, 26 April 1916.

19. William Arthur Winter, MD (b. 1869) lived at 17 Fitzwilliam Place, Dublin.

20. Mather Thomson's home was 37 Fitzwilliam Place; *Thom's Official*

Directory of the United Kingdom and Ireland for the Year 1915 (Dublin, 1915), p.1566.

21. Isabella (Ella) Gertrude Webb (née Ovenden) (1877–1946) studied at the Catholic University Medical School and graduated with a BA (1899), MB, B.Ch. and BAO (1904) and MD from the Royal University in 1906, later specializing in paediatrics. During Easter Week, under her direction (as district superintendant of the St John's Ambulance Brigade) the War Hospital Supply Depot in Merrion Square was converted into a temporary hospital. Her husband was George Randolph Webb (1877–1929), a mathematician and fellow of TCD. They lived in St Kevin's Park, Ranelagh.

22. Mabel Dickinson was a relative. Her brother Charlie Dickinson was a JP and a land agent. Their home was at Altan Grange, Foxrock; *Thom's Official Directory of the United Kingdom and Ireland for the Year 1915*, p.1896.

23. Lovick Brandsby Friend, Major General in charge of administration and General Officer commanding in 1916. He was on leave in England when the Easter Rising began.

24. Sir John Denton Pinkstone French. In 1916 he was in command of all forces on home service, including Ireland.

25. The Veteran Corps were a part-time volunteer corps of veterans, who wore armbands with GR (Georgius Rex) and were generally referred to in Dublin as the 'Gorgeous Wrecks'. They were carrying rifles but had no ammunition and had been on a route march on Easter Monday. A detachment of the corps was returning to their base at Beggars Bush Barracks when they were fired on and five were killed and eight wounded.

26. Constance Georgine Markievicz (née Gore-Booth) (1868–1927), republican and labour activist. She was a member of Sinn Féin and Inghinidhe na hÉireann (Daughters of Ireland) and she also helped to found and became a regular contributor to *Bean na hÉireann* and, together with Bulmer Hobson, founded Fianna Éireann in 1909. A member of the Irish Citizen Army, during the Easter Rising in 1916 she was second-in-command of a troop of Citizen Army combatants at St Stephen's Green and the Royal College of Surgeons. Originally sentenced to death for her part in the Rising, her sentence was commuted to life imprisonment and released under a general amnesty in June 1917. In 1918 she was the first woman to be elected to the British parliament, but like all Sinn Féin

MPs she refused to take her seat at Westminster.

27. The Beattys were neighbours of the Henrys in Ranelagh.

28. Sir David Prain (1857–1944), botanist and Director of the Royal Botanic Gardens at Kew from 1905 to 1922.

29. Elsie's uncle, Edward Adderley Stopford and his family were moving from St Mary's in Frankfort Road, Rathgar to Temple Road, Rathmines.

30. Carrisbrook House was at 124 Pembroke Road, and was an outpost for a detachment of men from de Valera's garrison in Boland's Mills.

31. Francis Sheehy Skeffington (1878–1916), a radical, feminist and pacifist. On 25 April 1916, he was arrested by an army detachment and taken to Portobello (later Cathal Brugha) barracks, Rathmines, Dublin. On the morning of 26 April 1916, Sheehy Skeffington and two other civilians were shot by firing squad on orders of Captain John Bowen-Colthurst, who was subsequently judged to have been insane.

32. The two men shot with Francis Sheehy Skeffington were journalists, Thomas Dickson and Patrick MacIntyre.

33. Roger Casement landed from a German submarine at Banna Strand, Co. Kerry on Friday 21 April 1916 and was arrested. Later convicted

of treason, he was hanged in August 1916.

34. Augustine Birrell (1850–1933), a London barrister and Liberal politician, was appointed Chief Secretary for Ireland in 1907 and resigned after the 1916 Rising.

35. Now Pearse Street.

36. Now O'Connell Street

37. James Connolly (1868–1916), a socialist and labour leader. In 1914 he became acting general secretary of the Irish Transport and General Workers Union, after the departure of James Larkin (1876–1947) to America. In 1916, as commandant of the Irish Citizen Army, he and his comrades took part in the Easter Rising. Connolly was the last of the fifteen men executed after the Rising, shot in Kilmainham Jail on 12 May 1916.

38. Thomas McDonagh (1878–1916) was a teacher and author. He was one of the signatories of the 1916 Proclamation. During the Rising he commanded a force of 150 volunteers that occupied Jacob's biscuit factory, Bishop Street, Dublin and was executed on 3 May 1916.

39. Harriet Emily Reed, a qualified nurse, who with Helen Schuter, also a qualified nurse, ran a private nursing home at 61 Landsdowne Road; *Thom's Official Directory of the United Kingdom and Ireland*

for the Year 1915, p.1821. She was also superintendant of the RCScI Sphagnum Moss Depot.

40. Wife of James H. Pollok, lecturer in physical and metallurgical chemistry at the RCScI.

41. This was the War Hospital Supply Depot. It was turned into an emergency hospital during the Easter Rising.

42. Nettie [Henriette] O'Brien, who was superintendant of a private hospital at 67 Lower Leeson Street; *Thom's Official Directory of the United Kingdom and Ireland for the Year 1915*, p.1618.

43. Richard Irvine Best (1872–1959), Celticist and librarian, and his wife Edith (née Oldham). An expert on Celtic philology and literature, R.I. Best joined the staff of the National Library of Ireland (NLI) in 1906, became chief librarian (1924) and subsequently director until his retirement (1940). They lived at 57 Upper Leeson Street, Dublin.

44. Thomas William Lyster (1855–1922). After graduating from TCD, in 1878 he joined the National Library of Ireland as an assistant librarian, becoming head librarian in 1895 and retiring in 1920. His home was at 10 Harcourt Terrace, Dublin.

45. William John Rice. He was 35.

46. Augustine's widowed sister Mary Kerley and her daughter.

47. A large bakery whose premises were in Ballsbridge.

48. Patrick A.E. Dowling, the Registrar of the RCScI lived at 39 Angelsea Road, Ballsbridge, *Thom's Official Directory of the United Kingdom and Ireland for the Year 1915*, p.1812.

49. Sir Matthew Nathan's sister-in-law, Mrs Estelle Nathan and her daughters, Maud and Pamela.

50. Elsie may mean the Sherwood Foresters, who relieved the garrison in Beggar's Bush barracks.

51. Augustine's brother, Thomas Henry, was a civil engineer.

52. Robert Lepper Valentine (1890–1916). He had been a student at the RCScI and subsequently employed in the Geological Survey of Ireland. He had joined the 'Pals' brigade of the Dublin Fusiliers. He died of wounds at Loos on 30 April 1916.

53. Holden Stoddart from Blackrock, Co. Dublin. He was superintendant of the St. John's Ambulance Brigade and was killed working with a stretcher party in Northumberland Road. He was 33.

54. *The Spark* was a newspaper published between 1915 and March 1916 by the Gaelic Press.

55. The Marquis MacSwiney, an Inspecting Officer with the National Volunteers, had been arrested on 8 May and detained in Dublin Castle overnight before being released, without charge.

56. Count George Noble Plunkett (1851–1948), a nationalist politician. In 1907 he became director of the National Museum of Ireland. The father of one of the executed leaders of the Rising, Joseph Mary Plunkett (1887–1916), he lost his position at the museum after 1916 and he and his wife were interned in England.

57. David Lloyd George (1863–1945), a member of the Liberal Party and Prime Minister of Britain 1916 to 1922.

58. Sir Thomas Henry Grattan Esmonde (1862–1935), a landowner in Wexford and a nationalist politician.

6. The 'flooding sorrow' of a World at War Continues: The Diaries 1917

1. Alice Brunton Henry Diaries, 14 December 1916–19 April 1917 (NLI MS 7985), 11 November 1917 – 20 June 1918 (NLI MS 7986).

2. Mrs Jardin was the 'Superintendant of the Tea Dept.' and in charge of catering, and a member of the management committee of the Sphagnum Moss Depot at the RCScI.

3. Mrs Hubert Lewis who had established a college of gardening for women (funded by DATI) at Ballingale house, Ballycarney, Co. Wexford in January 1917. Nance taught there. The first Irish School (later College) of Gardening for Women had been established in April 1916, following a meeting at the RCScI; *Irish Times*, 24 March 1916.

4. An Irish School of Gardening for women at Meeanee, Kimmage Road, Terenure, established in 1916; *Irish Times*, 13 September 1916.

5. Henry Homan Jeffcott (1877–1937), Professor of Engineering at the RCScI from 1910 to 1922.

6. Miss H.E. Reed, Commandant and Lady Superintendant of the Sub-depot.

7. During the First World War the British government's concern with food production and self sufficiency led to Compulsory Tillage Acts. In Dublin, the Corporation set up a Land Cultivation Committee to provide allotments with the intention of increasing food supplies. For more on this see Jonathan Bell and Mervyn Watson, *Rooted in the Soil: A History of Cottage Gardens and Allotments in Ireland since 1750* (Dublin, 2012), pp.74–84.

8. Grigori Rasputin (1869–1916) a Russian Orthodox mystic who exercised considerable influence on the Russian emperor Nicholas II and his wife Alexandra.

9. Sir William Huggins (1824–1910) and his wife, Margaret Huggins (née Murray) (1848–1915), astronomers and pioneer spectroscopists.

10. Companion to Margaret Huggins.

11. Lady Huggins bequeathed scientific instruments and some personal effects (including observatory notebooks) to Wellesley College, Massachusetts.

7. Crisis in Ireland but Peace at Last: The Diaries 1918–19

1. Alice Brunton Henry Diaries, 11 November 1917-20 June 1918 (NLI MS 7986) 24 June 1918 – 10 November 1918 (NLI MS 7987); 11 November 1918 – (NLI MS 7988).

2. On 10 October 1918 the R.M.S. *Leinster*, a City of Dublin Steampacket ship on the Holyhead to Dublin route, was torpedoed just off the Irish coast with the loss of at least 500 lives.

3. Joseph Dowling of the Connaught Rangers, who was one of the Irish prisoners of war in Germany who joined Casement's Irish Brigade.

4. Elsie's cousin Bob had been interned in Germany since the beginning of the war.

5. Probably May Starkie (née Walsh), wife of William Joseph Myles Starkie (1860–1920), resident commissioner of national education in Ireland 1888–1920.

6. Alice Wordsworth, Elsie's cousin and Dorothy Stopford's cousin.

7. The home of Edward ('Uncle Ned') and Aunt Lily Stopford.

8. The Irish Convention (July 1917–April 1918), with Sir Horace Plunkett as chairman, was an attempt by the British government to reach some agreement about a scheme of domestic self-government for Ireland. Nationalists, members of the Irish Parliamentary party and southern unionists attended but it was boycotted by Sinn Féin and opposed by Ulster unionists.

9. In April 1918 the British government decided to impose conscription on Ireland, thereby radicalizing nationalists and propelling large numbers into the ranks of Sinn Féin.

10. William Redmond (1886-1932) son of John Redmond (1856–1918).

11. Women's Auxiliary Army Corps, founded in 1917.

12. John Simon's first wife was Ethel Mary Venables, daughter of Gilbert Venables, and the niece of the historian J.R. Green. She died in 1901 and his second wife was

Kathleen Rochard Simon (née Harvey (1863/4–1955). She married John Simon in 1917 and during the period of the Black and Tans in Ireland, Kathleen Simon urged her husband to speak against the actions of the Black and Tans, which he did. Edie Stopford worked for John Simon during this period.

13. J.W. Hotson, University of Washington, who was a strong advocate for the use of sphagnum moss for surgical and medical purposes.

14. Sir Thomas Wallace Russell (1841–1920), vice-president of the Department of Agricultural and Technical Instruction for Ireland (1907–18).

15. Robert Mitchell Henry (1873–1950), classical scholar and university administrator. He was appointed Professor of Latin at Queen's College Belfast in 1917 and secretary to the academic council of the new Queen's University of Belfast in 1909, retiring from the university in 1938. A protestant and an Irish nationalist, he was the author of *The Evolution of Sinn Fein* (1920).

16. The artist Paul Henry (1876–1958).

17. In November 1918 the Parliament (Qualification of Women) Act, 1918 (8 & 9 Geo. V, c.47) entitled women to vote and to become members of parliament. In December 1918 there was a general election which in Ireland resulted in an overwhelming victory for Sinn Féin candidates and the election of Constance Markievicz as the first woman to be elected to the Westminster parliament, although she declined to take her seat there.

8. Postscript

1. The Four Courts in Dublin is the seat of Ireland's Supreme and High Courts. In 1922 the Four Courts was occupied by republican forces who were opposed to the Treaty, precipitating outright civil war. In the subsequent siege in June 1922 by the forces of the Irish provisional government (the Free State), Ireland's Public Record Office and the archives it held was destroyed.

2. Roderick ('Rory') O'Connor (1883–1922), a republican and member of the IRA, opposed the Anglo-Irish treaty and was a member of the republican Four Courts garrison. On the 8 December 1922, by order of the Free State cabinet, O'Connor and three other veterans of the Four Courts executive were executed.

3. Letter in the possession of Anne Kruming; quoted by Sheila Pim, *The Woods and the Trees: A Biography of Augustine Henry* (London, 1966), p.214.

4. Edie Stopford Papers (NLI MS 11,426).

5. Liam Price (1891–1967), a district justice and local historian. He practised in the republican courts during the War of Independence but was a supporter of the Anglo-Irish Treaty. He was assigned as district justice to the Wicklow circuit in 1924, a post he held until his retirement in 1960.

6. Alice Stopford Green to Mrs de Villiers, 21 June 1921 (NLI MS 8714 [6]).

7. The Society of Irish Foresters put up a memorial to Augustine in Avondale, Co. Wicklow (once the home of Charles Stewart Parnell) in 1951 and they organize an annual lecture in the RDS called the Augustine Henry lecture.

8. [Thomas J. Walsh], *The Augustine Henry Forestry Herbarium at the National Botanic Gardens Glasnevin, Dublin, Ireland: A Catalogue of the Specimens* (Dublin, 1957), pp.v–vi.

9. E. Charles Nelson and Eileen M. McCracken, *The Brightest Jewel: A History of the National Botanic Gardens Glasnevin, Dublin* (Kilkenny, 1987), pp.220, 226–7.

10. Information received from the family of Elsie Henry.

11. Maurice Fitzpatrick, *Roadside Trees in Town and Country* (Dublin [n.d.]).

12. Mrs Augustine [Alice] Henry, 'Some Remarkable Trees in the Glasnevin Botanical Gardens, Dublin', *The Irish Naturalists' Journal*, 8, no.1 (March 1942), pp.11–14; Dublin Naturalists' Field Club, *Report ... for the Year 1948 ... and List of Members Corrected up to February 1949* (Dublin, 1949), p.15.

13. Irish Society for the Protection of Birds, *Report to Annual Meeting, January 14th 1948* (Letterkenny, 1948).

14. Elsie Henry notebook on a visit to Kingly Vale, Sussex, August 1939 (Library of the National Botanic Gardens Glasnevin).

15. Sir Peter James Kerley (1900–79), a doctor and radiologist who was instrumental in establishing a national radiography service for the detection of tuberculosis in Britain, for which he was made CBE in 1951. In the 1940s he also advised the Irish government on setting up a mass radiographic service in Ireland

16. Information received from James Brunton, Nancy Willson, Barbara Phillips and Sandra Lefroy.

Select Bibliography

Primary Sources

National Library of Ireland

Diaries of Alice Helen Brunton (Elsie) Henry (1881–1956) 1913–1919 (NLI MS 7981–7988).

Diary of Thomas King Moylan [with sub-title 'An unfinished Diary of THE GREAT WAR: begun 5th August 1914; continued intermittently until 6th April 1918, and including account of some personal experiences in Dublin during Easter Week 1916'] (NLI MS 9,620).

Letters to Mrs Alice Stopford Green from Mrs D. de Villiers, 1901–1914 (NLI MS 10,233).

Manuscripts and typewritten letters from Mrs Alice Stopford Green to Mrs D. de Villiers, 1909–1930 (NLI MS 8,714).

Edie Stopford Papers (NLI MS 11,426).

Letters of Dr Augustine Henry to Miss Evelyn Gleeson, 1901–1930 (NLI MS 13,698).

Diary of Annie Brunton, afterwards Mrs Anne Kruming, January 1913–April 1915 (NLI MS 13,620 [1–2]).

Diary of Dorothy Stopford, Dublin April–May 1916 (NLI MS 16,063).

Papers of Robert J. Stopford (NLI MS 21,205 [1–4]).

Library of the National Botanic Gardens Glasnevin

Copy of Alice Henry's notes of Augustine Henry's Chinese activities (Original in the possession of Dr Barbara Phillips, Bath).

Elsie Henry notebook on a visit to Kingly Vale Sussex, August 1939.

Manuscript of a talk given to the Dublin Naturalists' Field Club on 8 December 1941 and later published as 'Some Remarkable Trees in the Glasnevin Botanical Gardens, Dublin', *The Irish Naturalists' Journal*, 8, no.1 (March 1942), pp.11–14.

Electronic Resources

Dictionary of Irish biography (http://dib.cambridge.org).

Irish Times Digital Archive, 1859–2010 (http://www.search.proquest.com).

National Archives of Ireland Census of Ireland 1901 and 1911 (http://www.census.nationalarchives.ie).

National Library of Ireland online exhibition *The 1916 Rising: Personalities and Perspectives* (http://www.nli.ie/1916).

Oxford Dictionary of National Biography (http://oxforddnb.com).

Published Works

[Anon.], 'Augustine Henry Herbarium', *Irish Naturalists' Journal*, 6, no.9 (May 1937), p.209

[Anon.], 'Sphagnum Moss in Ireland', *Irish Life* (26 July 1918), pp.29–32.

Boyce, David George, 'A First World War Transition: State and Citizen in Ireland 1914–19', in *Ireland in Transition 1867–1921*, ed. David George Boyce and Alan O'Day (London, 2004), pp.92–109.

Clear, Catriona, *Social Change and Everyday Life in Ireland, 1850–1922* (Manchester, 2007).

Connell, Joseph E.A., *Where's Where in Dublin. A Directory of Historic Locations, 1913–1923: The Great Lockout, the Easter Rising, the War of Independence, the Irish Civil War* (Dublin, 2006).

Cullen, Clara, '"A pure school of science": The Royal College of Science for Ireland (1867–1926) and Scientific Education in Victorian Ireland', in *Science and Technology in Nineteenth-Century Ireland*, ed. J. Adelman and E. Agnew (Dublin, 2011), pp.136–49.

Cullen, Clara and Orla Feely (eds), *The Building of the State: Science and Engineering with Government on Merrion Street* (Dublin, 2011).

Downes, Margaret, 'The Civilian Voluntary Aid Effort' in *Ireland and the First World War*, ed. David Fitzpatrick (Dublin, 1988), pp.27–37.

Dublin Naturalists' Field Club, *Report ... for the Year 1948 ... and List of Members Corrected up to February 1949* (Dublin, 1949).

Fannin, Alfred, *Letters from Dublin, Easter 1916: Alfred Fannin's Diary of the Rising*, ed. Adrian and Sally Warwick-Haller (Dublin, 1995).

Ferriter, Diarmaid, *The Transformation of Ireland, 1900–2000* (London, 2004).

Finn, Irene, 'Women in the Medical Profession in Ireland, 1876–1919', in *Women and Paid Work in Ireland, 1500–1930*, ed. Bernadette Whelan (Dublin, 2000), pp.102–19.

Fitzpatrick, Maurice, *Roadside Trees in Town and Country* (Dublin, [n.d.]).

Foster, R.F., *Modern Ireland, 1600–1972* (London, 1988).

Garvin, Tom, *Nationalist Revolutionaries in Ireland, 1858–1928* (Oxford, 1987).

Gould, Jenny, 'Women's Military Services in First World War Britain', in *Behind the Lines: Gender and the Two World Wars*, ed. Margaret Randolph Higonnet [et al.] (New Haven, CT, 1987), pp.114–25.

Hayes-McCoy, G.A., 'A Military History of the 1916 Rising', in *The Making of 1916: Studies in the History of the Rising*, ed. Kevin B. Nowlan (Dublin, 1969), pp.255–338.

Hegarty, Shane and Fintan O'Toole, *The Irish Times Book of the 1916 Rising* (Dublin, 2006).

Henry, Alice, 'Sphagnum Moss', *The Torch: Journal of the Royal College of Science for Ireland*, 1 (1916), pp.6–7.

Henry, Alice H., *Town Planting* (Glenageary, [n.d.]). (One of a series of pamphlets [4 pages] published by the Irish Road-side Tree Association. There is no date but published sometime after 1935.)

Henry, Mrs Augustine [Alice], 'Some Remarkable Trees in the Glasnevin Botanical Gardens, Dublin', *The Irish Naturalists' Journal*, 8, no.1 (March 1942), pp.11–14.

Hill, Myrtle, *Women in Ireland: A Century of Change* (Belfast, 2003).

Horgan-Ryan, Siobhan, 'Irish Military Nursing in the Great War', in *Care to Remember: Nursing and Midwifery in Ireland*, ed. Gerard M. Fealy (Cork, 2005), pp.89–101.

Horne, John (ed.), *Our War: Ireland and the Great War* (Dublin, 2008).

Irish Society for the Protection of Birds, *Report to Annual Meeting, January 14th 1948* (Letterkenny, 1948).

Irish War Hospital Supply Organisation. Royal College of Science Sub-Depot Sphagnum Department, *Annual Reports* (Dublin, [1917–1919]).

Jackson, Alvin, *Ireland, 1798–1998: Politics and War* (Oxford, 1999).

Jeffrey, Keith, 'The Great War in Modern Irish Memory', in *Men, Women and War*, ed. T.G. Frazer and Keith Jeffrey (Dublin, 1993), pp.136–57.

Jeffrey, Keith, *Ireland and the Great War* (Cambridge, 2000).

Jeffrey, Keith, *The GPO and the Easter Rising* (Dublin, 2006).

Johnson, Nuala C., *Ireland, the Great War and the Geography of Remembrance* (Cambridge, 2003).

Johnson, T., 'Sphagnum', in Irish War Hospital Supply Organisation. Royal College of Science Sub-Depot Sphagnum Department, *[3rd] Annual Report* (Dublin, [1918–1919]), pp.3–6.

Lee, J.J., *Ireland, 1912–1985: Politics and Society* (Cambridge, 1989).

Lyons, F.S.L., *Culture and Anarchy in Ireland 1890–1939* (Oxford, 1979).

Marlow, Joyce (ed.) *The Virago Book of Women and the Great War, 1914–1918* (London, 1998).

Marwick, Arthur, *Women at War, 1914–1918* (London, 1977).

Matthews, Ann, *Renegades: Irish Republican Women 1900–1922* (Cork, 2010).

Matthews, Ann, *Dissidents: Irish Republican Women 1923–1941* (Cork, 2012).

McDowell, R.B., *Alice Stopford Green: A Passionate Historian* (Dublin, 1967).

McGarry, Fearghal, *The Rising: Ireland; Easter 1916* (Oxford, 2010).

McIntosh, Gillian and Diane Urquhart (eds), *Irish Women at War: The Twentieth Century* (Dublin, 2010).

McLellan, Anne, 'Revolutionary Doctors', in *Lab Coats and Lace: The Lives and Legacies of Inspiring Irish Women Scientists and Pioneers*, ed. Mary Mulvihill (Dublin, 2009) pp. 86-101.

Nelson, E. Charles and Eileen M. McCracken, *The Brightest Jewel: A History of the National Botanic Gardens Glasnevin, Dublin* (Kilkenny, 1987).

O'Brien, Seamus, *In the Footsteps of Augustine Henry and his Chinese Plant Collectors* (London, 2011).

O Broin, Leon, *Protestant Nationalists in Revolutionary Ireland: The Stopford Connection* (Dublin, 1985).

Ó hÓgartaigh, Margaret, 'Dorothy Stopford-Price and the Elimination of Childhood Tuberculosis', in Margaret Ó hÓgartaigh, *Quiet Revolutionaries; Irish Women in Education, Medicine and Sport, 1861–1964* (Dublin, 2011), pp.106–20.

Ouditt, Sharon, *Fighting Forces: Writing Women: Identity and Ideology in the First World War* (London, 1994).

Owens, Rosemary Cullen, *A Social History of Women in Ireland, 1870–1970* (Dublin, 2005).

Pašeta, Senia, *Before the Revolution: Nationalism, Social Change and Ireland's*

Catholic Elite, 1879–1922 (Cork, 1999).

Pim, Sheila, *The Woods and the Trees: A Biography of Augustine Henry* (London, 1966).

Reilly, Eileen, 'Women and Voluntary War Work', in *Ireland and the Great War: 'a war to unite us all'?*, ed. Adrian Gregory and Senia Pašeta (Manchester, 2002), pp.49–72.

Riegler, Natalie N., 'Sphagnum Moss in World War I: The Making of Surgical Dressings by Volunteers in Toronto, Canada, 1917–1918', *Canadian Bulletin of Medical History/Bulletin Canadian d'histoire de la médicine*, 6 (1989), pp.27–43.

Smith, Angela K., *Women's Writing of the First World War; An Anthology* (Manchester, 2000).

Stephen, Rosamond, *An Englishwoman in Belfast: Rosamond Stephen's Record of the Great War*, ed. Oonagh Walsh (Cork, 2000).

Stephens, James, *The Insurrection in Dublin*; with an introduction and afterword by John A. Murphy (Gerrards Cross, 1992 [Originally published: Dublin; London, 1916]).

Swan, Alicia C., *Augustine Henry Report* [typescript] [1994].

The College of Science for Ireland: its origin and development, with notes on similar institutions in other countries, and a bibliography of the work published by the staff and students (1900–1923) (Dublin, 1923).

Thom's Official Directory of the United Kingdom and Ireland for the Year 1915 (Dublin, 1915)

Thom's Official Directory of the United Kingdom and Ireland for the Year 1916 (Dublin, 1916)

Townshend, Charles, *Easter 1916: The Irish Rebellion* (London, 2005).

Urquhart, Diane, '"Ora et labora": The Women's Legion, 1915–18', in *Irish Women at War: The Twentieth Century*, ed. Gillian McIntosh and Diane Urquhart (Dublin, 2010), pp.1–16.

[Walsh, Thomas J.], *The Augustine Henry Forestry Herbarium at the National Botanic Gardens Glasnevin, Dublin, Ireland: A Catalogue of the Specimens* (Dublin, 1957).

Who was Who: A Companion to Who's Who 1916–28 (London, 1929).

Yeates, Pádraig, *A City in Wartime; Dublin 1914–18* (Dublin, 2011).

Index